Refractive Surgery

Section 13

2011–2012

BASIC AND CLINICAL SCIENCE COURSE

AMERICAN ACADEMY
OF OPHTHALMOLOGY
The Eye M.D. Association

LEO

LIFELONG
EDUCATION FOR THE
OPHTHALMOLOGIST

The Basic and Clinical Science Course (BCSC) is one component of the Lifelong Education for the Ophthalmologist (LEO) framework, which assists members in planning their continuing medical education. LEO includes an array of clinical education products that members may select to form individualized, self-directed learning plans for updating their clinical knowledge. Active members or fellows who use LEO components may accumulate sufficient CME credits to earn the LEO Award. Contact the Academy's Clinical Education Division for further information on LEO.

The American Academy of Ophthalmology is accredited by the Accreditation Council for Continuing Medical Education to provide continuing medical education for physicians.

The American Academy of Ophthalmology designates this enduring material for a maximum of 10 *AMA PRA Category 1 Credits*™. Physicians should claim only credit commensurate with the extent of their participation in the activity.

The BCSC is designed to increase the physician's ophthalmic knowledge through study and review. Users of this activity are encouraged to read the text and then answer the study questions provided at the back of the book.

To claim *AMA PRA Category 1 Credits*™ upon completion of this activity, learners must demonstrate appropriate knowledge and participation in the activity by taking the post-test for Section 13 and achieving a score of 80% or higher. For further details, please see the instructions for requesting CME credit at the back of the book.

The Academy provides this material for educational purposes only. It is not intended to represent the only or best method or procedure in every case, nor to replace a physician's own judgment or give specific advice for case management. Including all indications, contraindications, side effects, and alternative agents for each drug or treatment is beyond the scope of this material. All information and recommendations should be verified, prior to use, with current information included in the manufacturers' package inserts or other independent sources, and considered in light of the patient's condition and history. Reference to certain drugs, instruments, and other products in this course is made for illustrative purposes only and is not intended to constitute an endorsement of such. Some material may include information on applications that are not considered community standard, that reflect indications not included in approved FDA labeling, or that are approved for use only in restricted research settings. **The FDA has stated that it is the responsibility of the physician to determine the FDA status of each drug or device he or she wishes to use, and to use them with appropriate, informed patient consent in compliance with applicable law.** The Academy specifically disclaims any and all liability for injury or other damages of any kind, from negligence or otherwise, for any and all claims that may arise from the use of any recommendations or other information contained herein.

Cover image courtesy of Jayne S. Weiss, MD.

Basic and Clinical Science Course

Gregory L. Skuta, MD, Oklahoma City, Oklahoma, *Senior Secretary for Clinical Education*

Louis B. Cantor, MD, Indianapolis, Indiana, *Secretary for Ophthalmic Knowledge*

Jayne S. Weiss, MD, Detroit, Michigan, *BCSC Course Chair*

Section 13

Faculty Responsible for This Edition

Christopher J. Rapuano, MD, *Chair,* Philadelphia, Pennsylvania
Brian S. Boxer Wachler, MD, Beverly Hills, California
Elizabeth A. Davis, MD, Bloomington, Minnesota
Eric D. Donnenfeld, MD, Rockville Centre, New York
M. Bowes Hamill, MD, Houston, Texas
J. Bradley Randleman, MD, Atlanta, Georgia
Steven I. Rosenfeld, MD, Delray Beach, Florida
Donald Tan, MD, *Consultant,* Singapore
William S. Clifford, MD, Garden City, Kansas
Practicing Ophthalmologists Advisory Committee for Education

The Academy wishes to acknowledge Holly Hindman, MD, *Committee on Aging,* for her review of this edition.

The Academy also wishes to acknowledge the American Society of Cataract and Refractive Surgeons for recommending faculty members to the BCSC Section 13 committee.

Financial Disclosures

The following Academy staff members state that they have no significant financial interest or other relationship with the manufacturer of any commercial product discussed in this course or with the manufacturer of any competing commercial product: Christine Arturo, Steve Huebner, Stephanie Tanaka, and Brian Veen.

The authors state the following financial relationships:

Dr Boxer Wachler: Addition Technology, consultant

Dr Davis: Abbott Medical Optics, consultant; Allergan, grant recipient; Bausch & Lomb, consultant; Inspire Pharmaceuticals, consultant; ISTA Pharmaceuticals, consultant; Refractec, equity ownership/stock options

Dr Donnenfeld: Abbott Medical Optics, consultant, lecturer, grant recipient; Advanced Vision Research, consultant, lecturer, grant recipient; Alcon Laboratories, consultant, lecturer, grant recipient; Allergan, consultant, lecturer, grant recipient; Aquesys, consultant; Bausch & Lomb Surgical, consultant, lecturer, grant recipient; CRST, consultant; Eyemaginations, consultant; Glaukos Corporation, consultant; Inspire, consultant; Lensx, consultant; Odyssey, consultant; Pfizer Ophthalmics, consultant; QLT Phototherapeutics, consultant; Sirion, consultant; TLC Laser Eye Centers, lecturer, equity ownership/stock options; Tru Vision, consultant, equity ownership/stock options; Wavetec, consultant

Dr Hamill: Alcon, grant recipient; OPHTEC BV, grant recipient; VisionCare, grant recipient

Dr Rapuano: Alcon Laboratories, lecturer; Allergan, consultant, lecturer; Bausch & Lomb, lecturer; EyeGate Pharma, consultant; Inspire, lecturer; Rapid Pathogen Screening, equity ownership/stock options; Vistakon Johnson & Johnson Vision Care, lecturer

Dr Rosenfeld: Allergan, lecturer; Inspire Pharmaceuticals, consultant

The other authors state that they have no significant financial interest or other relationship with the manufacturer of any commercial product discussed in the chapters that they contributed to this course or with the manufacturer of any competing commercial product.

Recent Past Faculty

Michael W. Belin, MD
Robert S. Feder, MD
Jayne S. Weiss, MD
Helen K. Wu, MD

In addition, the Academy gratefully acknowledges the contributions of numerous past faculty and advisory committee members who have played an important role in the development of previous editions of the Basic and Clinical Science Course.

American Academy of Ophthalmology Staff

Richard A. Zorab, *Vice President, Ophthalmic Knowledge*
Hal Straus, *Director, Publications Department*
Christine Arturo, *Acquisitions Manager*
Stephanie Tanaka, *Publications Manager*
D. Jean Ray, *Production Manager*
Brian Veen, *Medical Editor*
Steven Huebner, *Administrative Coordinator*

AMERICAN ACADEMY
OF OPHTHALMOLOGY
The Eye M.D. Association

655 Beach Street
Box 7424
San Francisco, CA 94120-7424

Contents

6 Photoablation: Complications and Side Effects 93

10 Refractive Surgery in Ocular and Systemic Disease . . . 163

11 Considerations After Refractive Surgery 187

12 International Perspectives in Refractive Surgery 197

General Introduction

The Basic and Clinical Science Course (BCSC) is designed to meet the needs of residents and practitioners for a comprehensive yet concise curriculum of the field of ophthalmology. The BCSC has developed from its original brief outline format, which relied heavily on outside readings, to a more convenient and educationally useful self-contained text. The Academy updates and revises the course annually, with the goals of integrating the basic science and clinical practice of ophthalmology and of keeping ophthalmologists current with new developments in the various subspecialties.

The BCSC incorporates the effort and expertise of more than 80 ophthalmologists, organized into 13 Section faculties, working with Academy editorial staff. In addition, the course continues to benefit from many lasting contributions made by the faculties of previous editions. Members of the Academy's Practicing Ophthalmologists Advisory Committee for Education serve on each faculty and, as a group, review every volume before and after major revisions.

Organization of the Course

The Basic and Clinical Science Course comprises 13 volumes, incorporating fundamental ophthalmic knowledge, subspecialty areas, and special topics:

1 Update on General Medicine
2 Fundamentals and Principles of Ophthalmology
3 Clinical Optics
4 Ophthalmic Pathology and Intraocular Tumors
5 Neuro-Ophthalmology
6 Pediatric Ophthalmology and Strabismus
7 Orbit, Eyelids, and Lacrimal System
8 External Disease and Cornea
9 Intraocular Inflammation and Uveitis
10 Glaucoma
11 Lens and Cataract
12 Retina and Vitreous
13 Refractive Surgery

In addition, a comprehensive Master Index allows the reader to easily locate subjects throughout the entire series.

References

Readers who wish to explore specific topics in greater detail may consult the references cited within each chapter and listed in the Basic Texts section at the back of the book.

These references are intended to be selective rather than exhaustive, chosen by the BCSC faculty as being important, current, and readily available to residents and practitioners.

Related Academy educational materials are also listed in the appropriate sections. They include books, online and audiovisual materials, self-assessment programs, clinical modules, and interactive programs.

Study Questions and CME Credit

Each volume of the BCSC is designed as an independent study activity for ophthalmology residents and practitioners. The learning objectives for this volume are given on page 1. The text, illustrations, and references provide the information necessary to achieve the objectives; the study questions allow readers to test their understanding of the material and their mastery of the objectives. Physicians who wish to claim CME credit for this educational activity may do so by following the instructions given at the end of the book.

Conclusion

The Basic and Clinical Science Course has expanded greatly over the years, with the addition of much new text and numerous illustrations. Recent editions have sought to place a greater emphasis on clinical applicability while maintaining a solid foundation in basic science. As with any educational program, it reflects the experience of its authors. As its faculties change and as medicine progresses, new viewpoints are always emerging on controversial subjects and techniques. Not all alternate approaches can be included in this series; as with any educational endeavor, the learner should seek additional sources, including such carefully balanced opinions as the Academy's Preferred Practice Patterns.

The BCSC faculty and staff are continuously striving to improve the educational usefulness of the course; you, the reader, can contribute to this ongoing process. If you have any suggestions or questions about the series, please do not hesitate to contact the faculty or the editors.

The authors, editors, and reviewers hope that your study of the BCSC will be of lasting value and that each Section will serve as a practical resource for quality patient care.

Objectives

Upon completion of BCSC Section 13, *Refractive Surgery*, the reader should be able to

- state the contribution of the cornea's shape and tissue layers to the optics of the eye and how these components are affected biomechanically by different types of keratorefractive procedures

- outline the basic concepts of wavefront analysis and its relationship to different types of optical aberrations

- identify the general types of lasers used in refractive surgeries

- outline the steps—including medical and social history, ocular examination, and ancillary testing—in evaluating whether a patient is an appropriate candidate for refractive surgery

- for incisional keratorefractive surgery (radial keratotomy, transverse keratotomy, arcuate keratotomy, and limbal relaxing incisions), describe the history, patient selection, surgical techniques, outcomes, and complications

- list the various types of corneal onlays and inlays that have been used for refractive correction

- for surface ablation procedures, describe patient selection, epithelial removal and laser calibration techniques, refractive outcomes, and complications

- describe patient selection, surgical techniques, outcomes, and complications for laser in situ keratomileusis (LASIK)

- describe the different methods for creating a LASIK flap using a microkeratome or a femtosecond laser as well as the instrumentation and possible complications associated with each

- explain recent developments in the application of wavefront technology to surface ablation and LASIK

- for conductive keratoplasty, provide a brief overview of history, patient selection, and safety issues

- describe how intraocular surgical procedures, including clear lens extraction with IOL implantation or phakic IOL implantation, can be used in refractive correction, with or without corneal intervention

- describe the different types of IOLs used for refractive correction

- explain the leading theories of accommodation and how they relate to potential treatment of presbyopia

- describe nonaccommodative and accommodative approaches to the treatment of presbyopia

- state considerations for, and possible contraindications to, refractive surgery in the setting of preexisting ocular and systemic disease

- list some of the effects of prior refractive procedures on later IOL calculations, contact lens wear, and ocular surgery

- describe the role of the FDA in the development and approval of ophthalmic devices used in refractive surgery

CHAPTER 1

The Science of Refractive Surgery

The goal of refractive surgery is to reduce dependence on contact lenses or spectacles for routine daily activities. A wide variety of surgical techniques and technologies are available, with appropriate presurgical evaluation matching the best technique and outcome for each individual.

Refractive surgical procedures can be generally categorized as *corneal* or *intraocular* (Table 1-1). Keratorefractive (corneal) procedures include incisional, laser ablation, lamellar implants, corneal collagen shrinkage, and collagen crosslinking techniques. Intraocular refractive procedures include phakic intraocular lens (PIOL) implantation and cataract surgery or refractive lens exchange (RLE) with implantation of a monofocal, toric, multifocal, or accommodative intraocular lens. Each of these techniques has advantages and disadvantages and should be specifically matched to the individual.

This chapter will review the fundamental corneal properties relevant to refractive surgery (focusing on keratorefractive procedures), corneal imaging for refractive surgery, and the effects of keratorefractive surgery on the cornea. This will include review of the optical principles discussed in BCSC Section 3, *Clinical Optics;* refractive errors (both lower- and higher-order aberrations); corneal biomechanics; corneal topography and tomography; wavefront analysis; laser biophysics and laser–tissue interactions; corneal biomechanical changes after surgery; and corneal wound healing.

Corneal Optics

The air–tear film interface provides the majority of the optical power of the eye. Although a normal tear film has minimal deleterious effect, an abnormal tear film can have a dramatic impact on vision. For example, either excess tear film (eg, epiphora) or altered tear film (eg, dry eye or blepharitis) can decrease visual quality.

The optical power of the eye derives primarily from the anterior corneal curvature, which produces about two-thirds of the eye's refractive power, approximately +48.00 diopters (D). The overall corneal power is less (approximately +42.00 D) as a result of the negative power (approximately –6.00 D) of the posterior corneal surface. Standard keratometers and Placido-based corneal topography instruments measure the anterior corneal radius of curvature and *estimate* total corneal power from these front surface measurements. These instruments extrapolate the central corneal power (K) by measuring the rate of change in curvature from the paracentral 4-mm zone; this factor takes on

Table 1-1 Overview of Refractive Procedures

Location	Type of Procedure	Specific Procedures	Common Abbreviations	Refractive Error Treated
Corneal	Incisional	Radial keratotomy	RK	Myopia (historical)
		Astigmatic keratotomy		
		Arcuate keratotomy	AK	Astigmatism
		Limbal relaxing incisions	LRI	Astigmatism
		Hexagonal keratotomy	Hex K	Hyperopia (historical)
	Excimer laser	Surface ablation		Myopia, hyperopia, astigmatism
		Photorefractive keratectomy	PRK	+6 to −14 D
		Laser subepithelial keratomileusis	LASEK	+6 to −14 D
		Epipolis LASIK	Epi-LASIK	+6 to −14 D
		Lamellar		
		Laser in situ keratomileusis	LASIK	+6 to −14 D
		Femtosecond	Femto-LASIK	Investigational
	Nonlaser lamellar	Epikeratophakia, epikeratoplasty		Myopia, hyperopia, astigmatism (historical)
		Myopic keratomileusis		Myopia (historical)
		Intrastromal corneal ring segments	ICRS	Myopia, keratoconus
	Collagen shrinkage	Laser thermokeratoplasty	LTK	Hyperopia, astigmatism (historical)
		Conductive keratoplasty	CK	Hyperopia, astigmatism +0.75 to +3.25 D
	Collagen crosslinking		CCL, CXL	Keratoconus (investigational)
Intraocular	Phakic	Anterior chamber phakic IOLs		Myopia (in development)
		Iris-fixated phakic IOLs		Myopia (−5 to −20 D)
		Posterior chamber phakic IOLs		Myopia (−3 to −20 D)
	Pseudophakic	Refractive lens exchange (multifocal/accommodating IOL)	RLE	Myopia, hyperopia, presbyopia
		Refractive lens exchange (toric IOL)		Myopia, hyperopia, astigmatism

critical importance in the determination of IOL power after keratorefractive surgery (see Chapter 11). The normal cornea flattens from the center to the periphery by up to 4.00 D and is flatter nasally than temporally.

Almost all keratorefractive surgical procedures change the refractive state of the eye by altering corneal curvature. The tolerances involved in altering corneal dimensions are relatively small. For instance, changing the refractive status of the eye by 2.00 D may require altering the cornea's thickness by less than 30 μm. Thus, achieving predictable results is sometimes problematic because minuscule changes in the shape of the cornea may produce large changes in refraction.

Refractive Error: Optical Principles and Wavefront Analysis

One of the major applications of the wave theory of light is in wavefront analysis. Currently, wavefront analysis can be performed clinically by 4 methods: Hartmann-Shack; Tscherning; thin-beam single-ray tracing; and optical path difference, which combines retinoscopy with corneal topography. Each method generates a detailed report of lower-order aberrations (sphere and cylinder) and higher-order aberrations (spherical aberration, coma, and trefoil, among others). This information is useful both in calculating custom ablations to enhance vision or correct optical problems and in explaining patients' visual symptoms.

Measurement of Wavefront Aberrations and Graphical Representations

Although several techniques are available for measuring wavefront aberrations, the most popular in clinical practice is based on the Hartmann-Shack wavefront sensor. With this device, a low-power laser beam is focused on the retina. A point on the retina acts as a point source, and the reflected light is then propagated back through the optical elements of the eye. In a perfect eye, all the rays would emerge in parallel, and the wavefront would be a flat plane. In reality, the wavefront is not flat. An array of lenses samples parts of the wavefront and focuses light on a detector (Fig 1-1). The wavefront shape can be determined from the

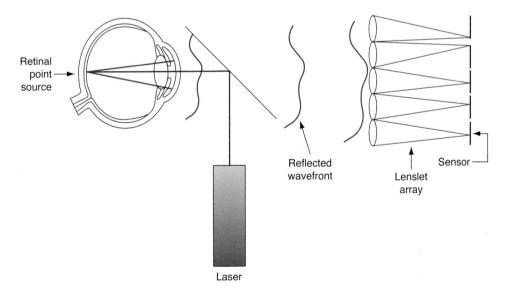

Figure 1-1   Schematic of a Hartmann-Shack wavefront sensor.

position of the focus on each detector. Optical aberrations can be resolved into a variety of basic shapes, the combination of which represents the total aberration of the system, just as conventional refractive error is a combination of sphere and cylinder.

Currently, wavefront aberrations are most commonly specified by *Zernike polynomials,* which are the mathematical formulas used to describe surfaces. Each aberration may be positive or negative in value and induces predictable alterations in the image quality. The magnitude of these aberrations is expressed as a root mean square (RMS) error, which is the deviation of the wavefront averaged over the entire wavefront. The majority of patients have total RMS values less than 0.3 μm. Most higher-order Zernike coefficients have mean values close to zero. The most important Zernike coefficients affecting visual quality are coma, spherical aberration, and trefoil.

Fourier reconstruction is an alternative method of analyzing the output from an aberrometer. Fourier is a sine wave–derived transformation of a complex shape. Compared with shapes derived from Zernike polynomial analysis, the shapes derived from Fourier analysis are more detailed, theoretically allowing for the measurement and treatment of more highly aberrant corneas.

Lower-Order Aberrations

Myopia, hyperopia, and regular astigmatism are all lower-order (second-order) aberrations that can be expressed as wavefront aberrations. Myopia produces *positive defocus* (Fig 1-2), while hyperopia produces *negative defocus.* Regular (cylindrical) astigmatism produces a wavefront aberration that has orthogonal and oblique components (Fig 1-3). Other lower-order aberrations are non–visually significant aberrations known as *first-order aberrations,* such as vertical and horizontal prisms and zero-order aberrations (piston).

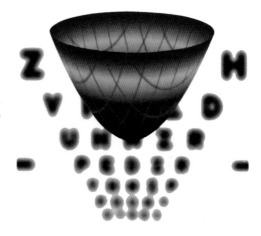

Figure 1-2 Zernike polynomial representation of defocus. *(Used with permission from Alcon Laboratories.)*

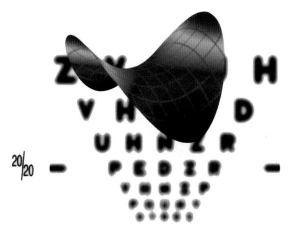

Figure 1-3 Zernike polynomial representation of astigmatism. *(Used with permission from Alcon Laboratories.)*

Higher-Order Aberrations

Wavefront aberration is a function of pupil size, with increased higher-order aberrations seen as the pupil dilates. Higher-order aberrations also increase with age, although the clinical effect is thought to be balanced by the increasing miosis of the pupil with age. Although lower-order aberrations decrease after laser vision correction, higher-order aberrations, particularly spherical aberration and coma, may increase after conventional surface ablation or laser in situ keratomileusis (LASIK) for myopia. This increase is correlated with the degree of preoperative myopia. After standard hyperopic laser vision correction, higher-order aberrations increase even more than they do in myopic eyes but in the opposite (toward negative values) direction. Compared with conventional treatments, customized excimer laser treatments may decrease the number of induced higher-order aberrations and provide a higher quality of vision, particularly in mesopic conditions.

Spherical aberrations

When peripheral light rays focus in front of more central rays, the effect is called *spherical aberration* (Fig 1-4). Clinically, this radially symmetric fourth-order aberration is the cause of night myopia and is commonly increased after myopic LASIK and surface ablation. It results in halos around point images. Spherical aberration is the most significant higher-order aberration. It may increase depth of field but decreases contrast sensitivity.

Coma and trefoil

With *coma,* a third-order aberration, rays at one edge of the pupil come into focus before rays at the opposite edge. The effective image resembles a comet, having vertical and horizontal components (Fig 1-5). Coma is common in patients with decentered corneal grafts, keratoconus, and decentered laser ablations.

Trefoil, also a third-order aberration seen after refractive surgery, produces less degradation in image quality compared with coma of similar RMS magnitude (Fig 1-6).

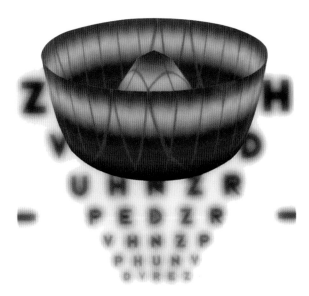

Figure 1-4 Zernike polynomial representation of spherical aberration. *(Used with permission from Alcon Laboratories.)*

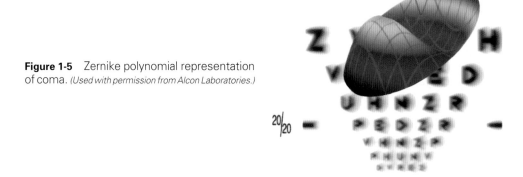

Figure 1-5 Zernike polynomial representation of coma. *(Used with permission from Alcon Laboratories.)*

Other higher-order aberrations

There are numerous other higher-order aberrations, of which only a small number are of clinical interest. Secondary astigmatism and quadrafoil are fourth-order aberrations with dramatically different effects on vision. As knowledge of surgically induced aberration increases, more of the basic types of aberrations may become clinically relevant.

Effect of excimer laser ablation on higher-order aberrations

While conventional (non–wavefront-guided) excimer laser ablations typically increase higher-order aberrations, both wavefront-optimized and wavefront-guided ablations tend to induce fewer higher-order aberrations and may, in principle, be able to reduce preexisting higher-order optical aberrations.

Figure 1-6 Zernike polynomial representation of trefoil. *(Used with permission from Alcon Laboratories.)*

Wavefront Analysis and Irregular Astigmatism

Irregular astigmatism is usually caused by irregularities of corneal shape resulting from such factors as keratoconus, previous refractive surgery, corneal transplantation, and corneal scars. Neither spectacles nor soft contact lenses nor routine keratorefractive surgery adequately corrects irregular astigmatism. Significant irregular astigmatism usually requires a rigid gas-permeable contact lens for optimal visual rehabilitation.

Klyce SD, Karon MD, Smolek MK. Advantages and disadvantages of the Zernike expansion for representing wave aberration of the normal and aberrated eye. *J Refract Surg.* 2004;20(5):S537–S541.

Salmon TO, van de Pol C. Normal-eye Zernike coefficients and root-mean-square wavefront errors. *J Cataract Refract Surg.* 2006;32(12):2064–2074.

Stonecipher KG, Kezirian GM. Wavefront-optimized versus wavefront-guided LASIK for myopic astigmatism with the ALLEGRETTO WAVE: three-month results of a prospective FDA trial. *J Refract Surg.* 2008;24(4):S424–S430.

Corneal Biomechanics

The cornea consists of collagen fibrils arranged in approximately 200 parallel lamellae that extend from limbus to limbus. The fibrils are oriented at angles to the fibrils in adjacent lamellae. This network of collagen is responsible for the mechanical strength of the cornea. The fibrils are more closely packed in the anterior two-thirds of the cornea and in the axial, or prepupillary, cornea compared with the peripheral cornea. (See BCSC Section 8, *External Disease and Cornea.*)

When the cornea is in a dehydrated state, stress is distributed principally to the posterior layers or uniformly over the entire structure. When the cornea is healthy or edematous, the anterior lamellae take up most of the strain. There are differences in glycosaminoglycans between the anterior and posterior stroma, as well as more lamellar interweaving in the anterior corneal stroma; thus, the anterior cornea swells far less than the posterior cornea. Stress within the tissue is partly related to intraocular pressure (IOP) but not in a linear manner under physiologic conditions (normal IOP range).

Most keratorefractive procedures alter corneal biomechanical properties either directly (eg, radial keratotomy weakening the cornea to induce refractive change) or indirectly (eg, excimer laser surgery weakening the cornea by means of tissue removal). The lack of uniformity of biomechanical load throughout the cornea explains the variation in corneal biomechanical response to different keratorefractive procedures. For instance, LASIK has a greater overall effect than photorefractive keratectomy (PRK) on corneal biomechanics not only because a lamellar flap is created but also because the laser ablation occurs in the deeper, weaker corneal stroma (a more detailed discussion of this can be found later in this chapter and in Chapter 5).

Corneal Imaging for Keratorefractive Surgery

Corneal shape, curvature, and thickness profiles can be generated from a variety of technologies, including Placido disk–based systems and elevation-based systems (including scanning-slit systems and Scheimpflug imaging). Each technology conveys different information about corneal curvature, anatomy, and biomechanical function. In addition, computerized topographic and tomographic systems may display other data: pupil size and location, indices estimating regular and irregular astigmatism, estimates of the probability of having keratoconus, simulated keratometry, and corneal asphericity. Other topography systems may integrate wavefront aberrometry data with topographic data. While this additional information can be additive in preoperative surgical evaluations, no automated screening system can supplant clinical experience in evaluating corneal imaging.

The asphericity of the cornea can be quantified by determining the Q value, with Q = 0 for spherical corneas, Q < 0 for prolate corneas, and Q > 0 for oblate corneas. A normal cornea is prolate, with an asphericity Q of –0.26. Prolate corneas minimize spherical aberrations by virtue of their relatively flat peripheral curve. Conversely, oblate corneal contours, in which the peripheral cornea is steeper than the center, increase the probability of having induced spherical aberrations. Following conventional refractive surgery for myopia, corneal asphericity increases in the oblate direction, which may cause degradation of the optics of the eye.

Corneal Topography

Corneal topography provides highly detailed information about corneal curvature. Topography is evaluated using keratoscopic images, which are captured from Placido disk patterns that are reflected from the corneal surface and then converted to computerized color scales (Fig 1-7). Placido-based systems are referenced from the line that the instrument makes to the corneal surface (vertex normal). This line is not necessarily the patient's line of sight nor the visual axis, which may lead to confusion in interpreting topographic maps. For a more extensive discussion of other uses of computerized corneal topography, refer to BCSC Section 3, *Clinical Optics,* and Section 8, *External Disease and Cornea.*

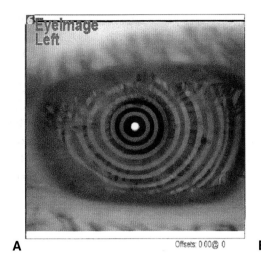

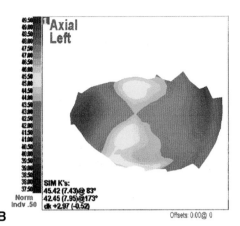

Figure 1-7 Placido imaging of the cornea. **A,** The raw Placido disk image; **B,** computer generated color map derived from data in **A.** *(Courtesy of J. Bradley Randleman, MD.)*

Axial power and curvature

Axial power provides a "smoother" picture of the cornea because the instrument used assumes a radius of curvature that intersects with the instrument axis. The curvature and power of the central 1–2 mm of the cornea can be closely approximated by the axial power and curvature indices (formerly called *sagittal curvature*); however, the central measurements are extrapolated and thus are potentially inaccurate. These indices also fail to describe the true shape and power of the peripheral cornea. Topographic maps displaying axial power and curvature provide an intuitive sense of the physiologic flattening of the cornea but do not represent the true refractive power or the true curvature of peripheral regions of the cornea (Fig 1-8).

Instantaneous power and curvature

A second method of describing the corneal curvature on Placido disk–based topography is the *instantaneous radius of curvature* (also called *meridional* or *tangential power*). The potential benefit of this method's increased sensitivity is balanced by its tendency to document excessive detail ("noise"), which may not be clinically relevant.

The instantaneous radius of curvature is determined by taking a perpendicular path through the point in question from a plane that intersects the point and the visual axis, but allowing the radius to be the length necessary to correspond to a sphere with the same curvature at that point. The curvature, which is expressed in diopters, is estimated by the difference between the corneal index of refraction and 1.000, divided by this tangentially determined radius. A tangential map typically shows better sensitivity to peripheral changes with less "smoothing" of the curvature than an axial map (see Fig 1-8). In these maps, diopters are relative units of curvature and are not the equivalent of diopters of corneal power.

For routine refractive screening, most surgeons have the topographic output in the axial (sagittal) curvature mode rather than the instantaneous (tangential) mode.

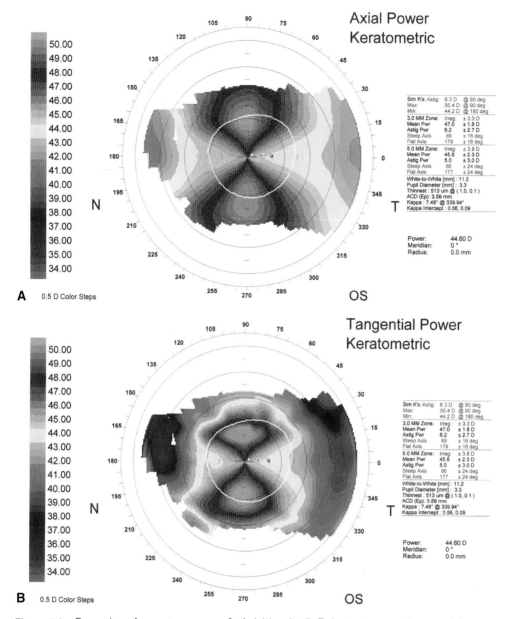

Figure 1-8 Examples of curvature maps. **A,** Axial (sagittal); **B,** instantaneous (tangential). *(Courtesy of J. Bradley Randleman, MD.)*

Corneal topography and astigmatism

A normal topographic image of a cornea without astigmatism demonstrates a relatively uniform color pattern centrally with a natural flattening in the periphery (Fig 1-9). *Regular astigmatism* is uniform steepening along a single corneal meridian that can be fully corrected with a cylindrical lens. Topographic imaging of regular astigmatism demonstrates a symmetric "bow-tie" pattern along a single meridian with a straight axis on both

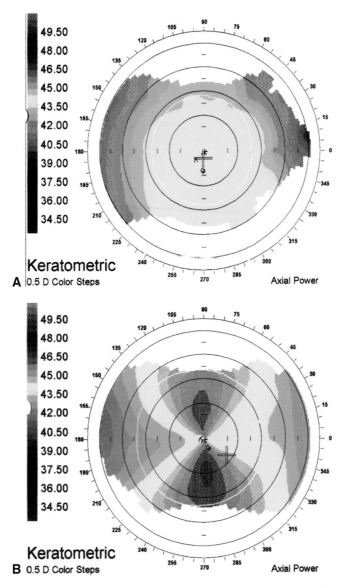

Figure 1-9 Normal corneal topographic patterns. **A,** Round; **B,** symmetric bow tie. *(Courtesy of J. Bradley Randleman, MD.)*

sides of center (see Fig 1-9). The bow-tie pattern on topographic maps is an artifact of Placido-based imaging: because the Placido image cannot detect curvature at the central measurement point, the corneal meridional steepening seems to disappear centrally and become enhanced as the imaging gets farther from center.

Irregular astigmatism is nonuniform corneal steepening from a variety of causes that cannot be corrected by cylindrical lenses. Irregular astigmatism decreases best spectacle-corrected visual acuity and may reduce contrast sensitivity and increase visual aberrations, depending on the magnitude of irregularity. Rigid gas-permeable and hard contact lenses can correct visual acuity reductions resulting from corneal irregular astigmatism by bridging the irregular corneal surface and the contact lens with the tear film. For more information on irregular astigmatism, see BCSC Section 3, *Clinical Optics*.

Corneal topography is very helpful in evaluating eyes with irregular astigmatism. Topographic changes include nonorthogonality of the steep and flat axes (Fig 1-10). Asymmetry between the superior and inferior or nasal and temporal halves of the cornea may also be seen on corneal topography, although these patterns are not necessarily indicative of corneal pathology. In contrast, wavefront analysis can demonstrate higher-order aberrations (such as coma, trefoil, quadrafoil, or secondary astigmatism). The ability to differentiate regular from irregular astigmatism has clinical significance in keratorefractive surgery. Traditional excimer laser ablation can treat spherocylindrical errors but does not effectively treat irregular astigmatism. Topography-guided ablation may be useful in treating irregular astigmatism not caused by early corneal ectatic disorders.

Limitations of corneal topography

In addition to the limitations of the specific algorithms and the variations in terminology among manufacturers, the accuracy of corneal topography may be affected by other potential problems:

- tear-film effects
- misalignment (misaligned corneal topography may give a false impression of corneal apex decentration suggestive of keratoconus)
- instability (test-to-test variation)
- insensitivity to focus errors
- area of coverage (central and limbal)
- decreased accuracy of corneal power simulation measurements (Sim K) after refractive surgical procedures
- decreased accuracy of posterior surface elevation values in the presence of corneal opacities or, often, after refractive surgery (with scanning-slit technology)

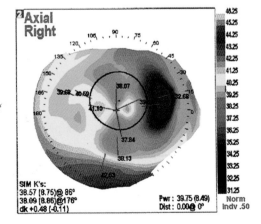

Figure 1-10 Irregular astigmatism. *(Courtesy of J. Bradley Randleman, MD.)*

Corneal Tomography

While surface corneal curvature (power) is best expressed by Placido imaging, overall corneal shape, including spatial thickness profiles, is best expressed by computed tomography. A variety of imaging systems are available that take multiple slit images and reconstruct them into a corneal shape profile, including anterior and posterior corneal elevation data. These include scanning-slit technology and Scheimpflug-based imaging systems (Fig 1-11). To represent shape directly, color maps may be used to display a *z-height*

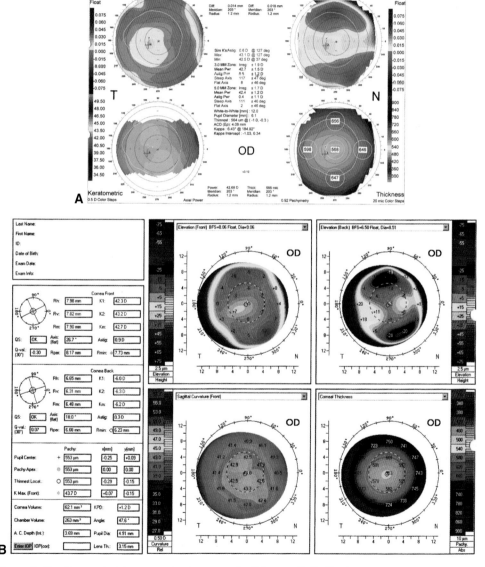

Figure 1-11 Computed tomography images. **A,** Orbscan II; **B,** Pentacam. *(Courtesy of J. Bradley Randleman, MD.)*

from an arbitrary plane such as the iris plane; however, in order to be clinically useful, corneal surface maps are plotted to show differences from best-fit spheres or other objects that closely mimic the normal corneal shape (Fig 1-12).

Elevation-based tomography is especially helpful in refractive surgery for depicting the anterior and posterior surface shapes of the cornea and lens. With such information, alterations to the shape of the ocular structures can be determined with greater accuracy, especially postoperative changes.

Indications for Corneal Imaging in Refractive Surgery

Corneal topography is essential in the preoperative evaluation of refractive surgery candidates. About two-thirds of patients with normal corneas have a symmetric astigmatism pattern that is round, oval, or bow-tie shaped (see Fig 1-9). Asymmetric patterns include asymmetric bow-tie patterns, inferior steepening, superior steepening, skewed radial axes, or other nonspecific irregularities.

Corneal topography detects irregular astigmatism, which may result from dry eye, contact lens warpage, keratoconus and other corneal ectatic disorders, corneal surgery, trauma, scarring, and postinflammatory or degenerative conditions. Repeated topographic examinations may be helpful when the underlying etiology is in question, especially in cases of suspicious steepening patterns in patients who wear contact lenses or who have dry eye. Contact lens wearers with irregular astigmatism often benefit from extended periods without contact lens wear prior to refractive surgery to allow the corneal map and refraction to stabilize. Patients with keratoconus or other ectatic disorders are not routinely considered for ablative keratorefractive surgery, because the thin cornea has an unpredictable response, and reducing its thickness may lead to progressive ectasia. Forme fruste, or subclinical, keratoconus identified by Placido disk–based and elevation-based tomography requires caution

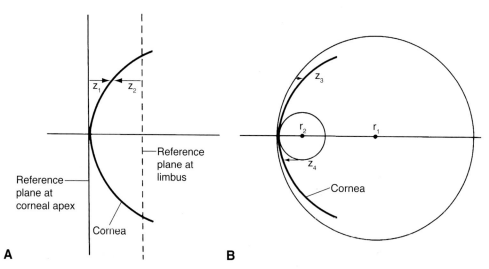

Figure 1-12 Height maps (typically in μm). **A,** Height relative to plane surface; z_1 is below the surface parallel to the corneal apex. z_2 is above the surface parallel to the corneal limbus. **B,** Height relative to reference sphere. z_3 is below a flat sphere of radius r_1. z_4 is above a steep sphere of radius r_2. *(Illustration by Christine Gralapp.)*

on the part of the ophthalmologist and is considered a contraindication to LASIK; the safety and efficacy of surface ablation in these cases remains to be determined. Studies are under way to determine the suitability of some keratorefractive procedures in combination with corneal collagen crosslinking as alternative therapeutic modalities for these patients.

Corneal topography and tomography can also be used to demonstrate the effects of keratorefractive procedures. Preoperative and postoperative maps may be compared to determine the refractive effect achieved (*difference map;* Fig 1-13). Corneal mapping can also help to explain unexpected results, including undercorrection and overcorrection, induced astigmatism, and induced aberrations from small optical zones, decentered ablations, or central islands (Fig 1-14).

De Paiva CS, Harris LD, Pflugfelder SC. Keratoconus-like topographic changes in keratoconjunctivitis sicca. *Cornea.* 2003;22(1):22–24.

Rabinowitz YS, Yang H, Brickman Y, et al. Videokeratography database of normal human corneas. *Br J Ophthalmol.*1996;80(7):610–616.

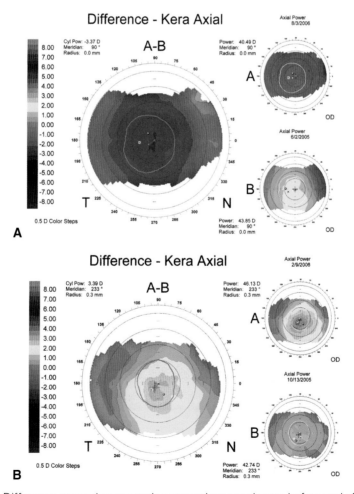

Figure 1-13 Difference maps demonstrating corneal power change before and after **(A)** myopic and **(B)** hyperopic LASIK. *(Courtesy of J. Bradley Randleman, MD.)*

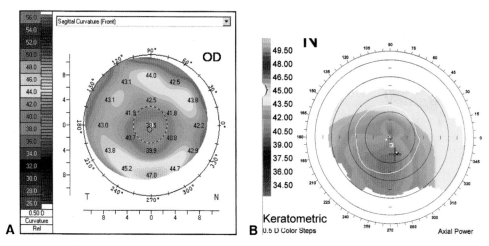

Figure 1-14 **A,** Small optical zone after excimer laser ablation; **B,** decentered ablation. *(Courtesy of J. Bradley Randleman, MD.)*

Clinical Situations Illustrating the Role of Corneal Topography in Refractive Surgery

Corneal ectatic disorders (keratoconus and pellucid marginal degeneration)

Keratoconus (KC) and pellucid marginal degeneration (PMD) are generally progressive conditions in which thinning occurs in the central, paracentral, or peripheral cornea, resulting in asymmetric corneal steepening and reduced spectacle-corrected visual acuity. These 2 conditions may be separate entities or different clinical expressions of the same ectatic process; in either case, they are currently contraindications for excimer laser surgery. (See BCSC Section 8, *External Disease and Cornea,* for further discussion.) The topographic pattern in keratoconic eyes usually demonstrates significant inferonasal or inferotemporal steepening, although severe central steepening, and even superior steepening, patterns may occur (Fig 1-15). The classic topographic pattern in PMD is inferior steepening, which is most dramatic between the 4 and 8 o'clock positions, with superior flattening. This inferior steepening often extends centrally, coming together in what has been described as a "crab-claw" shape (Fig 1-16). There may be significant overlap in the topographic patterns of KC and PMD.

It is the patient who will ultimately develop KC but shows no obvious clinical signs at the time of examination who poses the greatest difficulty in preoperative evaluation for refractive surgery. Corneal topography may reveal subtle abnormalities that should alert the surgeon to this problem. Although newer screening indices take into account a variety of topographic factors that may indicate a higher likelihood of subclinical KC, none of these indices are definitive. Inferior–superior (I–S) values are useful in screening for KC. The I–S value is derived by calculating the difference between inferior and superior corneal curvature measurements at a defined set of 5 points above and below the horizontal meridian. I–S values greater than 1.4, central corneal powers greater than 47.2 D, and skewed radial axes are all suggestive of corneal ectatic disorders; but there is some overlap between normal and abnormal eyes.

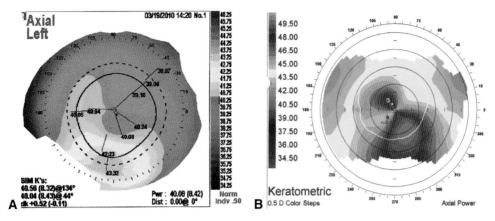

Figure 1-15 Keratoconus. Suspected case **(A)** and topography of confirmed case **(B)**. *(Courtesy of J. Bradley Randleman, MD.)*

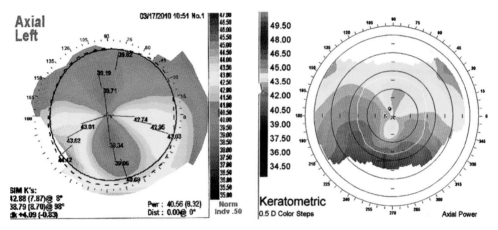

Figure 1-16 Pellucid marginal corneal degeneration. Examples of topographies. *(Courtesy of J. Bradley Randleman, MD.)*

In addition to these topographic metrics, significant displacement of the thinnest area of the cornea from the center as seen with corneal tomography is also suggestive of KC. Normal corneas are significantly thicker peripherally than centrally (by approximately 50–60 μm), and corneas that are not thicker peripherally suggest an ectatic disorder. Some clinicians utilize posterior elevation measurements to quantitate the extent of anterior bulging of the posterior corneal surface as indicative of KC.

Ambrosio R Jr, Alonso RS, Luz A, Coca Velarde LG. Corneal-thickness spatial profile and corneal-volume distribution: tomographic indices to detect keratoconus. *J Cataract Refract Surg.* 2006;32(11):1851–1859.

Lee BW, Jurkunas UV, Harissi-Dagher M, Poothullil AM, Tobaigy FM, Azar DT. Ectatic disorders associated with a claw-shaped pattern on corneal topography. *Am J Ophthalmol.* 2007;144(1):154–156.

Rabinowitz YS. Videokeratographic indices to aid in screening for keratoconus. *J Refract Surg.* 1995;11(5):371–379.

Rabinowitz YS, McDonnell PJ. Computer-assisted corneal topography in keratoconus. *Refract Corneal Surg.* 1989;5(6):400–408.

Post–penetrating keratoplasty

Corneal topography is very helpful in managing postoperative astigmatism following penetrating keratoplasty (PKP). Complex peripheral patterns may result in a refractive axis of astigmatism that is not aligned with the topographic axis. It is important to remove all the sutures in the graft prior to performing refractive surgery, as the presence of sutures may affect the refractive error. It is also important to operate on the appropriate axis in this situation; otherwise, an unexpected result may occur. The appropriate axis depends on the type of surgery (incisional surgery is performed on the steep axis; compression sutures and wedge resections are placed on the flat axis). In addition, after PKP, corneal topography may identify a component of irregular astigmatism. Conventional, wavefront-optimized, wavefront-guided, or topography-guided ablations may be considered in PKP eyes after all sutures have been removed and the refraction has stabilized, depending on the resulting refractive error and corneal shape.

Corneal Effects of Keratorefractive Surgery

All keratorefractive procedures induce refractive changes by altering corneal curvature; however, the method by which this is accomplished varies by procedure and by the refractive error being treated. Treatment of myopia requires a *flattening,* or decrease, in central corneal curvature, while treatment of hyperopia requires a *steepening,* or increase, in central corneal curvature.

Overall patient satisfaction after refractive surgery depends on the successful correction of refractive error and creation of a corneal shape that maximizes visual quality. The natural shape of the cornea is *prolate,* or steeper centrally than peripherally. In contrast, an *oblate* cornea is steeper peripherally than centrally. The natural prolate corneal shape results in an aspheric optical system, which reduces spherical aberration and therefore minimizes fluctuations in refractive error as the pupil changes size. Oblate corneas increase spherical aberrations. Common complaints in patients with significant spherical aberration include glare, halos, and decreased night vision.

Corneal refractive procedures can be performed using a variety of techniques, including incisional, tissue addition or subtraction, alloplastic material addition, collagen shrinkage, and laser ablation (the latter technique is discussed later in the chapter under Laser Biophysics).

Incisional Techniques

Incisions perpendicular to the corneal surface predictably alter its shape, depending on direction, depth, location, and number (see Chapter 4). All incisions cause a local flattening

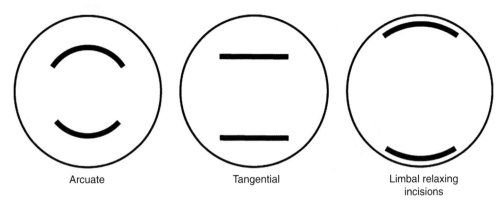

Arcuate

Tangential

Limbal relaxing incisions

Figure 1-17 Astigmatic keratotomy. Flattening is induced in the axis of the incisions (at 90° in this case) and steepening is induced 90° away from the incisions (at 180° in this case). *(Illustration by Cyndie C. H. Wooley.)*

of the cornea. Radial incisions lead to flattening in both the meridian of the incision and 90° away. Tangential (arcuate or linear) incisions (Fig 1-17) lead to flattening in the meridian of the incision and steepening in the meridian 90° away that may be equal to or less than the magnitude of the decrease in the primary meridian; this phenomenon is known as *coupling* (see Chapter 3, Fig 3-5).

The closer that radial incisions approach the visual axis (ie, the smaller the optical zone), the greater their effect; similarly, the closer that tangential incisions are placed to the visual axis, the greater the effect. The longer a radial incision, the greater its effect until approximately an 11-mm diameter is achieved, and then the effect reverses. The larger the angle severed by the tangential incision, the greater the effect.

For optimum effect, an incision should be 85%–90% deep to retain an intact posterior lamella and maximum anterior bowing of the other lamellae. Nomograms for numbers of incisions and optical zone size can be calculated based on finite element analysis, but surgical nomograms are typically generated empirically. The important variables for radial and astigmatic surgery include patient age and number, depth, and length of incisions. The same incision has greater effect in older patients than in younger patients. IOP and preoperative corneal curvature are not significant predictors of effect.

Tissue Addition or Subtraction Techniques

With the exception of laser ablation techniques (discussed later in this chapter under Laser Biophysics), lamellar procedures that alter corneal shape through tissue addition or subtraction are of historical interest only. Myopic *keratomileusis* was originated by Barraquer as "carving" of the anterior surface of the cornea. It is defined as a method of modifying the spherical or meridional surfaces of a healthy cornea by tissue subtraction. *Epikeratoplasty* (sometimes called *epikeratophakia*) adds carved donor tissue to the surface to cause hyperopic or myopic changes. *Keratophakia* requires the addition of a tissue lenticule or synthetic inlay intrastromally (see Chapter 4).

Alloplastic Material Addition Techniques

The shape of the cornea can be altered by adding alloplastic material such as hydrogel on the surface or into the corneal stroma to produce a change in the anterior shape or the refractive index of the cornea. For example, the 2 arc segments of an intrastromal corneal ring can be placed in 2 pockets of the stroma to directly alter the surface contour based on the profile of the individual rings (Fig 1-18).

Collagen Shrinkage Techniques

Alteration in corneal biomechanics can also be achieved by collagen shrinkage. Heating collagen to a critical temperature of 58°–76°C causes it to shrink, inducing changes in the corneal curvature. *Thermokeratoplasty* and *conductive keratoplasty (CK)* are avoided in the central cornea because of scarring but can be used in the midperiphery (Fig 1-19; also see Chapter 7) to cause local collagen contraction with concurrent central corneal steepening. Corneal collagen can be heated with a holmium laser (noncontact) in thermokeratoplasty (although this technique is not commonly used) or with a radiofrequency diathermy probe inserted in the cornea (contact) in CK (Refractec, Bloomington, MN).

If the temperature is too high, local necrosis will occur; and if the source of heat is not uniform or not uniformly applied, irregular astigmatism will be induced.

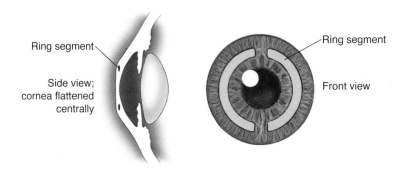

Figure 1-18 Intrastromal corneal ring segments. *(Illustration by Jeanne Koelling.)*

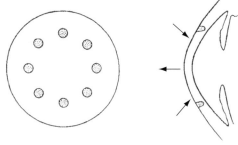

Figure 1-19 Thermokeratoplasty and conductive keratoplasty. Heat shrinks the peripheral cornea, causing central steepening.

Laser Biophysics

Laser–Tissue Interactions

Three different types of laser–tissue interactions are used in keratorefractive surgery: photoablation, photodisruption, and photothermal. *Photoablation,* the most important laser–tissue interaction in refractive surgery, breaks chemical bonds using excimer (for "excited dimer") lasers or other lasers of the appropriate wavelength. Laser energy of more than 4 eV per photon is sufficient to break carbon–nitrogen or carbon–carbon tissue bonds. Argon-fluoride (ArF) lasers are excimer lasers that use electrical energy to stimulate argon to form dimers with the caustic fluorine gas. They generate a wavelength of 193 nm with 6.4 eV per photon. The 193-nm light is in the ultraviolet C (high ultraviolet) range, approaching the wavelength of x-rays. In addition to having high energy per photon, light at this end of the electromagnetic spectrum also has very low tissue penetrance and thus is suitable for operating on the surface of tissue. This laser energy is capable of great precision, with little thermal spread in tissue; moreover, its lack of penetrance or lethality to cells makes the 193-nm laser nonmutagenic, enhancing its safety. (DNA mutagenicity occurs in the range of 250 nm.) Solid-state lasers have been designed to generate wavelengths of light near 193 nm without the need for toxic gas, but the technical difficulties in manufacturing these lasers have limited their clinical use.

The femtosecond laser is approved by the US Food and Drug Administration (FDA) for creating corneal flaps for LASIK and may also be used to create channels for intrastromal ring segments and for lamellar keratoplasty and PKP. It uses a 1053-nm infrared beam that causes *photodisruption,* a process by which tissue is transformed into plasma, and high pressure and temperature lead to rapid tissue expansion and formation of microscopic cavities within the corneal stroma. Contiguous photodisruption allows for creation of the corneal flap, channel, or keratoplasty incision.

Photothermal effects are achieved by focusing a holmium:YAG laser with a wavelength of 2.13 μm into the anterior stroma. The laser beam is absorbed by water, causing collagen shrinkage from heat. This technique is approved by the FDA for treating low hyperopia but is not commonly used today.

Fundamentals of Excimer Laser Photoablation

The amount of tissue removed centrally for myopic treatments is estimated by the Munnerlyn formula:

Ablation depth in micrometers (μm) ≈ diopters (D) of myopia
multiplied by the square of the optical zone diameter (mm), divided by 3

Clinical experience has confirmed that the effective change is independent of the initial curvature of the cornea. The Munnerlyn formula also highlights some of the problems and limitations of laser vision correction. The amount of ablation increases by the square of the optical zone; but the complications of glare, halos, and regression increase when the optical zone decreases. To reduce these side effects, the optical zone should be 6 mm or larger.

With surface ablation, the laser treatment is applied to the Bowman layer and the anterior stroma, while LASIK combines an initial lamellar incision with ablation of the cornea, typically in the stromal bed (see Chapter 5 for further details of surgical technique). The same theoretical limits for residual posterior cornea apply as with PRK. Flaps range in thickness from ultra-thin (80–100 μm) to standard (130–180 μm) flaps. The thickness and diameter of the LASIK flap depend on instrumentation, corneal diameter, corneal curvature, and corneal thickness.

Myopic treatments remove central corneal tissue, whereas hyperopic treatments steepen the cornea by removing a doughnut-shaped portion of midperipheral tissue. *Multizone keratectomies* use several concentric optical zones to generate the total refraction required. This method can provide the full correction centrally, while the tapering peripheral zones reduce symptoms and allow higher degrees of myopia to be treated. For an extreme example, 12.00 D of myopia can be treated as follows: 6.00 D are corrected with a 4.5-mm optical zone, 3.00 D with a 5.5-mm optical zone, and 3.00 D with a 6.5-mm optical zone (Fig 1-20). Thus, the total 12.00 D correction is achieved in the center using a shallower ablation depth than would be necessary for a single pass (103 μm instead of 169 μm). Hyperopic surface ablation and LASIK use a similar formula for determining the maximum ablation depth, but the ablation zone for hyperopia is much larger than the optical zone. The zone of maximal ablation coincides with the outer edge of the optical zone. A transition zone of ablated cornea is necessary to blend the edge of the optical zone with the peripheral cornea.

Care must be taken to ensure that adequate stromal tissue remains after ablation and creation of the LASIK flap to maintain an adequate corneal structure. The historical standard has been to leave a minimum of 250 μm of tissue in the stromal bed, although the exact amount of remaining tissue required to ensure biomechanical stability is not known and likely varies among individuals.

Types of Photoablating Lasers

Photoablating lasers can be divided into broad-beam lasers, scanning-slit lasers, and flying spot lasers. *Broad-beam lasers* have larger-diameter beams and slower repetition rates and rely on optics or mirrors to create a smooth and homogeneous multimode laser beam of up to approximately 7 mm in diameter. These lasers have very high energy per pulse

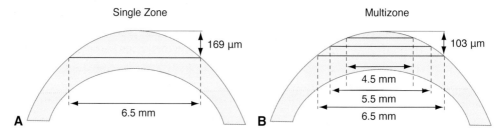

Figure 1-20 Multizone keratectomies. **A,** Depth of ablation required to correct 12 D of myopia in a single pass. **B,** Figure demonstrates how use of multiple zones reduces the ablation depth required. *(Illustration by Cyndie C. H. Wooley.)*

and require a small number of pulses to ablate the cornea. *Scanning-slit lasers* use excimer technology to generate a narrower slit beam that is scanned over the surface of the tissue to alter the photoablation profile, thus improving the smoothness of the ablated cornea and allowing for larger-diameter ablation zones. *Flying spot lasers* use smaller-diameter beams (approximately 0.5–2.0 mm) that are scanned at a higher repetition rate; they require a tracking mechanism for precise placement of the desired pattern of ablation. Broad-beam lasers and some scanning-slit lasers require a mechanical iris diaphragm or ablatable mask to create the desired shape in the cornea, while the rest of the scanning-slit lasers and the flying spot lasers use a pattern projected onto the surface to guide the ablation profile without masking. The majority of excimer lasers in clinical use today utilize some form of variable or flying spot ablation profile.

Wavefront-optimized and wavefront-guided laser ablations

Because conventional laser treatment profiles have small blend zones and create a more oblate corneal shape postoperatively, they are likely to induce some degree of higher-order aberration, especially spherical aberration and coma. These aberrations occur because the corneal curvature is relatively more angled peripherally in relation to laser pulses emanating from the central location; thus, the pulses hitting the peripheral cornea are relatively less effective than central pulses.

Wavefront-optimized laser ablation improves the postoperative corneal shape by taking the curvature of the cornea into account and increasing the number of peripheral pulses; this approach minimizes the induction of higher-order aberrations and often results in better-quality vision and fewer night vision complaints. As in conventional procedures, the patient's refraction alone is used to program the wavefront-optimized laser ablation. This technology does not directly address preexisting higher-order aberrations; however, recent studies have found that the vast majority of patients do not have significant preoperative higher-order aberrations. It also has the advantage of being quicker than wavefront-guided technology and avoids the additional expense of the aberrometer.

In *wavefront-guided laser ablation,* information obtained from a wavefront-sensing aberrometer (which quantifies the aberrations) is transferred electronically to the treatment laser to program the ablation. This is distinct from conventional excimer laser and wavefront-optimized laser treatments, in which the subjective refraction is used to program the laser ablation. The wavefront-guided laser attempts to treat both lower-order (myopia or hyperopia and/or astigmatism) and higher-order aberrations by applying complex ablation patterns to the cornea to correct the wavefront deviations. The correction of higher-order aberrations requires non–radially symmetric patterns of ablation (which are often much smaller in magnitude than ablations needed to correct defocus and astigmatism). The difference between the desired and the actual wavefront is used to generate a 3-dimensional map of the planned ablation. Accurate registration is required to ensure that the ablation treatment actually delivered to the cornea matches the intended pattern. Such registration is achieved by using marks at the limbus prior to obtaining the wavefront patterns or by iris registration, which matches reference points in the natural iris pattern to compensate for cyclotorsion and pupil centroid shift. The wavefront-guided laser then uses a pupil-tracking system, which helps to maintain centration during treatment and allows the accurate delivery of the customized ablation profile.

The results for both wavefront-optimized and wavefront-guided ablations for myopia, hyperopia, and astigmatism are excellent, with well over 90% of eyes achieving 20/40 or better uncorrected visual acuity. Although most Snellen acuity parameters are similar between conventional and customized treatments (including both wavefront-optimized and wavefront-guided treatments), the majority of recent reports demonstrate improved visual quality when customized treatment profiles are used. Outcomes with wavefront-optimized treatments are comparable to those of wavefront-guided treatments for most patients, except those who have significant preoperative higher-order aberrations.

Myrowitz EH, Chuck RS. A comparison of wavefront-optimized and wavefront-guided ablations. *Curr Opin Ophthalmol.* 2009;20(4):247–250.

Netto MV, Dupps W Jr, Wilson SE. Wavefront-guided ablation: evidence for efficacy compared to traditional ablation. *Am J Ophthalmol.* 2006;141(2):360–368.

Padmanabhan P, Mrochen M, Basuthkar S, Viswanathan D, Joseph R. Wavefront guided versus wavefront-optimized laser in situ keratomileusis: contralateral comparative study. *J Cataract Refract Surg.* 2008;34(3):389–397.

Perez-Straziota CE, Randleman JB, Stulting RD. Visual acuity and higher-order aberrations with wavefront-guided and wavefront-optimized laser in situ keratomileusis. *J Cataract Refract Surg.* 2010;36(3):437–441.

Schallhorn SC, Farjo AA, Huang D, et al; American Academy of Ophthalmology. Wavefront-guided LASIK for the correction of primary myopia and astigmatism: a report by the American Academy of Ophthalmology. *Ophthalmology.* 2008;115(7):1249–1261.

Schallhorn SC, Tanzer DJ, Kaupp SE, Brown M, Malady SE. Comparison of night driving performance after wavefront-guided and conventional LASIK for moderate myopia. *Ophthalmology.* 2009;116(4):702–709.

Stonecipher KG, Kezirian GM. Wavefront-optimized versus wavefront-guided LASIK for myopic astigmatism with the ALLEGRETTO WAVE: three-month results of a prospective FDA trial. *J Refract Surg.* 2008;24(4):S424–S430.

Corneal Wound Healing

All forms of keratorefractive surgery are exquisitely dependent on corneal wound healing to achieve the desired results. Satisfactory results require either modifying or reducing wound healing or exploiting normal wound healing for the benefit of the patient. For example, astigmatic keratotomy requires initial weakening of the cornea followed by permanent corneal healing, with replacement of the epithelial plugs with collagen and remodeling of the collagen to ensure stability and avoid long-term hyperopic drift. PRK requires the epithelium to heal quickly, with minimal stimulation of the underlying keratocytes, to avoid corneal scarring and haze. Lamellar keratoplasty requires intact epithelium and healthy endothelium early in the postoperative period to seal the flap. Later, the cornea must heal in the periphery to secure the flap in place and avoid late-term displacement while minimizing irregular astigmatism but remain devoid of significant healing centrally to maintain a clear visual axis.

Our understanding of corneal wound healing has advanced tremendously with recognition of the multiple factors involved in the cascade of events initiated by corneal wounding. The cascade is somewhat dependent on the nature of the injury. Injury to the epithelium can lead to loss of underlying keratocytes from apoptosis. The remaining keratocytes respond by generating new glycosaminoglycans and collagen, to a degree dependent on the duration of the epithelial defect and the depth of the stromal injury. Corneal haze is localized in the subepithelial anterior stroma and may last for several years after surface ablation. Clinically significant haze, however, is present only in a small percentage of eyes. The tendency toward haze formation is greater with deeper ablations, surface irregularity, and prolonged absence of the epithelium. Despite loss of the Bowman layer, normal or even enhanced numbers of hemidesmosomes and anchoring fibrils form to secure the epithelium to the stroma.

Controversy persists over the value of different agents for modulating wound healing in surface ablation. Typically, clinicians in the United States use corticosteroids in a tapering manner following surgery to reduce inflammation. Mitomycin C has been applied to the stromal bed after excimer surface ablation to attempt to decrease haze formation (see Chapter 6). It has been proposed that vitamin C may play a role in protecting the cornea from ultraviolet light damage by the excimer laser, but no randomized, prospective clinical trial has yet been performed. A number of growth factors that have been found to promote wound healing after PRK, including transforming growth factor β, may be useful in the future.

Haze formation does not seem to occur in the central flap interface following LASIK, which may be related either to lack of significant epithelial injury and consequent subcellular signaling or to maintenance of some intact surface neurons. LASIK shows very little long-term evidence of healing between the disrupted lamellae and only typical stromal healing at the peripheral wound. The lamellae are initially held in position by negative stromal pressure generated by the endothelial cells aided by an intact epithelial surface. Even years after treatment, the lamellar interface can be broken and the flap lifted, indicating that only a minimal amount of healing occurs. LASIK flaps can also be dislodged secondary to trauma many years postoperatively.

Dupps WJ Jr, Wilson SE. Biomechanics and wound healing in the cornea. *Exp Eye Res.* 2006; 83(4):709–720.

Netto MV, Mohan RR, Sinha S, Sharma A, Dupps W, Wilson SE. Stromal haze, myofibroblasts, and surface irregularity after PRK. *Exp Eye Res.* 2006;82(5):788–797.

Schmack I, Dawson DG, McCarey BE, Waring GO III, Grossniklaus HE, Edelhauser HF. Cohesive tensile strength of human LASIK wounds with histologic, ultrastructural, and clinical correlations. *J Refract Surg.* 2005;21(5):433–445.

CHAPTER 2

Patient Evaluation

A thorough preoperative patient evaluation is critically important in achieving a successful outcome following refractive surgery. It is during this encounter that the physician begins to develop an impression as to whether the patient is a good candidate for refractive surgery.

Patient History

The evaluation actually begins before the physician sees the patient. Receptionists or refractive surgical coordinators who speak with a patient prior to the visit may get a sense of the patient's goals and expectations regarding refractive surgery. If the patient is quarrelsome about the time or date of the appointment or argues about cost, the surgeon should be informed. Such a patient may be too demanding to be a good candidate for surgery.

Important parts of the preoperative evaluation include an assessment of the patient's expectations; his or her social, medical, and ocular history; manifest and cycloplegic refractions; a complete ophthalmic evaluation, including slit-lamp and fundus examinations; and ancillary testing (Table 2-1). If the patient is a good candidate for surgery, the appropriate refractive surgery procedures, benefits, and risks need to be discussed, and informed consent must be obtained.

Because accurate testing results are critical to the success of refractive surgery, the refractive surgeon must closely supervise office staff members who are performing the various tests (eg, corneal topography or pachymetry) in the preoperative evaluation. Likewise, the surgeon should make sure the instruments used in the evaluation are properly calibrated, as miscalibrated instruments can result in faulty data and poor surgical results.

Patient Expectations

One of the most crucial aspects of the entire evaluation is assessing the patient's expectations. Inappropriate patient expectations are probably the leading cause of patient dissatisfaction after refractive surgery. The results may be exactly what the surgeon expected, but if those expectations were not conveyed adequately to the patient before surgery, the patient may be quite disappointed.

The surgeon should explore expectations relating to both the refractive result (eg, uncorrected visual acuity [UCVA]) and the emotional result (eg, improved self-esteem). Patients need to understand that they should not expect refractive surgery to improve

---

Table 2-1 Important Parts of the Preoperative Refractive Surgery Evaluation

Patient expectations and motivations
Assessment of specific patient expectations
Discussion of uncorrected distance versus reading vision

History
Social history, including visual requirements of profession and hobbies, tobacco and alcohol use
Medical history, including systemic medications and diseases such as diabetes and rheumatologic diseases
Ocular history, including history of contact lens wear

Ocular examination
Uncorrected near and distance vision
Manifest refraction (pushing plus)
Monovision demonstration, if indicated
External evaluation
Pupillary evaluation
Motility
Slit-lamp examination, including IOP measurement
Corneal topography
Wavefront analysis, if indicated
Pachymetry
Cycloplegic refraction (refining sphere, not cylinder)
Dilated fundus examination

Informed consent
Discussion of findings
Discussion of medical and surgical alternatives and risks
Answering of patient questions
Having patient read informed consent document when undilated and unsedated, ideally before the day of procedure, and sign prior to surgery

---

their best-corrected visual acuity (BCVA). In addition, refractive surgery will not prevent possible future ocular problems such as cataract, glaucoma, or retinal detachment. If the patient has obviously unrealistic desires, such as a guarantee of 20/20 uncorrected visual acuity or perfect uncorrected reading *and* distance vision, even though he or she is presbyopic, the patient may need to be told that refractive surgery cannot currently fulfill his or her needs. The refractive surgeon should exclude patients with unrealistic expectations.

Social History

The social history and medical history can identify the visual requirements of the patient's profession. Certain jobs require that best vision be at a specific distance. For example, a preacher may desire that best uncorrected vision be at arm's length, so that reading can be done at the pulpit without glasses. Military personnel, firefighters, or police may have restrictions on minimal UCVA and BCVA and also on the type of refractive surgery they can have. The type of sports and recreational activities a patient prefers may help select the best refractive procedure or determine whether that patient is even a good candidate for refractive surgery. For example, a surface laser procedure may be preferable to a lamellar procedure for a patient who wrestles, boxes, or rides horses and is at high risk of ocular trauma. A highly myopic and presbyopic stamp collector or jeweler, who is used to examining objects without glasses a few inches from the eyes, may not be happy with postoperative emmetropia. Tobacco and alcohol use should be documented.

Medical History

The medical history should include systemic conditions, prior surgeries, and current and prior medications. Certain systemic conditions, such as connective tissue disorders, can lead to poor healing after refractive surgery. An immunocompromised state—for example from cancer or HIV/AIDS—may increase the risk of infection after refractive surgery (see Chapter 10). Medications that affect healing or the ability to fight infection, such as systemic corticosteroids or chemotherapeutic agents, should be specifically noted. The use of corticosteroids and some diseases, such as diabetes, increase the risk of cataract development, which could compromise the long-term postoperative visual outcome. Certain medications—for example, isotretinoin (eg, Sotret, Claravis) and amiodarone (eg, Cordarone, Pacerone)—have been traditionally thought to increase the risk of poor results with photorefractive keratectomy (PRK) and laser in situ keratomileusis (LASIK) due to a potentially increased risk of poor corneal healing; however, there is no evidence for this in the peer-reviewed literature. Previous use of isotretinoin can damage the meibomian glands and predispose to dry-eye symptoms postoperatively. In addition, caution needs to be taken with patients using sumatriptan (eg, Imitrex, Imigran) who are undergoing PRK and LASIK and with patients using hormone replacement therapy or antihistamines who are undergoing PRK because of a possible increased risk of delayed epithelial healing.

Although laser manufacturers do not recommend excimer laser surgery in patients with cardiac pacemakers and implanted defibrillators, many such patients have undergone the surgery without problems. It may be best to check with the pacemaker and defibrillator manufacturer before laser surgery. Refractive surgery is also generally contraindicated in pregnant and nursing women, because of possible changes in refraction and corneal hydration status. Many surgeons recommend waiting at least 3 months after delivery and cessation of nursing before performing the refractive surgery evaluation and procedure.

Pertinent Ocular History

The ocular history should focus on previous and current eye problems such as dry-eye symptoms, blepharitis, recurrent erosions, and retinal tears or detachments. Ocular medications should be noted. A history of previous methods of optical correction, such as glasses and contact lenses, should be taken. The stability of the current refraction is very important. Have the glasses or the contact lens prescription changed significantly in the past few years? A significant change is generally thought to be greater than 0.50 D in either sphere or cylinder over the past year. A contact lens history should be taken. Important information includes the type of lens (eg, soft, rigid gas-permeable [RGP], polymethylmethacrylate [PMMA]); the wearing schedule (eg, daily-wear disposable, daily-wear frequent replacement, overnight wear indicating number of nights worn in a row); the type of cleaning, disinfecting, and enzyming agents; and how old the lenses are. Occasionally, a patient may have been happy with contact lens wear and only need a change in lens material or wearing schedule to eliminate a recent onset of uncomfortable symptoms.

Because contact lens wear can change the shape of the cornea (corneal warpage), it is recommended that patients discontinue contact lens wear before the refractive surgery evaluation and also before the surgery. The exact amount of time the patient should be out of contact lenses has not been established. Current clinical practice typically involves discontinuing soft contact lenses for at least 3 days to 2 weeks and rigid contact lenses for at least 2–3 weeks. Some surgeons keep patients out of rigid contact lenses for 1 month for every decade of contact lens wear. Patients with irregular or unstable corneas should discontinue their contact lenses for a longer period and then be rerefracted every few weeks until the refraction and corneal topography stabilize before being considered for refractive surgery. For patients who wear RGP lenses and find glasses a significant hardship, some surgeons suggest changing to soft lenses for a period to aid stabilization and regularization of the corneal curvature.

Patient Age, Presbyopia, and Monovision

The age of a patient is very important in predicting postoperative patient satisfaction. The loss of near vision with aging should be discussed with all patients. Before age 40, emmetropic individuals generally do not require reading adds to see a near target. After this age, patients need to understand that if they are made emmetropic with refractive surgery, they will require reading glasses for near vision. They must also understand that "near vision" tasks include all tasks performed up close, such as applying makeup, shaving, or seeing the computer screen—not just reading. These points cannot be overemphasized for myopic patients who are approaching age 40. Before refractive surgery, these patients can read well with and without their glasses. Some may even read well with their contact lenses. If they are emmetropic after surgery, many will not read well without reading glasses. The patient needs to understand this phenomenon and must be willing to accept this result prior to undergoing any refractive surgery that aims for emmetropia. In patients wearing glasses, a trial with contact lenses will approximate the patient's reading ability after surgery.

A discussion of monovision (1 eye corrected for distance and the other eye for near) often fits well into the evaluation at this point. The alternative of monovision correction should be discussed with all patients in the prepresbyopic and presbyopic age groups. Many patients have successfully used monovision in contact lenses and want it after refractive surgery. Others have never tried it but would like to, and still others have no interest. If a patient has not used monovision before but is interested, the attempted surgical result should be demonstrated with glasses at near and distance. Generally, the dominant eye is corrected for distance and the nondominant eye is corrected to approximately –1.50 to –1.75 D. For most patients, such a refraction allows good uncorrected distance and near vision without intolerable anisometropia. Some surgeons prefer a "mini-monovision" procedure, where the near-vision eye is corrected to approximately –0.75 D, which allows some near vision with better distance vision and less anisometropia. The exact amount of monovision depends on the desires of the patient. Higher amounts of monovision (up to –2.50 D) can be used successfully in selected patients who want excellent postoperative near vision. However, in some patients with a higher degree of postoperative myopia, improving near vision may lead to the unwanted side effects of loss of depth perception and anisometropia. It is often advisable to have a patient try monovision with contact lenses before surgery to ensure that distance and near vision and stereovision are acceptable to him or her and also to ensure that no muscle imbalance is present, especially with higher degrees of monovision.

Although typically the nondominant eye is corrected for near, some patients prefer that the dominant eye be corrected for near. There are several methods for testing ocular dominance. One of the simplest is to have the patient point to a distant object, such as a small letter on an eye chart, and then close each eye to determine which eye he or she was using when pointing; this is the dominant eye. Another is to have a patient make an "okay sign" with one hand and look at the examiner through the opening.

Examination

Uncorrected Visual Acuity and Manifest and Cycloplegic Refraction Acuity

The refractive elements of the preoperative examination are critically important because they directly determine the amount of surgery that is performed. UCVA at distance and near should be measured. The current glasses prescription and vision with those glasses should also be measured, and a manifest refraction should be performed. The sharpest visual acuity with the least amount of minus ("pushing plus") should be the final endpoint (see BCSC Section 3, *Clinical Optics*). The duochrome test should not be used as the final endpoint because it tends to overminus patients. Document the best visual acuity obtainable, even if it is better than 20/20. An automated refraction with an autorefractor or wavefront aberrometer may be helpful in refining the manifest refraction. A cycloplegic refraction is also necessary; sufficient waiting time must be allowed between the time the patient's eyes are dilated with appropriate cycloplegic drops—tropicamide 1% or cyclopentolate 1% is generally used—and the refraction. For full cycloplegia, waiting at least 30 minutes (with tropicamide 1%) or 60 minutes (with cyclopentolate 1%) is recommended. The cycloplegic refraction should refine the sphere and not the cylinder from the manifest refraction, as it is done to neutralize accommodation. For eyes with greater than 5.00 D of refractive error, a vertex distance measurement should be performed to obtain the most accurate refraction. When the difference between the manifest and cycloplegic refractions is large (eg, >0.5 D), a postcycloplegic manifest refraction may be helpful to recheck the original. In myopic patients, such a large difference is often caused by an overminused manifest refraction. In hyperopic patients, significant latent hyperopia may be present, and in such cases the surgeon and patient need to decide exactly how much hyperopia to treat. If there is significant latent hyperopia, a pushed-plus spectacle or contact lens correction can be worn for several weeks preoperatively to reduce the postoperative adjustment from treating the true refraction.

Refractive surgeons have their own preferences on whether to program the laser using the manifest or cycloplegic refraction, based on their own individual nomogram and technique and on the patient's age. Many surgeons plan their laser input based on the manifest refraction, especially in younger patients, if that refraction has been performed with a careful pushed-plus technique.

Pupillary Examination

After the manifest refraction (but before dilating drops are administered), the external and anterior segment examinations are performed. Specific attention should be given to the pupillary examination; the pupil size should be evaluated in bright room light and dim illumination, and the surgeon should look for any afferent pupillary defect. A variety of techniques are available for measuring pupil size in dim illumination, including use of a near card with pupil sizes on the edge (with the patient fixating at distance), a light amplification pupillometer (eg, Colvard pupillometer), and an infrared pupillometer. The actual amount of light entering the eye during the dim-light measurement should closely approximate that entering the eye at night during normal nighttime activities, such as night driving; it should not necessarily be completely dark.

It is important to try to standardize pupil size measurements as much as possible. Large pupil size may be one of the risk factors for postoperative glare and halo symptoms after refractive surgery. Other risk factors for postoperative glare include higher degrees of myopia or astigmatism. As a rule, pupil size greater than the effective optical zone (usually 6–8 mm) increases the risk of glare, but large pupil size is not the only determinant of glare. When asked, patients often note that they had glare under dim-light conditions even before refractive surgery. It is important that patients become aware of their glare and halo symptoms preoperatively, as this may minimize postoperative complaints.

Measuring the low-light pupil diameter preoperatively and using that measurement to direct surgery remains controversial. Conventional wisdom suggests that the optical zone should be larger than the pupil diameter to minimize visual disturbances such as glare and halos. However, it is not clear that pupil size can be used to predict which patients are more likely to have such symptoms. It is possible that the size of the effective optical zone, which is related to the ablation profile and the level of refractive error, is more important in minimizing visual side effects than the low-light pupil diameter.

Edwards JD, Burka JM, Bower KS, Stutzman RD, Sediq DA, Rabin JC. Effect of brimonidine tartrate 0.15% on night-vision difficulty and contrast testing after refractive surgery. *J Cataract Refract Surg.* 2008;34(9):1538–1541.

Lee JH, You YS, Choe CM, Lee ES. Efficacy of brimonidine tartrate 0.2% ophthalmic solution in reducing halos after laser in situ keratomileusis. *J Cataract Refract Surg.* 2008;34(6):963–967.

Pop M, Payette Y. Risk factors for night vision complaints after LASIK for myopia. *Ophthalmology.* 2004;111(1):3–10.

Schallhorn SC, Kaupp SE, Tanzer DJ, Tidwell J, Laurent J, Bourque LB. Pupil size and quality of vision after LASIK. *Ophthalmology.* 2003;110(8):1606–1614.

Schmidt GW, Yoon M, McGwin G, Lee PP, McLeod SD. Evaluation of the relationship between ablation diameter, pupil size, and visual function with vision-specific quality-of-life measures after laser in situ keratomileusis. *Arch Ophthalmol.* 2007;125(8):1037–1042.

Ocular Motility, Confrontation Fields, and Ocular Anatomy

Ocular motility should also be evaluated. Patients with an asymptomatic tropia or phoria may develop symptoms after refractive surgery if the change in refraction causes the motility status to break down. If there is a history of strabismus (see Chapter 10) or a concern regarding ocular alignment postoperatively, a trial with contact lenses before surgery should be considered. A sensory motor evaluation can be obtained preoperatively if strabismus is an issue.

Confrontation fields should be considered, if clinically indicated.

The general anatomy of the orbits should also be assessed. Patients with small palpebral fissures and/or large brows may not be ideal candidates for LASIK or epipolis LASIK (epi-LASIK) because there may be inadequate exposure and difficulty in achieving suction with the microkeratome or laser suction ring.

Intraocular Pressure

The intraocular pressure (IOP) should be checked after the manifest refraction is done and corneal topography measurements are taken. Patients with glaucoma (see Chapter 10) should be advised that during certain refractive surgery procedures the IOP is dramatically elevated, potentially aggravating optic nerve damage. Also, topical corticosteroids are used after most refractive surgery procedures and, after a surface ablation procedure, may be used for months. Long-term topical corticosteroids may cause a marked elevation of IOP in corticosteroid responders. Laser refractive surgery procedures such as surface ablation procedures and LASIK thin the cornea and typically cause a falsely low Goldmann applanation measurement of IOP postoperatively. Patients and surgeons need to be aware of this issue, especially if the patient has glaucoma or is a glaucoma suspect.

Samuelson TW. Refractive surgery in glaucoma. *Curr Opin Ophthalmol.* 2004;15(2):112–118.

Slit-Lamp Examination

A complete slit-lamp examination of the eyelids and anterior segment should be performed. The eyelids should be checked for significant blepharitis and meibomitis, and the tear lake should be assessed for aqueous tear deficiency. The conjunctiva should be examined, specifically for conjunctival scarring, which may cause problems with microkeratome suction. The cornea should be evaluated for surface abnormalities such as decreased tear breakup time (Fig 2-1) and punctate epithelial erosions (Fig 2-2). Significant blepharitis (Fig 2-3), meibomitis, and dry-eye syndrome should be addressed before refractive surgery, as they are associated with increased postoperative discomfort and decreased vision. A careful examination for epithelial basement membrane dystrophy (Fig 2-4) is required, because its presence increases the risk of flap complications during LASIK. Patients with epithelial basement membrane dystrophy are not ideal candidates for LASIK and may be better candidates for a surface ablation procedure. Signs of keratoconus, such as corneal thinning and steepening, may also be found. Keratoconus is typically a contraindication to refractive surgery (see Chapter 5). The endothelium should be examined carefully for signs of cornea guttata and Fuchs and other dystrophies. Corneal edema is generally considered a contraindication to refractive surgery. Poor visual results have been reported in patients with cornea guttata and a family history of Fuchs dystrophy. The deposits of granular and Avellino corneal dystrophies may increase significantly in size and in number in the flap interface after LASIK, resulting in poor vision.

The anterior chamber, iris, and crystalline lens should also be examined. A shallow anterior chamber depth may be a contraindication for insertion of certain phakic

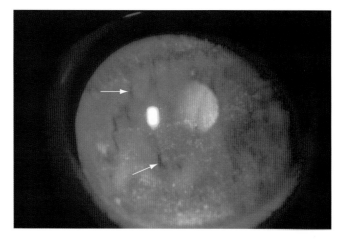

Figure 2-1 Decreased tear breakup time. After instillation of fluorescein dye, the patient keeps the eye open for 10 seconds and the tear film is examined with cobalt blue light. Breaks, or dry spots, in the tear film can be seen in this patient *(arrows)*. Punctate epithelial erosions are also present. *(Courtesy of Christopher J. Rapuano, MD.)*

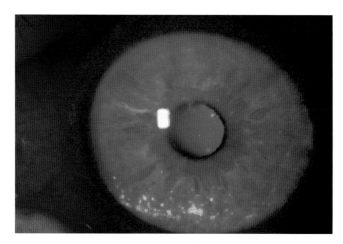

Figure 2-2 Punctate epithelial erosions. Inferior punctate fluorescein staining is noted in this patient with moderately dry eyes. *(Courtesy of Christopher J. Rapuano, MD.)*

intraocular lenses (IOLs) (see Chapter 8). Careful undilated and dilated evaluation of the crystalline lens for clarity is essential, especially in patients older than 50 years. Surgeons should be wary of progressive myopia due to nuclear sclerosis. Patients with mild lens changes that are visually insignificant should be informed of these findings and advised that the changes may become more significant in the future, independent of refractive surgery. They should also be told that IOL power calculations are not as accurate when performed after keratorefractive surgery. In patients with moderate lens opacities, cataract extraction may be the best form of refractive surgery. Patients with cataracts should be informed that if they do not undergo refractive surgery at this time, significant refractive error can be addressed at the time of future cataract surgery. Some surgeons give patients

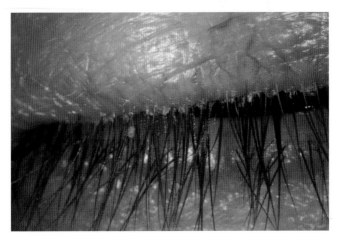

Figure 2-3 Blepharitis. Moderate crusting at the base of the lashes is found in this patient with seborrheic blepharitis. *(Courtesy of Christopher J. Rapuano, MD.)*

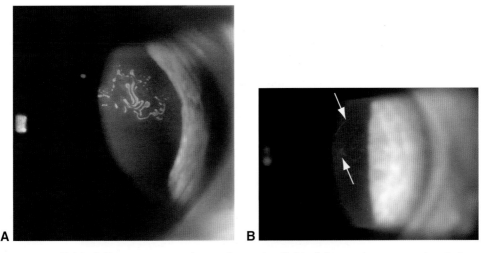

Figure 2-4 Epithelial basement membrane dystrophy. Epithelial map changes can be obvious **(A)** or more subtle **(B)**. *Arrows* show geographic map lines. *(Part A courtesy of Vincent P. deLuise, MD; part B courtesy of Christopher J. Rapuano, MD.)*

a record of their preoperative refractions and keratometry measurements along with the amount of laser ablation performed and the postoperative refraction. This information should help improve the accuracy of the IOL calculation should cataract surgery be required at a future date.

Kim TI, Kim T, Kim SW, Kim EK. Comparison of corneal deposits after LASIK and PRK in eyes with granular corneal dystrophy type II. *J Refract Surg.* 2008;24(4):392–395.

Moshirfar M, Feiz V, Feilmeier MR, Kang PC. Laser in situ keratomileusis in patients with corneal guttata and family history of Fuchs endothelial dystrophy. *J Cataract Refract Surg.* 2005;31(12):2281–2286.

Dilated Fundus Examination

A dilated fundus examination is also important prior to refractive surgery to ensure that the posterior segment is normal. Special attention should be given to the optic nerve (glaucoma, optic nerve drusen) and peripheral retina (retinal breaks, detachment). Patients and surgeons should realize that highly myopic eyes are at increased risk for retinal detachment (see Chapter 10), even after the refractive error has been corrected.

Ancillary Tests

Corneal Topography

The corneal curvature must be evaluated. Although manual keratometry readings can be quite informative, they have largely been replaced by computerized corneal topographic analyses. Several different methods are available to analyze the corneal curvature, including Placido disk, scanning-slit-beam, rotating Scheimpflug photography, high-frequency ultrasound, and ocular coherence tomography. (See also the discussion of corneal topography in Chapter 1.) These techniques image the cornea and provide color maps showing corneal power and/or elevation. The analysis gives a "simulated keratometry" reading and an overall evaluation of the corneal curvature. Eyes with visually significant irregular astigmatism are generally not good candidates for corneal refractive surgery. Curvature analysis should reveal a spherical cornea or regular astigmatism. Early keratoconus, pellucid marginal degeneration (Fig 2-5), and contact lens warpage should be considered as possible causes of visually significant irregular astigmatism. Irregular astigmatism secondary to contact lens warpage usually reverses over time, although it may take months.

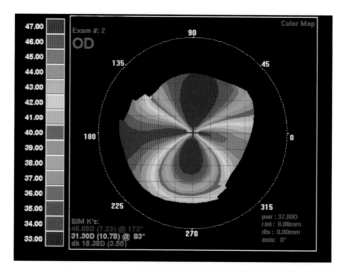

Figure 2-5 A corneal topographic map of the typical irregular against-the-rule astigmatism that is seen in eyes with pellucid marginal degeneration. Note that the steepening nasally and temporally connects inferiorly. *(Courtesy of Christopher J. Rapuano, MD.)*

Serial corneal topography should be performed to document the disappearance of visually significant irregular astigmatism prior to any refractive surgery.

Unusually steep or unusually flat corneas can increase the risk of poor flap creation with the microkeratome. Flat corneas (flatter than 40.00 D) increase the risk of small flaps and free caps, and steep corneas (steeper than 48.00 D) increase the risk of button-hole flaps. Femtosecond laser flap creation theoretically may avoid these risks. Excessive corneal flattening (flatter than approximately 34.00 D) or excessive corneal steepening (steeper than approximately 50.00 D) after refractive surgery may increase the risk of poor-quality vision. Postoperative keratometry for myopic patients is estimated by subtracting approximately 80% of the refractive correction from the average preoperative keratometry reading. For example, if the preoperative keratometry reading is 42.00 D, and 5.00 D of myopia is being corrected, an estimated postoperative keratometry reading would be 42.00 D – (0.8 × 5.00 D) = 38.00 D. Postoperative keratometry for hyperopic patients is estimated by adding 100% of the refractive correction to the average preoperative keratometry reading. For example, if the preoperative keratometry reading is 42.00 D, and 3.00 D of hyperopia is being corrected, the estimated postoperative keratometry reading would be 42.00 D + (1 × 3.00 D) = 45.00 D.

When keratometric or corneal topographic measurements reveal an amount or an axis of astigmatism significantly different from that seen at refraction, the refraction should be rechecked for accuracy. Lenticular astigmatism or posterior corneal curvature may account for the difference between refractive and keratometric/topographic astigmatism. Most surgeons will treat the amount and axis of the refractive astigmatism, as long as the patient understands that following future cataract surgery, some astigmatism may reappear (after the astigmatism contributed by the natural lens has been eliminated).

Pachymetry

Corneal thickness should be measured to determine whether the cornea is of adequate thickness for keratorefractive surgery. This procedure is usually performed with ultrasound pachymetry; however, certain non–Placido disk corneal topography systems can also be used if properly calibrated. Most newer systems can provide a map showing the relative thickness of the cornea at various locations. The accuracy of the pachymetry measurements of scanning-slit systems decreases markedly after keratorefractive surgery is performed. Because the thinnest part of the cornea is typically located centrally, a central measurement should always be performed. Unusually thin corneas may reveal early keratoconus. Some surgeons also check the midperipheral corneal thickness for inferior thinning, which may also suggest early keratoconus. Unusually thick corneas may suggest mild Fuchs dystrophy. The thickness of the cornea is an important factor in determining whether the patient is a candidate for refractive surgery and which procedure may be best. In a study of 896 eyes undergoing LASIK, the mean central corneal thickness was 550 μm ± 33 μm, with a range of 472 μm to 651 μm. It is possible that an unusually thin cornea (beyond perhaps 2 standard deviations) suggests inherent instability that would not be ideal for any refractive surgery. Consequently, even if there is adequate stromal tissue for an excimer ablation, most refractive surgeons will not consider LASIK below a certain lower limit of corneal thickness. If LASIK is performed and results in a relatively thin residual stromal bed—for example around 250 µm—future enhancement surgery that further thins the stromal bed may not be possible. If there is a question of endothelial integrity causing an abnormally thick cornea, specular microscopy may be helpful in assessing the health of the endothelium.

> Price FW Jr, Koller DL, Price MO. Central corneal pachymetry in patients undergoing laser in situ keratomileusis. *Ophthalmology*. 1999;106(11):2216–2220.

Wavefront Analysis

Wavefront analysis is a technique that can provide an objective refraction measurement (see also discussion of this topic in Chapters 1 and 5). Certain excimer lasers can use this wavefront analysis information directly to perform the ablation, a procedure called *wavefront-guided,* or *custom, ablation*. Some surgeons use wavefront analysis to document levels of preoperative higher-order aberrations. Refraction data from the wavefront analysis unit can also be used to refine the manifest refraction. If the manifest refraction and the wavefront analysis refraction are very dissimilar, the patient may not be a good candidate for wavefront treatment. Note that a custom wavefront ablation generally removes more tissue than a standard ablation in the same eye.

Calculation of Residual Stromal Bed Thickness After LASIK

A lamellar laser refractive procedure such as LASIK involves creation of a corneal flap, ablation of the stromal bed, and replacement of the flap. The strength and integrity of the cornea postoperatively depend greatly on the thickness of the residual stromal bed. Residual stromal bed thickness (RSBT) is calculated by taking the preoperative central corneal thickness and subtracting the flap thickness and the calculated laser ablation depth for the particular refraction. For example, if the central corneal thickness is 550 µm, the flap thickness is estimated to be 140 µm, and the ablation depth for the patient's refraction is 50 µm, the RSBT would be 550 µm – (140 µm + 50 µm) = 360 µm. When the surgeon calculates the RSBT, the amount of actual tissue removed should be based on the actual intended refractive correction, not on the nomogram-adjusted number entered into the laser computer. For example, if a –10.00 D myopic patient is being fully corrected, the amount of tissue removed is 128 µm for a 6.5-mm ablation zone for the VISX laser. Even if the surgeon usually takes off 15% of the refraction for a conventional ablation and enters that number into the laser computer, approximately 128 µm of tissue will be removed, not 85% of 128 µm.

Exactly how thick the residual stromal bed needs to be is unclear. However, most surgeons believe it should be at least 250 µm thick. Others want the RSBT to be greater than 50% of the original corneal thickness. If the calculation reveals an RSBT that is thinner than desired, LASIK may not be the best surgical option. In these cases, a surface ablation procedure may be a better option because no stromal flap is required; this results in a thicker residual stromal bed postoperatively.

Discussion of Findings and Informed Consent

Once the evaluation is complete, the surgeon must analyze all the information and discuss the findings with the patient. If the patient is a candidate for refractive surgery, the risks and benefits of the various medical and surgical alternatives must be discussed. (Table 2-2 provides an overview of the most common refractive surgery procedures, their typical refractive ranges, and their key limitations.) Important aspects of this discussion are the expected UCVA results for the amount of refractive error (including the need for distance and/or reading glasses, the chance of needing an enhancement, and whether maximal

Table 2-2 Limitations of the Most Common Refractive Surgery Procedures

Procedure	Typical Spherical Range	Typical Cylinder Range	Limitations
LASIK	−10.00 to +4.00 D	Up to 4.00 D	Thin corneas (thin residual stromal bed); epithelial basement membrane dystrophy; small palpebral fissures; microkeratome flap complications, especially with flat and steep corneas; preoperative severe dry-eye syndrome; certain medications; wavefront-guided ablations may have more restricted FDA-approved treatment parameters
Surface ablation	−10.00 to +4.00 D	Up to 4.00 D	Postoperative haze at high end of treatment range but range may be extended with the use of mitomycin C; preoperative severe dry-eye syndrome; certain medications
Intrastromal corneal ring segments	−1.00 to −3.00 D	None	Not FDA approved to correct cylinder; glare symptoms; white opacities at edge of ring segments; not after radial keratotomy
Intrastromal corneal ring segments	FDA approved to treat myopia in keratoconus	NA	Approved for patients 21 years or older; contact lens intolerance; corneal thickness ≥450 μm at incision site; no corneal scarring
Phakic intraocular lenses	−3.00 to −20.00 D	None	FDA approved for myopia; intraocular surgery; long-term complications such as glaucoma, iritis, cataract, pupil distortion, corneal edema
Refractive lens exchange	All ranges	Up to 3.00 D	Not FDA approved; same complications as with cataract extraction with a lens implant

surgery is being performed during the initial procedure), the risk of decreased BCVA or severe vision loss, the side effects of glare and halos or dry eyes, the change in vision quality, and the rare need to revise a corneal flap (eg, for flap displacement, significant striae, or epithelial ingrowth). The patient should understand that the laser ablation might need to be aborted if there is an incomplete, decentered, or buttonholed flap. The pros and cons of surgery on 1 eye versus both eyes on the same day should also be discussed, and patients allowed to decide which is best for them. Although the risk of bilateral infection may be higher with bilateral surgery, serial unilateral surgery may result in temporary anisometropia and is more inconvenient. Nonsurgical alternatives, such as glasses and contact lenses, should also be discussed.

If a patient is considering refractive surgery, he or she should be given the informed consent document before dilation or after dilation has worn off to take home and review. The patient should be given an opportunity to discuss any questions related to the surgery or the informed consent form with the surgeon preoperatively. The consent form should be signed before surgery and never when the patient is dilated and/or sedated. For sample informed consent forms, see Appendix 2, as well as the website of the Ophthalmic Mutual Insurance Company (OMIC; http://www.omic.com/resources/risk_man/forms.cfm).

CHAPTER 3

Incisional Corneal Surgery

Incisional surgery for myopia and hyperopia has been replaced by excimer laser procedures and intraocular lens implantation, but astigmatic keratotomy still has a role in the treatment of primary and residual astigmatism after both cataract and keratorefractive surgery (limbal relaxing incisions) and following penetrating keratoplasty (arcuate keratotomy).

The first organized examination of incisional keratotomy has been attributed to a Dutch ophthalmologist, Lans, working in the 1890s. Lans examined astigmatic changes induced in rabbits after partial-thickness corneal incisions and thermal cautery. A Japanese ophthalmologist, Sato, made significant contributions to incisional refractive surgery in the 1930s and 1940s. He observed central corneal flattening and improvement in vision after the healing of spontaneous ruptures of the Descemet membrane (hydrops) in advanced keratoconus patients, which led him to develop a technique to induce artificial ruptures of the Descemet membrane. His long-term results in humans were poor, because incisions were made posteriorly through the Descemet layer, inducing late corneal edema in 75% of patients. In the 1960s and 1970s, the Russian ophthalmologist Fyodorov, using radial incisions on the anterior cornea, established that the diameter of the central optical clear zone was inversely related to the amount of refractive correction: smaller central clear zones yield greater myopic corrections.

Incisional Correction of Myopia

Radial Keratotomy in the United States

Radial keratotomy (RK) is now largely considered an obsolete procedure, but it did play an important role in the history of refractive surgery and was the primary procedure for treating patients with −1.00 to −4.00 D of myopia. The excimer laser was originally applied to the cornea to produce more accurate RK incisions, not for surface ablation or laser in situ keratomileusis (LASIK), for which the excimer laser is now used. Radial keratotomy differs from surface ablation and LASIK in that it does not involve removal of tissue from the central cornea.

To evaluate the safety and efficacy of RK, the Prospective Evaluation of Radial Keratotomy (PERK) study was undertaken in 1982 and 1983 for patients with myopia from −2.00 to −8.75 D (mean: −3.875 D). The sole surgical variable was the diameter of the central optical clear zone (3.00, 3.50, or 4.00 mm), based on the level of preoperative myopia.

It was later found that the older the patient, the greater the effect achieved with the same surgical technique. In the PERK study, 8 radial incisions were used for all patients; repeat surgery, if necessary, involved an additional 8 incisions. Ten years after the procedure, 53% of the 435 study patients had 20/20 or better uncorrected visual acuity (UCVA) and 85% were 20/40 or better. Of the patients who had bilateral surgery, only 30% reported the use of spectacles or contact lenses for distance refractive correction at 10 years. Complications related to the procedure included loss of best-corrected visual acuity (BCVA; 3%), delayed bacterial keratitis, corneal scarring, irregular astigmatism, and epithelial erosions.

The most important finding in the 10-year PERK study was the continuing long-term instability of the procedure. A hyperopic shift of 1.00 D or greater was found in 43% of eyes between 6 months and 10 years postoperatively. There was an association between length of the incision and hyperopic shift, particularly if the incisions extended into the limbus.

> Waring GO III, Lynn MJ, McDonnell PJ; PERK Study Group. Results of the Prospective Evaluation of Radial Keratotomy (PERK) study 10 years after surgery. *Arch Ophthalmol.* 1994; 112(10):1298–1308.

Surgical technique

Radial corneal incisions sever collagen fibrils in the corneal stroma. This produced a wound gape with midperipheral bulging of the cornea, compensatory central corneal flattening, and decreased refractive power, thereby decreasing myopia (Fig 3-1).

The design of the diamond-blade knife (angle and sharpness of cutting edge, width of blade, and design of footplate) influenced both the depth and the contour of incisions (Fig 3-2). The length of the knife blade and the associated depth of the incisions were set based on the corneal thickness, which was usually measured with an ultrasonic pachymeter. The ideal depth of RK incisions was 85%–90% of the corneal thickness.

Postoperative refraction, visual acuity, and corneal topography

Radial keratotomy changed not only the curvature of the central cornea but also its overall topography, creating a multifocal cornea—flatter in the center and steeper in the periphery. The result was less correlation among refraction, central keratometry, and UCVA, presumably because the new corneal curvature created a more complex optical system. Thus, keratometric readings, which sample a limited number of points approximately 3.0 mm apart, might show amounts of astigmatism different from those detected by refraction. Similarly, UCVA might vary, particularly depending on pupil diameter: the smaller the pupil, the less the multifocal effect from postoperative corneal contour and the better the quality of vision. Also, the central corneal flattening may affect intraocular lens (IOL) power calculation for cataract surgery (discussed later in this chapter).

Stability of refraction

Most eyes were generally stable by 3 months after RK surgery. However, 2 phenomena of postoperative refractive instability—diurnal fluctuation of vision and a progressive flattening effect of surgery—have been known to persist for several years.

Diurnal fluctuation of vision could occur because the cornea was flatter upon awakening and gradually steepened during the patient's waking hours. This was thought to be due to local edema of the incisions with the eyelids closed during sleep. In a subset of

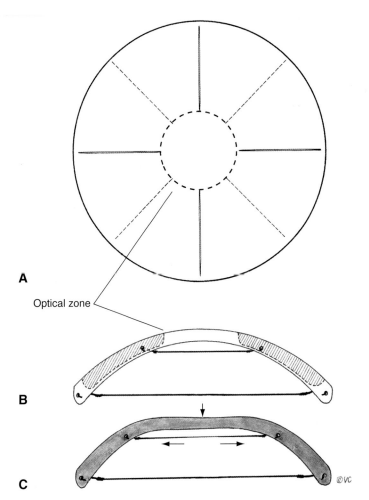

Figure 3-1 Effect of radial incisions. **A,** 8-incision radial keratotomy (RK) with circular central optical zone *(dashed line)*, which shows the limit of the inner incision length. **B,** Cross-sectional view of the cornea, showing RK incisions *(shaded areas)*. **C,** Flattening is induced in the central cornea. *(Modified from Troutman RC, Buzard KA.* Corneal Astigmatism: Etiology, Prevention, and Management. *St Louis: Mosby-Year Book; 1992.)*

the PERK study at 10 years, the mean change in the spherical equivalent of refraction between the morning (waking) and evening examinations was an increase of 0.31 ± 0.58 D in minus power.

The *progressive flattening effect of surgery* was one of the major untoward results with RK. The refractive error in 43% of eyes in the PERK study changed in the hyperopic direction by 1.00 D or more between 6 months and 10 years postoperatively. The hyperopic shift was statistically associated with decreasing diameter of the central optical clear zone.

Complications
After RK surgery, 1%–3% of eyes lost 2 or more Snellen lines. Mild to moderate irregular astigmatism can cause visual distortion and glare, especially in patients who had more

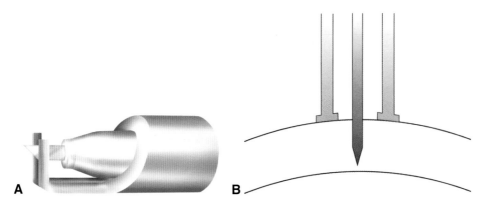

Figure 3-2 **A,** The guarded diamond knife used in RK surgery. Note the footplates and blade between them. The distance from the tip of the blade to the footplates is adjustable. **B,** Diagram of RK diamond blade with footplates that rest on the cornea, reducing the risk of penetration into the anterior chamber. *(Part A courtesy of KMI Surgical; redrawn by Cyndie C. H. Wooley.)*

than 8 incisions, incisions extending inside a 3.0-mm central clear zone, or intersecting radial and transverse incisions (Fig 3-3A, B), and in patients with hypertrophic scarring.

Many patients reported seeing a starburst pattern around lights at night after RK. This presumably resulted from light scattering off the radial incisions and/or scars. Although most patients found the starburst effect comparable to looking through dirty spectacles or contact lenses, some patients could not drive at night because of this complication. Miotic agents such as brimonidine (eg, Alphagan) or pilocarpine could temporarily reduce symptoms by shrinking the pupil, which blocked light from the peripheral cornea. Side effects that did not reduce BCVA included postoperative pain, undercorrection and overcorrection, increased astigmatism, high induced astigmatism due to epithelial plugs and wound gape (see Fig 3-3), vascularization of stromal scars, and nonprogressive endothelial disruption beneath the incisions.

Potentially blinding complications occurred only rarely after RK. These included perforation of the cornea, which can lead to endophthalmitis, epithelial downgrowth, and traumatic cataract.

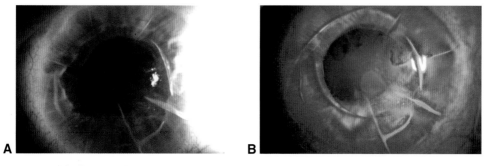

Figure 3-3 **A,** Crossed RK and arcuate keratotomy incisions with epithelial plugs in a patient who had intraoperative corneal perforation. **B,** Fluorescein demonstrates gaping of the incisions, causing persistent ocular irritation. *(Courtesy of Jayne S. Weiss, MD.)*

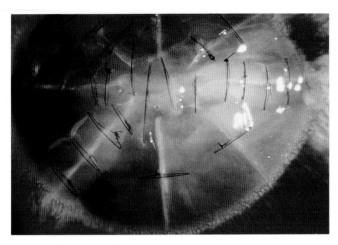

Figure 3-4 Traumatic rupture of an 8-incision RK, showing communication between 2 horizontal RK incisions. Interrupted 10-0 nylon sutures were used to close the incision. *(Reprinted with permission from* External Disease and Cornea: A Multimedia Collection. *San Francisco: American Academy of Ophthalmology; 2000.)*

RK incisions remain a point of weakness, and traumatic rupture of RK wounds has been reported up to 13 years after the procedure (Fig 3-4).

Ocular surgery after radial keratotomy

It is not uncommon for RK patients to present years later with hyperopia, which may be related to the corneal incisions, naturally occurring crystalline lens changes, or both. LASIK and surface ablation have been shown to be effective in correcting hyperopia and myopia after RK. LASIK after RK engenders an increased risk of epithelial ingrowth, which can prove very challenging to treat and which can occur when epithelium is implanted as a result of the original RK incision and extends under the flap. Creating and manipulating a LASIK flap can cause the original RK incisions to splay apart; this is even more likely when the surgeon performs a LASIK enhancement after RK by attempting to lift the original LASIK flap. Splaying of the incision can change corneal shape unpredictably. Surface ablation avoids the LASIK-related risks after RK but does increase the risk of postoperative corneal haze. The off-label use of mitomycin C 0.02% (0.2 mg/mL) applied to the cornea with a circular sponge for 2 minutes has dramatically reduced surface ablation haze after RK and other prior cornea surgeries (eg, corneal transplant and LASIK). The drug should be copiously irrigated from the eye so that toxic effects are reduced. The refractive correction is often reduced by 5%–15% when mitomycin C is used prophylactically.

Patients undergoing laser vision correction for refractive errors after RK should understand that laser correction will not remove scars caused by RK incisions, so glare or fluctuation symptoms will remain after the laser surgery. In addition, obtaining accurate wavefront analysis may not be possible due to complex optical irregularities associated with RK. Because of the progressive hyperopia that can occur with RK, it is prudent to aim for slight myopia with laser vision correction, as some patients may still progress to hyperopia in the future. Finally, because of RK-related flattening, a nomogram adjustment must be made to reduce programmed laser correction in order to minimize the chance of significant overcorrection if the laser is programmed for myopia (risk of hyperopic outcome) or hyperopia (risk of myopic outcome).

In patients with endothelial dystrophy, corneal infection, irregular astigmatism, severe visual fluctuations, or starburst effects, penetrating keratoplasty may be needed to restore visual functioning. It should be avoided if the patient's visual problems can be corrected with glasses or contact lenses. If penetrating keratoplasty is deemed necessary, the RK incisions may need to be sutured before trephination in order to minimize the chance of their opening and to allow adequate suturing of the donor corneal graft to the recipient bed.

Cataract extraction with IOL implantation may lead to variable results following RK. In the early postoperative period, corneal edema may be present that can flatten the central cornea and cause temporary hyperopia. In addition, IOL power calculation may be problematic and may result in undercorrection and hyperopia. Calculation of implant power for cataract surgery after RK should be done using a third-generation formula (eg, Haigis, Hoffer Q, Holladay 2, or SRK/T) rather than a regression formula (eg, SRK I or SRK II) and then choosing the highest resulting IOL power. Keratometric power is determined in 1 of 3 ways: direct measurement using corneal topography; application of pre-RK keratometry value minus the refractive change; or adjustment of the base curve of a plano contact lens by the overrefraction (see Chapter 11).

When approaching cataract surgery in a patient who had RK, the surgeon should carefully consider incision placement and construction. Scleral tunnel incisions are often preferred, because clear corneal incisions increase the risk of the blade transecting the RK incision, which can induce irregular astigmatism. To help reduce preoperative corneal astigmatism, the surgeon may consider placing the incision in the steep astigmatic meridian of the cornea; in addition, toric IOLs can be used. At the conclusion of cataract surgery, care should be taken to prevent overhydrating the cataract incision in order to avoid rupture of the RK incision.

Hill WE, Byrne SF. Complex axial length measurements and unusual IOL power calculations. *Focal Points: Clinical Modules for Ophthalmologists.* San Francisco: American Academy of Ophthalmology; 2004, module 9.

Joyal H, Grégoire J, Faucher A. Photorefractive keratectomy to correct hyperopic shift after radial keratotomy. *J Cataract Refract Surg.* 2003;29(8):1502–1506.

Linebarger EJ, Hardten DR, Lindstrom RL. Laser-assisted in situ keratomileusis for correction of secondary hyperopia after radial keratotomy. *Int Ophthalmol Clin.* 2000;40(3):125–132.

Salamon SA, Hjortdal JO, Ehlers N. Refractive results of radial keratotomy: a ten-year retrospective study. *Acta Ophthalmol Scand.* 2000;78(5):566–568.

Seitz B, Langenbucher A. Intraocular lens calculations status after corneal refractive surgery. *Curr Opin Ophthalmol.* 2000;11(1):35–46.

Waring GO III. Radial keratotomy for myopia. *Focal Points: Clinical Modules for Ophthalmologists.* San Francisco: American Academy of Ophthalmology; 1992, module 5.

Incisional Correction of Astigmatism

Several techniques of incisional surgery have been used to correct astigmatism, including transverse (straight) keratotomy and arcuate (curved) keratotomy (AK), in which incisions are typically placed in the cornea at the 7-mm optical zone; and limbal relaxing incisions (LRIs), which are curved at the limbus. Transverse keratotomy was frequently used in the past in combination with RK to correct myopic astigmatism, but it is seldom used today. Arcuate keratotomy was also used to correct naturally occurring astigmatism, but it is now used primarily to correct postkeratoplasty astigmatism. LRIs are used to help manage astigmatism during or after cataract surgery and IOL implantation and after refractive surgery procedures such as LASIK and photorefractive keratectomy.

Coupling

When 1 meridian is flattened from an astigmatic incision, an amount of steepening occurs in the meridian 90° away (Fig 3-5). This phenomenon is known as *coupling*. When the coupling ratio (the amount of flattening in the meridian of the incision divided by the induced steepening in the opposite meridian) is 1.0, the spherical equivalent remains unchanged. When there is a positive coupling ratio (greater than 1.0), a hyperopic shift occurs. The type of incision (arcuate vs tangential) and the length and number of parallel incisions can influence the coupling ratio. Long, straight, and tangential incisions tend to induce more positive coupling (greater than 1.0), and therefore more hyperopia, than do

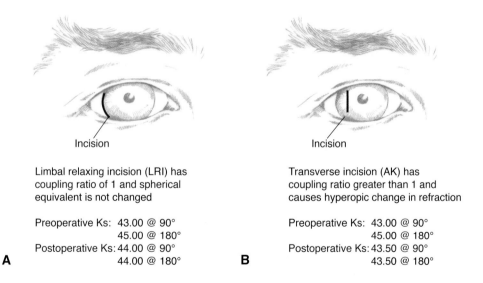

Incision   Incision

Limbal relaxing incision (LRI) has   Transverse incision (AK) has
coupling ratio of 1 and spherical   coupling ratio greater than 1 and
equivalent is not changed   causes hyperopic change in refraction

Preoperative Ks: 43.00 @ 90°   Preoperative Ks: 43.00 @ 90°
                  45.00 @ 180°   45.00 @ 180°
Postoperative Ks: 44.00 @ 90°   Postoperative Ks: 43.50 @ 90°
A   44.00 @ 180°   **B**   43.50 @ 180°

Figure 3-5 Coupling effect of astigmatic incisions. **A,** A limbal relaxing incision (LRI) has a coupling ratio of 1.0, and the spherical equivalent and average corneal power are not changed. **B,** A transverse incision has a coupling ratio greater than 1.0, which causes a hyperopic change in refraction by making the average corneal power flatter. *(Illustration by Cyndie C.H. Wooley.)*

short, arcuate incisions. When a correction is less than 2.00 D of astigmatism, coupling is typically 1.0, whereas when a correction is greater than 2.00 D of astigmatism, coupling tends to be greater than 1.0. In general, LRIs do not change the spherical equivalent.

Rowsey JJ, Fouraker BD. Corneal coupling principles. *Int Ophthalmol Clin.* 1996;36(4):29–38.

Arcuate Keratotomy and Limbal Relaxing Incisions

Arcuate keratotomy is an incisional surgical procedure in which arcuate incisions of approximately 95% depth are made in the steep meridians of the midperipheral cornea at the 7-mm optical zone. LRIs are incisions set at approximately 600 μm depth, or 50 μm less than the thinnest pachymetry at the limbus, and placed just anterior to the limbus (Fig 3-6). Arcuate keratotomy differs from LRIs by its midperipheral location and its greater relative depth. Due to the concomitant steepening of the orthogonal meridian (coupling), AK and LRIs correct astigmatism without inducing a substantial hyperopic shift of the spherical equivalent of the preoperative refraction. Increased effect in LRIs is achieved primarily by increasing the length of the incision. For AK, cylindrical correction can be increased by increasing the length or depth of the incision, using multiple incisions, or reducing the distance between the AK incisions (Table 3-1). The longer the incision, the deeper the incision, and the more central the incision, the greater the astigmatic correction.

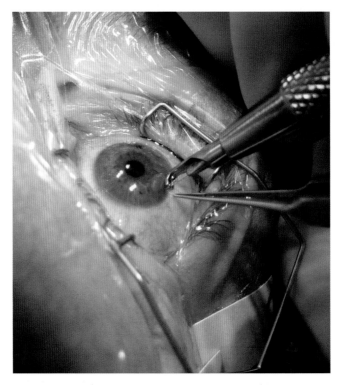

Figure 3-6 Limbal relaxing incision (LRI). A relaxing incision is made at the limbus with the use of a diamond knife. The coupling ratio is typically 1.0 and does not change the spherical equivalent. *(Courtesy of Brian S. Boxer Wachler, MD.)*

Table 3-1 Sample Nomogram for Limbal Relaxing Incisions to Correct Keratometric Astigmatism During Cataract Surgery

Preoperative Astigmatism (D)	Age (Years)	Number	Length (Degrees)
With-the-rule			
0.75–1.00	<65	2	45
	≥65	1	45
1.01–1.50	<65	2	60
	≥65	2	45 (or 1 × 60)
>1.50	<65	2	80
	≥65	2	60
Against-the-rule/oblique*			
1.00–1.25†	–	1	35
1.26–2.00	–	1	45
>2.00	–	2	45

*Combined with temporal corneal incision.
†Especially if cataract incision is not directly centered on the steep meridian.

From Wang L, Misra M, Koch DD. Peripheral corneal relaxing incisions combined with cataract surgery. *J Cataract Refract Surg.* 2003;29:712–722.

Instrumentation

The instruments used in AK and LRIs are similar. Front-cutting diamond blades are more often used in AK, and back-cutting diamond blades are more often used in LRI surgery. A mechanized trephine, the Hanna arcuate trephine, has been shown to make smooth curvilinear AK incisions of specified optical zone and arc length. Recently, the femtosecond laser has been adapted to create peripheral arcuate incisions.

Surgical Techniques

With any astigmatism correction system, accurate determination of the steep axis is essential. The plus cylinder axis of the manifest refraction is used, as this accounts for corneal and lenticular astigmatism, which are "manifest" in the refraction. If the crystalline lens is to be removed at the time of the astigmatic incisional surgery (ie, LRI), the correction should be based on the steep meridian and magnitude as measured with corneal topography or keratometry. The amount of treatment for a given degree of astigmatism can be determined from a nomogram, such as Table 3-1.

It is prudent to make horizontal reference marks using a surgical marking pen, with the patient sitting up, preferably at the slit lamp. Marking with the patient in this position avoids reference mark error due to cyclotorsion of the eyes. Studies have demonstrated that up to 15° of cyclotorsion can occur when patients move from an upright to a supine position. AK incisions may be placed in pairs along the steep meridian and, because of induced glare and aberrations, no closer than 3.5 mm from the center of the pupil. LRIs are placed in the peripheral cornea, near the limbus. They result in lower amounts of astigmatic correction than do AK incisions. AK incisions used to correct post–penetrating keratoplasty astigmatism are often made in the graft or in the graft–host junction. When AK incisions are made in the host, the effect is significantly reduced.

Outcomes

The outcome of AK and LRIs depends on several variables, including patient age; the distance separating the incision pairs; and the length, depth, and number of incisions. Few large prospective trials have been performed. The ARC-T trial of AK, which used a 7-mm optical zone and varying arc lengths, showed a reduction in astigmatism of 1.6 ± 1.1 D in patients with preoperative naturally occurring astigmatism of 2.8 ± 1.2 D. Other studies of AK have shown a final UCVA of 20/40 in 65%–80% of eyes. Overcorrections have been reported in 4%–20% of patients.

Studies of LRIs are limited, but these incisions are frequently used with seemingly good results in astigmatic patients undergoing cataract surgery. One study showed an absolute change in refractive astigmatism of 1.72 ± 0.81 D after LRIs in patients with mixed astigmatism. Astigmatism was decreased by 0.91 D, or 44%, in another series of LRIs in 22 eyes of 13 patients. Incisions in the horizontal meridian have been reported to cause approximately twice as much astigmatic correction as those in the vertical meridian (see Table 3-1).

Complications

Irregular astigmatism may occur following both AK and LRIs; however, it is more common with AK than with LRIs, probably because LRIs are farther from the corneal center, thus mitigating any effects of irregular incisions. Off-axis AK can lead to undercorrection or even worsening of preexisting astigmatism. To avoid creating an edge of cornea that swells and cannot be epithelialized, arcuate incisions and LRIs should not intersect other incisions (see Fig 3-3). Corneal infection and perforation have been reported.

Ocular Surgery After Arcuate Keratotomy and Limbal Relaxing Incisions

Arcuate keratotomy and LRIs can be combined with or done after cataract surgery, surface ablation, or LASIK surgery. Penetrating keratoplasty can be done after extensive AK, but the wounds may have to be sutured before trephination, as discussed earlier for RK. A prerequisite for combining LRIs with cataract surgery is the use of astigmatically predictable, small-incision phacoemulsification.

Bayramlar HH, Dağlioğlu MC, Borazan M. Limbal relaxing incisions for primary mixed astigmatism and mixed astigmatism after cataract surgery. *J Cataract Refract Surg.* 2003; 29(4):723–728.

Budak K, Yilmaz G, Aslan BS, Duman S. Limbal relaxing incisions in congenital astigmatism: 6 month follow-up. *J Cataract Refract Surg.* 2001;27(5):715–719.

Faktorovich EG, Maloney RK, Price FW Jr. Effect of astigmatic keratotomy on spherical equivalent: results of the Astigmatism Reduction Clinical Trial. *Am J Ophthalmol.* 1999;127(3): 260–269.

Nichamin LD. Astigmatism control. *Ophthalmol Clin North Am.* 2006;19(4):485–493.

Price FW, Grene RB, Marks RG, Gonzales JS; ARC-T Study Group. Astigmatism Reduction Clinical Trial: a multicenter prospective evaluation of the predictability of arcuate keratotomy. Evaluation of surgical nomogram predictability. *Arch Ophthalmol.* 1995;113(3):277–282.

CHAPTER 4

Onlays and Inlays

Refractive errors, including presbyopia, can be corrected by placing preformed tissue or synthetic material onto or into the cornea. This alters the optical power of the cornea by changing the shape of the anterior corneal surface or by creating a lens with a higher index of refraction than that of the corneal stroma. Tissue addition procedures, such as epikeratoplasty, have fallen out of favor because of the poor predictability of the refractive and visual results, loss of best-corrected visual acuity (BCVA), and difficulty in obtaining donor tissue. Synthetic material can be shaped to greater precision than donor tissue and can be mass-produced. Because of problems with re-epithelialization of synthetic material placed on top of the cornea, synthetic material generally has to be placed within the corneal stroma. This requires a partial or complete lamellar dissection with specialized instruments. Early work using lenticules of glass and plastic resulted in necrosis of the overlying stroma because these substances are impermeable to water, oxygen, and nutrients. Current techniques use lenticule inlays made of more permeable substances such as hydrogel, with or without microperforations in the lenticule, to increase the transmission of nutrients. Another type of inlay indirectly alters the shape of the central cornea using midperipheral corneal ring segments of polymethylmethacrylate (PMMA; Intacs [Addition Technology, Des Plaines, IL] and Ferrara rings [Ferrara Ophthalmics, Belo Horizonte, Brazil]). Because the ring segments are narrow, the overlying stroma can receive nutrients from surrounding tissue.

Keratophakia

In keratophakia, a plus-powered lens is placed intrastromally to increase the curvature of the anterior cornea for the correction of hyperopia and presbyopia. After a central lamellar keratectomy with a microkeratome or femtosecond laser, the flap is lifted, the lenticule is placed onto the host bed, and the flap is replaced and adheres without sutures. The lenticule can be prepared either from donor cornea (homoplastic) or synthetic material (alloplastic). The homoplastic lenticule is created from a donor cornea by a lamellar keratectomy after removal of the epithelium and Bowman layer. The lenticule (fresh or frozen) is then shaped into a lens with an automated lathe. The lens of tissue can be preserved fresh in refrigerated tissue-culture medium, frozen at subzero temperatures, or freeze-dried.

53

Homoplastic Corneal Inlays

Keratophakia has been used to correct aphakia and hyperopia of up to 20 D, but few studies have been published on this procedure. Troutman and colleagues reported on 32 eyes treated with homoplastic keratophakia, 29 of which also underwent cataract extraction. Even when the surgeons were more experienced, in their second series, predictability was still low: 25% of patients were more than 3 D from the intended correction. Complications included irregular lamellar resection, wound dehiscence, and postoperative corneal edema. Although the procedure was originally intended to be used in conjunction with cataract extraction for the correction of aphakia, the complexity of the procedure and the unpredictable refractive results could not compete with aphakic contact lenses or the improved technology of intraocular lens (IOL) implantation in the early 1980s. Homoplastic keratophakia is largely obsolete.

Alloplastic Corneal Inlays

Synthetic inlays offer several potential advantages over homoplastic inlays, such as the ability to be mass-produced in a wide range of sizes and powers that can be measured and verified. Synthetic material may have optical properties superior to those of tissue lenses.

For insertion of the inlay, a LASIK-type flap or stromal pocket dissection can be performed; this is technically easier than a complete lamellar keratectomy. Experiments in the early 1980s had disappointing results because of corneal opacities, nonhealing epithelial erosions, and diurnal fluctuations in vision. These results led to the incorporation of microperforations into the inlay for the transfer of fluid and nutrients to the anterior cornea. Although fenestrated polysulfone (35-μm fenestrations) showed increased safety in cat corneas, it proved to be optically unsatisfactory. Smaller fenestrations (10 μm) may preserve the optical properties of implanted polysulfone and still provide adequate nourishment to the anterior cornea.

Knowles and many subsequent investigators demonstrated the importance of the implant's fluid and nutrient permeability to the nourishment of the overlying anterior stroma. Because of their work, most succeeding studies used water-permeable hydrogel implants. Hydrogel lenses have an index of refraction similar to that of the corneal stroma, so they have little intrinsic optical power when implanted. To be effective, they must change the curvature of the anterior cornea.

Currently, 3 companies are beginning to commercialize products: AcuFocus, ReVision Optics, and Presbia, Inc. The Kamra Inlay, formerly known as the *AcuFocus Corneal Inlay* (AcuFocus Inc, Irvine, CA), is undergoing FDA clinical trials for the treatment of presbyopia. This device is composed of an ultrathin (5 μm), biocompatible polymer that is microperforated to allow improved near vision and perhaps nutrient flow. The 3.8-mm-diameter inlay has a central aperture of 1.6 mm. In the nondominant eye, a corneal flap that is 200 μm thick is created, and the inlay is placed on the stromal bed, centered on the pupil. Although the inlay has no refractive power, the goal of the device is to have the central aperture function as a pinhole to increase depth of focus and improve near vision without changing distance vision. See Chapter 12 for further discussion of corneal inlays.

Ismail MM. Correction of hyperopia with intracorneal implants. *J Cataract Refract Surg.* 2002;28(3):527–530.

Jankov M, Mrochen MC, Bueeler M, Seiler T. Experimental results of preparing laser-shaped stromal implants for laser-assisted intrastromal keratophakia in extremely complicated laser in situ keratomileusis cases. *J Refract Surg.* 2002;18(5):S639–S643.

Epikeratoplasty

To eliminate the complexity of the lamellar dissection and intraoperative lathing of early keratomileusis procedures, in which a corneal cap was dissected from the eye, shaped on a cryolathe, and then repositioned with sutures, Kaufman and Werblin developed *epikeratoplasty* (also called *epikeratophakia*) in the early 1980s. A largely obsolete procedure now, epikeratoplasty involved suturing a preformed lenticule of human donor corneal tissue directly onto the Bowman layer of the host cornea (Fig 4-1). Because no viable cells existed in the donor tissue, classic graft rejection did not occur. Epikeratoplasty was originally intended as a "living contact lens" for aphakic patients who were unable to wear contact lenses. Epikeratoplasty was later expanded to include the treatment of hyperopia, myopia, and keratoconus.

Werblin TP, Kaufman HE, Friedlander MH, Sehon KL, McDonald MB, Granet NS. A prospective study of the use of hyperopic epikeratophakia grafts for the correction of aphakia in adults. *Ophthalmology.* 1981;88(11):1137–1140.

Intrastromal Corneal Ring Segments

Background

Intrastromal corneal ring segments (ICRS; Intacs and Ferrara rings) can treat low amounts of myopia by displacing the lamellar bundles and shortening the corneal arc length. These circular arcs of PMMA are placed in the midperipheral corneal stroma in a lamellar

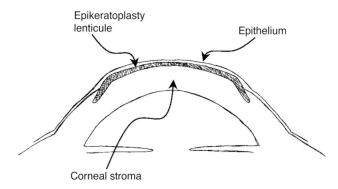

Epikeratoplasty
lenticule

Epithelium

Corneal stroma

Figure 4-1 The lenticule in epikeratoplasty is sutured onto the cornea after removal of the epithelium. The edge of the lenticule is placed into a shallow lamellar dissection and tucked under the peripheral cornea.

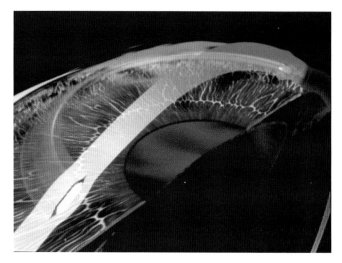

Figure 4-2 Cross section of the cornea with an intrastromal corneal ring segment. The ring segment displaces the lamellar bundles, which shortens the corneal arc length and reduces the myopia. *(Courtesy of Addition Technology.)*

channel (Figs 4-2, 4-3). The thicker the segment, the greater the flattening of the cornea and the greater the reduction in myopia. Ferrara rings have a smaller optical zone and more of a flattening effect than Intacs. This section discusses Intacs, because Ferrara rings, though commonly used in South America, are not FDA approved in the United States.

Ring segments have several potential advantages over other forms of refractive surgery. The ring segments can be explanted, making the refractive result of the procedure potentially reversible, and the ring segments can be replaced with ring segments of a different thickness to titrate the refractive result. However, the results with Intacs for the correction of myopia are not as predictable as those with LASIK.

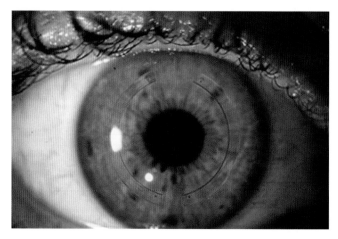

Figure 4-3 Ring segments implanted in an eye to treat low myopia. Note the vertical placement of the ring segments with a clear central zone. *(Courtesy of Steven C. Schallhorn, MD.)*

Patient Selection for Myopia

Intacs are approved by the FDA to treat low levels of myopia (−1.00 to −3.00 D spherical equivalent) and are not indicated for patients with astigmatism. However, Intacs surgery is no longer commonly performed for myopia. Additional selection criteria are for patients

- 21 years or older
- with documented stability of refraction, as demonstrated by a change of ≤0.50 D for at least 12 months prior to the preoperative examination
- with 1.00 D of astigmatism or less

Intacs are typically contraindicated in

- patients with collagen vascular, autoimmune, or immunodeficiency diseases
- pregnant or nursing women
- the presence of ocular conditions (such as recurrent corneal erosion syndrome, or corneal dystrophy) that may predispose the patient to future complications

Instrumentation

Initially, a 1-piece 330° Intacs segment was used in the procedure, but this was difficult to insert. The 1-piece segment was changed to 2 segments of 150° of arc. The segments have a fixed outer diameter of 8.10 mm and are available in numerous thicknesses: 0.210, 0.250, 0.275, 0.300, 0.325, 0.350, 0.400 and 0.450 mm. The amount of correction achieved is related to the thickness of the ring segments; the thicker ring segments are used for higher amounts of correction.

Manually operated surgical equipment or a femtosecond laser can be used to create the channels.

Technique

The ring segment procedure involves creating a lamellar channel at approximately 68%–70% stromal depth and then inserting the ring segments. The procedure usually takes 10–15 minutes per eye to complete.

The geometric center of the cornea or pupil is marked with a blunt hook. An ultra-sound pachymeter is used to measure the thickness of the cornea over the entry mark. A diamond knife is set to 68%–70% of the stromal depth and then used to create a 1.0-mm radial incision. Specially designed mechanical instruments are then used to create the channels for the Intacs segments (Fig 4-4). Similar entry incisions and channels may be created by a femtosecond laser. The channels are created in an arc pattern at a desired inner and outer diameter. Once the channels are created, by either technique, an Intacs forceps is used to insert the first ring segment, rotating it into position, and then the second. One or two 10-0 nylon sutures or tissue glue may be used to close the radial incision at the corneal surface.

Figure 4-4 The Intacs dissector tool is being rotated to create the intrastromal channel. *(Courtesy of Addition Technology.)*

Outcomes

The FDA clinical trials provided the most complete outcome analysis of Intacs for myopia. A total of 452 patients enrolled in these trials. The patients received the 0.25-, 0.30-, or 0.35-mm ring segments to correct an average preoperative mean spherical equivalent of –2.240 D, with a range of –0.750 to –4.125 D. At 12 months postoperatively, 97% of eyes had 20/40 or better uncorrected vision and 74% had achieved 20/20 or better. In addition, 69% and 92% of eyes were within ±0.50 and 1.00 D of emmetropia, respectively. These clinical outcomes were similar to early PRK and LASIK results, although excimer laser studies generally had a broader range of preoperative myopia.

The removal or exchange rate has been reported to vary between 3% and 15%. The most common reason for a ring segment exchange is residual myopia. Ring segment removal is most often performed for disabling visual symptoms such as glare, double vision, or photophobia. Few complications are associated with ring segment removal. In one series of 684 eyes that received Intacs, 46 underwent removal (6.7%). Most patients returned to their original preoperative myopia by 3 months postremoval (73% returned to within 0.50 D of preoperative mean spherical equivalent). No patient had a loss of BCVA of more than 2 lines. However, up to 15% of patients reported new or worsening symptoms after removal.

Intacs and Keratoconus

Until recently, other than penetrating and lamellar keratoplasty, very few surgical options were available for keratoconus. Excimer laser procedures, which correct ametropia by removing tissue, are generally not recommended in treating keratoconus because of the risk of exacerbating corneal structural weakening and ectasia.

In 2004, Intacs received a Humanitarian Device Exemption (HDE; see Appendix 1) from the FDA for use in reducing or eliminating myopia and astigmatism in certain patients with keratoconus, specifically those who are no longer able to achieve adequate vision with their contact lenses or spectacles. The intent is to restore functional vision and defer the need for a corneal transplant. Labeled selection criteria for patients include

- experience with a progressive deterioration in vision such that the patient can no longer achieve adequate functional vision on a daily basis with contact lenses or spectacles
- age 21 years or older
- clear central corneas
- a corneal thickness of 450 μm or greater at the proposed incision site
- corneal transplantation is the only remaining option for improving functional vision

Although these are FDA labeling parameters, many surgeons perform Intacs insertion outside these criteria. In one study of 26 keratoconus patients, the ring segments were oriented horizontally, with a thick ring (0.450 mm) in the inferior cornea and a thinner one (0.250 mm) in the superior cornea. In another study of 50 patients (74 eyes), the orientation of the ring segments was adjusted according to the refractive cylinder. Based on the level of myopia, either the 0.300-mm or the 0.350-mm ring (the largest available in the United States at that time) was placed inferiorly, and the 0.250-mm ring was placed superiorly. Patients had mild to severe keratoconus with or without scarring. A superficial channel with perforation of the Bowman layer in 1 eye was the only operative complication. A total of 6 rings were explanted for segment migration and externalization (1 ring) and foreign-body sensation (5 rings).

The visual improvement was significant. With an average follow-up of 9 months, the mean UCVA improved from approximately 20/200 (1.05 logMAR) to 20/80 (0.61 logMAR) ($P < .01$). The mean BCVA also improved, from approximately 20/50 (0.41 logMAR) to 20/32 (0.24 logMAR) ($P < .01$). Most patients still required optical correction to achieve their best-corrected vision. Eyes with corneal scarring had a similar improvement in UCVA and BCVA. Inferior steepening was reduced on topography. The dioptric power of the inferior cornea relative to the superior (I–S value) was reduced from a preoperative mean of 25.62 to 6.60 postoperatively.

One or two Intacs segments?

There are several algorithms and approaches that can help determine whether 1 or 2 Intacs segments should be used. Data indicate that when the keratoconus is peripheral (similar to pellucid marginal degeneration), not central, it may be preferable to place a single segment instead of 2 segments. The reason is that the keratoconic cornea has 2 optical areas of distortion within the pupil: a steep lower area and flat upper area. For peripheral keratoconus, instead of flattening the entire cornea, it is better to flatten the steep area and steepen the flat area. Single-segment placement can achieve that result (Fig 4-5). When a single segment is placed, it flattens the adjacent cornea but causes steepening of the cornea 180° away—the "bean bag effect" (when one sits on a bean bag, the bag flattens in one area and pops up in another area). This yields a more physiologic improvement than a global flattening effect from double segments. Intacs can also be combined

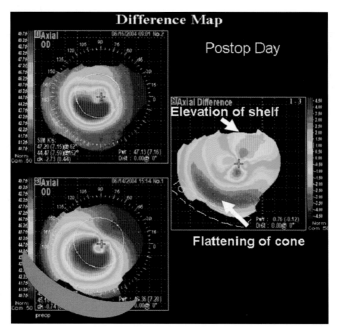

Figure 4-5 Corneal topography analysis before and after single-segment Intacs *(purple)*. The preoperative topography *(lower left)* shows oblique steepening, and the postoperative topography *(upper left)* shows contraction of a steep cone after a single-segment Intacs was placed outside the cone. The difference map (subtraction of preoperative and postoperative topography) *(at right)* shows flattening over the cone *(blue)* and steepening *(red)* in the overly flat area. *(Courtesy of Brian S. Boxer Wachler, MD.)*

with corneal collagen crosslinking to yield additional flattening and improved corneal strength. Corneal collagen crosslinking is not yet FDA approved.

Chan CC, Sharma M, Boxer Wachler BS. Effect of inferior-segment Intacs with and without C3-R on keratoconus. *J Cataract Refract Surg.* 2007;33(1):75–80.

Sharma M, Boxer Wachler BS. Comparison of single-segment and double-segment Intacs for keratoconus and post-LASIK ectasia. *Am J Ophthalmol.* 2006;141(5):891–895.

Wollensak G, Spörl E, Seiler T. Riboflavin/ultraviolet-A-induced collagen crosslinking for the treatment of keratoconus. *Am J Ophthalmol.* 2003;135(5):620–627.

Complications

The loss of BCVA (≥2 lines of vision) after Intacs insertion is approximately 1% at 1 year postoperatively. Adverse events (defined as events that, if left untreated, could be serious or result in permanent sequelae) occur in approximately 1% of patients. Reported adverse events include

- anterior chamber perforation
- microbial keratitis
- implant extrusion (Fig 4-6)
- shallow ring segment placement
- corneal thinning over Intacs (Fig 4-7)

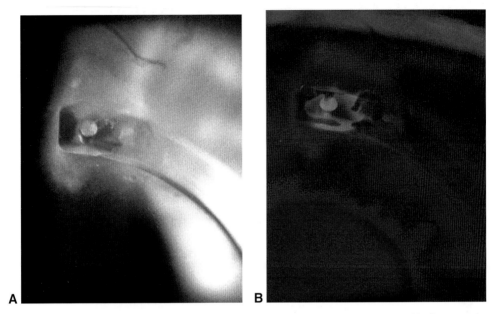

Figure 4-6 Intacs extrusion. **A,** Tip extrusion. **B,** Tip extrusion easily seen with fluorescein. *(Courtesy of Brian S. Boxer Wachler, MD.)*

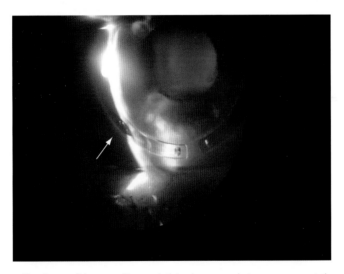

Figure 4-7 Complications of Intacs. Corneal thinning over Intacs segment *(arrow)* from non-steroidal anti-inflammatory drug abuse. *(Courtesy of Brian S. Boxer Wachler, MD.)*

Ocular complications (defined as clinically significant events that will not result in permanent sequelae) have been reported in 11% of patients at 12 months postoperatively. These include

- reduced corneal sensitivity (5.5%)
- induced astigmatism between 1 and 2 D (3.7%)

- deep neovascularization at the incision site (1.2%)
- persistent epithelial defect (0.2%)
- iritis/uveitis (0.2%)

Visual symptoms rated as always present and severe in nature have been reported in approximately 14% of patients and include

- difficulty with night vision (4.8%)
- blurred vision (2.9%)
- diplopia (1.6%)
- glare (1.3%)
- halos (1.3%)
- fluctuating distance vision (1.0%)
- fluctuating near vision (0.3%)
- photophobia (0.3%)

Fine white deposits occur frequently within the lamellar ring channels after Intacs placement (Fig 4-8). The incidence and density of the deposits increase with the thickness of the ring segment and the duration of implantation. Deposits do not seem to alter the optical performance of the ring segments or to result in corneal thinning or necrosis, although some patients are bothered by their appearance.

Intacs achieve the best results in eyes with mild to moderate keratoconus. The goals are generally to improve vision and reduce distortions and are based on degree of keratoconus. For example, a patient with mild keratoconus and best-corrected spectacle visual acuity (BCSVA) of 20/30 may have the goal of improved quality of vision in glasses or soft contact lenses. On the other hand, a contact lens–intolerant patient with more advanced keratoconus and BCSVA of 20/60 may have the goal of improved ability to wear a rigid gas-permeable contact lens. For some advanced cases of keratoconus, such as eyes with

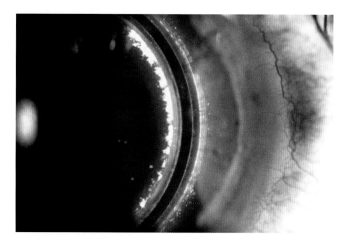

Figure 4-8 Grade 4 deposits around ring segments. The deposits can be graded on a 0 (none) to 4 (confluent) scale. These channel deposits are typically not seen until weeks or months after surgery. Although the corneal opacities may cause cosmetic complaints, they usually do not cause other ocular problems. *(Courtesy of Addition Technology.)*

keratometry values over 60.00 D, the likelihood of functional vision improvement is less compared to that for eyes with flatter keratometry values. In such cases, despite Intacs, a corneal transplant may not be avoided.

Ectasia After LASIK

Ring segments have also been used for the postoperative management of corneal ectasia after LASIK. As in the treatment of keratoconus, few surgical options are available to treat corneal ectasia. Use of the excimer laser to remove additional tissue is, in general, considered contraindicated. A lamellar graft or penetrating keratoplasty can have significant morbidity, such as irregular astigmatism, delayed visual recovery, and tissue rejection. In limited early trials using Intacs to treat post-LASIK ectasia, myopia was reduced and UCVA was improved. However, the long-term effect of such an approach for managing post-LASIK ectasia is still being evaluated. Use of Intacs for post-LASIK ectasia is off-label.

> Kymionis GD, Tsiklis NS, Pallikaris AI, et al. Long-term follow-up of Intacs for post-LASIK corneal ectasia. *Ophthalmology.* 2006;113(11):1909–1917.

Uses for Intrastromal Corneal Ring Segments After LASIK

Corneal ring segments have been used to correct residual myopia following LASIK with good initial results. In such cases, a nomogram adjustment is necessary to reduce the risk of overcorrection. This procedure may be useful in patients whose stromal bed would not support a second excimer laser ablation. Conversely, after ring segments have been removed from patients whose vision did not improve to a satisfactory level (eg, due to undercorrection or induced astigmatism), LASIK has been performed with good success. The flap is created in a plane superficial to the previous ring segment channel.

> Boxer Wachler BS, Christie JP, Chandra NS, Chou B, Korn T, Nepomuceno R. Intacs for keratoconus. *Ophthalmology.* 2003;110(5):1031–1040.
>
> Holmes-Higgin DK, Burris TE; Intacs Study Group. Corneal surface topography and associated visual performance with Intacs for myopia: phase III clinical trial results. *Ophthalmology.* 2000;107(11):2061–2071.
>
> Kymionis GD, Siganos CS, Kounis G, Astyrakakis N, Kalyvianaki MI, Pallikaris IG. Management of post-LASIK corneal ectasia with Intacs inserts: one-year results. *Arch Ophthalmol.* 2003;121(3):322–326.
>
> Rapuano CJ, Sugar A, Koch DD, et al. Intrastromal corneal ring segments for low myopia: a report by the American Academy of Ophthalmology. *Ophthalmology.* 2001;108(10):1922–1928.
>
> Siganos CS, Kymionis GD, Kartakis N, Theodorakis MA, Astyrakakis N, Pallikaris IG. Management of keratoconus with Intacs. *Am J Ophthalmol.* 2003;135(1):64–70.

Orthokeratology

Orthokeratology, or corneal refractive therapy, refers to the overnight use of rigid gas-permeable contact lenses to temporarily reduce myopia. The goal of this nonsurgical method of temporary myopia reduction is to achieve functional UCVA during the day. The contact lens is fitted at a base curve flatter than the corneal curvature. Temporary corneal flattening results from the flattening of corneal epithelium.

In 2002, the FDA approved a rigid contact lens (Paragon CRT, Paragon Vision Sciences, Mesa, AZ) for overnight orthokeratology for a temporary reduction of naturally occurring myopia of from –0.50 to –6.00 D of sphere, with up to 1.75 D of astigmatism.

Orthokeratology is most appropriate for highly motivated patients with low myopia who do not want refractive surgery but who want to be free of contact lenses and spectacles during the day. The contact lens does not treat astigmatism or hyperopia. Prospective patients should be informed that in clinical trials, approximately one-third of patients discontinued contact lens use and most patients (75%) experienced discomfort at some point during contact lens wear. Complications of orthokeratology include induced astigmatism, induced higher-order aberrations, recurrent erosions, and infectious keratitis, the most serious complication. Infectious keratitis can be bilateral and seems to be more common in children and teenagers. It may be caused by a number of pathogens, including *Pseudomonas, Acanthamoeba, Staphylococcus,* and *Nocardia.*

See BCSC Section 3, *Clinical Optics,* for further discussion of orthokeratology.

Berntsen DA, Barr JT, Mitchell GL. The effect of overnight contact lens corneal reshaping on higher-order aberrations and best-corrected visual acuity. *Optom Vis Sci.* 2005;82(6): 490–497.

Mascai MS. Corneal ulcers in two children wearing Paragon corneal refractive therapy lenses. *Eye Contact Lens.* 2005;31(1):9–11.

Saviola JF. The current FDA view on overnight orthokeratology: how we got here and where we are going. *Cornea.* 2005;24(7):770–771.

Schein OD. Microbial keratitis associated with overnight orthokeratology: what we need to know. *Cornea.* 2005;24(7):767–769.

US Food and Drug Administration. Paragon CRT. PMA P870024/S043. June 13, 2002. http://www.fda.gov/cdrh/PDF/p870024s043b.pdf.

Van Meter WS, Musch DC, Jacobs DS, et al. Safety of overnight orthokeratology for myopia: a report by the American Academy of Ophthalmology. *Ophthalmology.* 2008;115(12): 2301–2313.

Watt K, Swarbrick HA. Microbial keratitis in overnight orthokeratology: review of the first 50 cases. *Eye Contact Lens.* 2005;31(5):201–208.

CHAPTER 5

Photoablation: Techniques and Outcomes

The 193-nm argon-fluoride (ArF) excimer laser treats refractive error by ablating the anterior corneal stroma to create a new radius of curvature. Two major refractive surgical techniques use excimer laser ablation. In *surface ablation*, including photorefractive keratectomy (PRK), laser subepithelial keratomileusis (LASEK), and epipolis LASIK (epi-LASIK), the Bowman layer is exposed either by debriding the epithelium through various methods or by loosening and moving, but ultimately preserving, the epithelium. In laser in situ keratomileusis (LASIK), the excimer laser ablation is performed under a lamellar flap that is created with either a mechanical microkeratome or femtosecond laser. Currently available excimer laser ablation algorithms can be generally classified as conventional, wavefront-optimized, or wavefront-guided.

Excimer Laser

Background

The excimer laser uses a high-voltage electrical charge to transiently combine atoms of excited argon and fluorine; when the molecule, or dimer, reverts back to its separate atoms, a charged photon is emitted. The word *excimer* comes from "excited dimer." Srinivasan, an IBM engineer, was studying the far-UV (193-nm) argon-fluoride excimer laser for photoetching of computer chips. He and Trokel, an ophthalmologist, not only showed that the excimer laser could remove corneal tissue precisely with minimal adjacent corneal damage—*photoablation*—but also recognized the potential for refractive and therapeutic corneal surgery.

Photoablation occurs because the cornea has an extremely high absorption coefficient at 193 nm. A single 193-nm photon has sufficient energy to directly break carbon–carbon and carbon–nitrogen bonds that form the peptide backbone of the corneal collagen molecules. Excimer laser radiation ruptures the collagen polymer into small fragments, expelling a discrete volume and depth of corneal tissue from the surface with each pulse of the laser (Fig 5-1) without significantly damaging adjacent tissue.

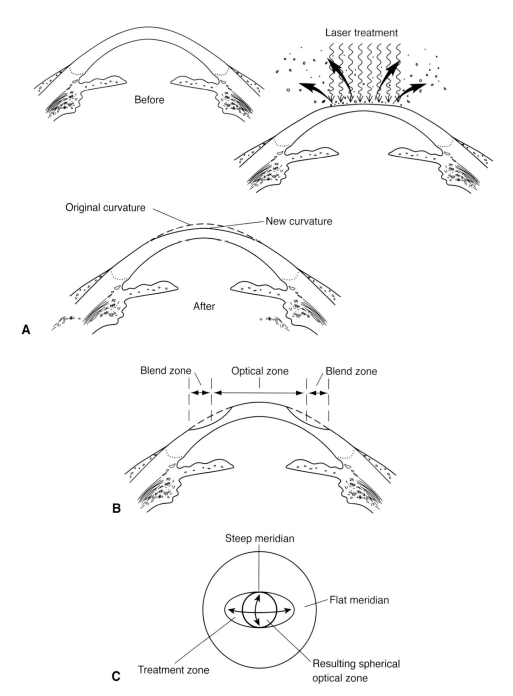

Figure 5-1 Schematic representation of corneal recontouring by the excimer laser. **A,** Correction of myopia by flattening the central cornea. **B,** Correction of hyperopia by steepening the central corneal optical zone and blending the periphery. **C,** Correction of astigmatism by differential tissue removal 90° apart. Note that in correction of myopic astigmatism, the steeper meridian with more tissue removal corresponds to the smaller dimension of the ellipse. **D,** In LASIK, a flap is reflected back, the excimer laser ablation is performed on the exposed stromal bed, and the flap is then replaced. The altered corneal contour of the bed causes the same alteration in the anterior surface of the flap. *(Illustration by Jeanne Koelling.)* *(continued)*

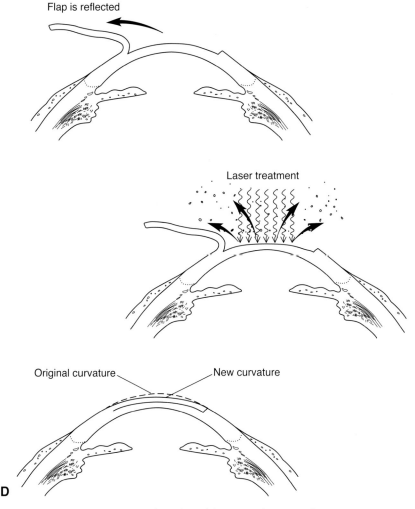

Figure 5-1 *(continued from previous page)*

Surface Ablation

PRK, the sculpting of the de-epithelialized corneal surface to alter refractive power, underwent extensive preclinical investigation before it was applied to sighted human eyes. Results of early animal studies provided evidence for relatively normal wound healing in laser-ablated corneas. McDonald and colleagues treated the first sighted human eye in 1988.

The popularity of PRK initially decreased when LASIK began to be performed in the late 1990s because of LASIK's faster visual recovery and decreased postoperative discomfort. LASIK combines 2 refractive technologies: excimer laser stromal ablation and creation of a stromal flap by a microkeratome and more recently by a femtosecond laser. Although more LASIK than surface ablation procedures are still performed, the number of surface ablations has increased. The latter technique remains an especially attractive alternative for specific indications, including irregular or thin corneas; epithelial basement membrane disease (often called *map-dot-fingerprint dystrophy*); previous corneal surgery, such as penetrating keratoplasty and radial keratotomy; and treatment of some LASIK flap complications, such as incomplete or buttonholed flaps. Surface ablation eliminates the potential for stromal flap–related complications and may have a decreased incidence of dry eye. Corneal haze, the major risk of PRK, has decreased markedly with the use of adjunctive mitomycin C; and, subsequently, the use of PRK for higher levels of myopia has increased.

Majmudar PA, Forstot SL, Dennis RF, et al. Topical mitomycin-C for subepithelial fibrosis after refractive corneal surgery. *Ophthalmology*. 2000;107(1):89–94.

Srinivasan R. Ablation of polymers and biological tissue by ultraviolet lasers. *Science*. 1986; 234(4776):559–565.

Trokel SL, Srinivasan R, Braren B. Excimer laser surgery of the cornea. *Am J Ophthalmol*. 1983;96(6):710–715.

LASIK

The term *keratomileusis* comes from the Greek words for "cornea" *(kerato)* and "to carve" *(mileusis). Laser in situ keratomileusis (LASIK),* which combines keratomileusis with excimer laser stromal ablation, is currently the most popular keratorefractive procedure because of its safety, efficacy, quick visual recovery, and minimal patient discomfort.

Barraquer first described corneal lamellar surgery for the correction of refractive error in 1949. The microkeratomes in use today employ many of the same general principles as Barraquer's original design of a manually advancing electric microkeratome for creating a corneal cap. Barraquer and colleagues initially devoted attention to reshaping and then replacing a free corneal cap. In the late 1980s, Ruiz and Rowsey introduced the concept of removing tissue from the stromal bed rather than from the free corneal cap, a concept referred to as *in situ keratomileusis*. In this technique, the microkeratome removed the corneal cap in a first pass. With a second pass of the microkeratome, a free lenticule of tissue was removed from the stromal bed. The diameter of the suction ring opening used in the second pass determined the thickness and, thus, the dioptric power of the lenticule removed. Although this technique produced less trauma to the corneal cap, the results remained suboptimal because of unpredictable refractive changes and irregular astigmatism. To improve the predictability of the microkeratome cut, Ruiz developed an automated microkeratome in the late 1980s. *Automated lamellar keratoplasty (ALK)* combined the advantages of an automated advancement of the microkeratome head with an adjustable suction ring for control of the second microkeratome cut. However, unacceptable optical aberrations often resulted from ALK because the amount of tissue removed in the second pass could not be predicted and the optical zone of the excised refractive lenticule was small.

In 1990, Pallikaris performed the first LASIK procedure when he used the excimer laser instead of the second microkeratome pass to remove tissue and induce refractive change. The excimer laser produced better optical results for 3 main reasons:

- The excimer laser ablates tissue with submicron accuracy.
- The laser does not deform the tissue during the refractive reshaping.
- Larger optical zones are achieved.

Modification in the microkeratome to stop the pass just short of creating a full free cap further improved results. With a narrow hinge of tissue, the outer corneal cap becomes a flap, which is reflected out of the way during the laser ablation. After the flap is returned to its original position, natural corneal dehydration from endothelial pump function causes it to adhere to the underlying stromal bed. The hinge allows for easier and more accurate repositioning of the flap, avoids the distortion induced by sutures, and reduces irregular astigmatism.

Wavefront-Optimized and Wavefront-Guided Ablations

Conventional excimer laser ablation treats lower-order, or spherocylindrical, aberrations such as myopia, hyperopia, and astigmatism. These lower-order aberrations constitute approximately 90% of all aberrations. Higher-order aberrations make up the remainder; such aberrations cannot be treated with spectacles. We are still learning about the visual impact of higher-order aberrations in the normal population. In fact, the small amounts found in this population may not adversely affect vision. Higher-order aberrations are also a by-product of excimer laser ablation. Some higher-order aberrations can cause symptoms, such as loss of contrast sensitivity and nighttime halos and glare, that decrease the quality of vision. The aberration most commonly associated with these visual complaints is spherical aberration. See Chapter 1 for more detailed discussion of higher-order aberrations.

In an effort to reduce preexisting aberrations and minimize the induction of new aberrations, *wavefront-guided ablation* creates ablation profiles that are customized for individual patients. In addition to addressing higher-order aberrations, wavefront-guided treatments can correct the lower-order aberrations of spherical error and astigmatism. *Wavefront-optimized lasers* have changed the ablation profile of conventional treatments by adding more prolate peripheral ablation, thereby reducing spherical aberration; however, they have no effect on other higher-order aberrations.

When compared with conventional excimer laser ablation, wavefront-guided ablations and wavefront-optimized ablations appear to offer better contrast sensitivity and induce fewer postoperative higher-order aberrations. However, although advances in aberrometry and registration systems have led to improved outcomes, patients who undergo photoablation may still have more higher-order aberrations postoperatively than they did preoperatively.

Wavefront-guided ablation is not suitable for all patients and may not be appropriate for use after cataract surgery, particularly with multifocal IOLs. In addition, wavefront data may be impossible to obtain in very irregular corneas or in eyes with small pupils. In the future, patients with very irregular corneas that cannot be treated with wavefront technology may be treated with topography-based ablations. In general, wavefront-guided ablations remove more tissue than conventional ablations.

Nuijts RM, Nabar VA, Hament WJ, Eggink FA. Wavefront-guided versus standard laser in situ keratomileusis to correct low to moderate myopia. *J Cataract Refract Surg.* 2002;28(11): 1907–1913.

Patient Selection for Photoablation

The preoperative evaluation of patients considering refractive surgery is presented in detail in Chapter 2. Table 5-1 reviews potential contraindications to photoablation.

Special Considerations for Surface Ablation

In general, any condition that significantly delays epithelial healing is a relative contraindication to surface ablation. Although keloid scar formation was listed as a contraindication to PRK in the FDA trials, 1 study found that African Americans with a history of keloid formation did well after PRK; and keloid formation is no longer considered a contraindication to surface ablation or LASIK. PRK may be contraindicated in patients actively taking isotretinoin when they have ocular surface disease or amiodarone hydrochloride, which may affect corneal wound healing.

Patients with epithelial basement membrane dystrophy (EBMD) are better candidates for surface ablation than for LASIK because surface ablation may be therapeutic, reducing epithelial irregularity and improving postoperative quality of vision while enhancing epithelial adhesion. In contrast, LASIK may cause a frank epithelial defect in eyes with EBMD. If the surgeon is in doubt as to which procedure to use, he or she can perform a simple test for EBMD after the patient has received topical anesthesia by gently rubbing a moistened cotton-tipped applicator over the corneal surface. If there is epithelial movement over the stroma, surface ablation is usually preferred.

Any patient undergoing excimer laser photoablation should have a pachymetric and topographic evaluation (see Chapter 2). Younger patients and patients with thin corneas,

---

Table 5-1 Potential Contraindications to Excimer Laser Photoablation

Connective tissue disease
  Rheumatoid arthritis
  Systemic lupus erythematosus
  Sjögren syndrome
  Wegener granulomatosis
Dry-eye syndrome
Neurotrophic corneas
Previous herpes simplex
Previous herpes zoster ophthalmicus
Fuchs corneal dystrophy
Corneal stromal dystrophies
Corneal ectatic disorders
Medications
  Isotretinoin
  Amiodarone hydrochloride (eg, Cordarone, Pacerone)
Uncontrolled systemic diabetes
Diabetic retinopathy
Thyroid eye disease
Monocular patients
Patients who are pregnant or nursing
Patients with unreasonable expectations
Patients younger than 18–21 years

low predicted residual stromal bed thickness, or irregular topography may be at increased risk for the development of ectasia with LASIK. These patients may be better candidates for surface ablation. Patients with topographic pattern abnormalities who are stable may be offered surface ablation but with a clear acknowledgment, as well as a signed informed consent form, that they understand there may still be a risk of progression to corneal ectasia or keratoconus.

Special Considerations for LASIK

The preoperative evaluation of patients prior to LASIK is similar to that for surface ablation. A narrow palpebral fissure and a prominent brow with deep-set globes both increase the difficulty of creating a successful corneal flap, and the presence of either may lead a surgeon to consider surface ablation over LASIK.

Many reports indicate that postoperative dry eye due to corneal denervation is more common with LASIK than with surface ablation. This is important to remember when considering refractive surgery in a patient with known dry-eye syndrome.

When evaluating the cornea prior to LASIK, it is particularly important that the surgeon look for signs of EBMD that could predispose the patient to epithelial defects with the microkeratome pass, as well as to postoperative epithelial ingrowth. Fewer epithelial defects may occur with a femtosecond laser flap than with a microkeratome; however, patients with EBMD are usually best served by having surface ablation, if their refractive error permits.

Corneal topography must be performed to assess corneal cylinder and rule out the presence of forme fruste keratoconus, pellucid marginal degeneration, or contact lens–induced corneal warpage. Corneas steeper than 48.00 D are more likely to have thin flaps or frank buttonholes (central perforation of the flap) with mechanical microkeratomes. Corneas flatter than 40.00 D are more likely to have smaller-diameter flaps and are at increased risk for creation of a free cap due to transection of the hinge with mechanical microkeratomes. These problems may be reduced by using a smaller or larger suction ring, which changes the flap diameter; modifying the hinge length; slowing passage of the microkeratome to create a thicker flap or using a microkeratome head designed to create thicker flaps; applying higher suction levels and creating a higher IOP; or selecting a femtosecond laser to create the lamellar flap. If a patient is having both eyes treated in a single session, the surgeon must be aware that using the same blade to create the flap in the second eye typically results in a flap that is often 10–20 µm thinner than the flap in the first eye.

Preoperative pachymetric measurement of corneal thickness is mandatory because an adequate stromal bed must remain to decrease the possibility of postoperative corneal ectasia, although the definition of what constitutes an adequate residual stromal bed remains controversial. The following formula is used to calculate residual stromal bed thickness (RSBT):

Central corneal thickness – thickness of flap – depth of ablation = RSBT

In calculating the likely RSBT, the surgeon must use the ablation depth based on the intended total correction, not the value of the nomogram-adjusted refractive error that is programmed into the laser. The true tissue ablation depth is closer to the value needed to achieve the refractive shift. A nomogram adjustment to a lower refractive error that is programmed into the laser does not mean that less tissue is removed.

Although most practitioners use a minimum RSBT of 250 μm as a guideline, this figure is clinically derived rather than based on any definitive laboratory investigations or controlled prospective studies. A thicker stromal bed after ablation does not guarantee that postoperative corneal ectasia will not develop. In a retrospective study of 10 eyes from 7 patients who developed corneal ectasia after LASIK, 30% had a predicted RSBT of ≥250 μm. In this series, 88% of patients had previously undiagnosed forme fruste keratoconus. Moreover, the actual LASIK flap may be thicker than that noted on the label of the microkeratome head, making the stromal bed thinner than the calculated minimum of 250 μm. Consequently, an increasing number of surgeons are using intraoperative pachymetry, especially for high myopic corrections, enhancements, or thin corneas, to determine actual flap thickness.

Although many practitioners do not routinely measure intraoperative pachymetry and instead use an estimated flap thickness based on plate markings, the most accurate method for determining flap thickness and RSBT is to measure the central corneal thickness at the beginning of the procedure, create the LASIK flap with the surgeon's instrument of choice, lift the flap, measure the untreated stromal bed, and subtract the intended thickness of corneal ablation from the stromal bed to ascertain whether the RSBT will be ≥250 μm or whatever safe threshold is desired. Flap thickness is then calculated by subtracting the untreated stromal bed measurement from the initial central corneal thickness.

The surgeon should preoperatively inform patients with thinner corneas or higher corrections that future LASIK enhancement may not be possible because of inadequate RSBT. These patients may be better candidates for surface ablation enhancements if needed.

Many ophthalmologists believe that excessive corneal flattening or steepening after LASIK may reduce visual quality and increase aberrations. Although no controlled studies have established specific limits, many surgeons avoid creating a postoperative corneal power less than approximately 34.00 D or more than approximately 50.00 D. The surgeon can predict the postoperative keratometry by estimating a flattening of 0.80 D for every diopter of myopia treated and a steepening of 1.00 D for every diopter of hyperopia treated (see Chapter 2).

If wavefront-guided laser ablation is planned, wavefront error is measured preoperatively, as discussed in Chapter 1. Although wavefront data are used to program the laser, the surgeon must still compare these data to the manifest refraction prior to surgery to prevent data input errors. In general, one needs to be wary of significant differences between the manifest refraction and the wavefront refraction.

Binder PS, Lindstrom RL, Stulting RD, et al. Keratoconus and corneal ectasia after LASIK. *J Cataract Refract Surg.* 2005;31(11):2035–2038.

Flanagan G, Binder PS. Estimating residual stromal thickness before and after laser in situ keratomileusis. *J Cataract Refract Surg.* 2003;29(9):1674–1683.

Randleman JB, Russell B, Ward MA, Thompson KP, Stulting RD. Risk factors and prognosis for corneal ectasia after LASIK. *Ophthalmology.* 2003;110(2):267–275.

Randleman JB, Woodward M, Lynn MJ, Stulting RD. Risk assessment for ectasia after corneal refractive surgery. *Ophthalmology.* 2008;115(1):37–50.

Salib GM, McDonald MB, Smolek M. Safety and efficacy of cyclosporine 0.05% drops versus unpreserved artificial tears in dry-eye patients having laser in situ keratomileusis. *J Cataract Refract Surg.* 2006;32(5):772–778.

Schallhorn SC, Kaupp SE, Tanzer DJ, Tidwell J, Laurent J, Bourque LB. Pupil size and quality of vision after LASIK. *Ophthalmology.* 2003;110(8):1606–1614.

Smith RJ, Maloney RK. Laser in situ keratomileusis in patients with autoimmune diseases. *J Cataract Refract Surg.* 2006;32(8):1292–1295.

Surgical Technique for Photoablation

Many of the steps in keratorefractive surgery are identical for surface ablation and LASIK. These include laser calibration and programming and patient preparation. The major difference between surface ablation and LASIK is preparation for ablation by exposure of the Bowman layer for surface ablation and the midstroma for LASIK. A list of FDA-approved lasers for refractive surgery can be found on the FDA website (http://www.fda.gov/MedicalDevices/ProductsandMedicalProcedures/SurgeryandLifeSupport/LASIK/ucm168641.htm).

Calibration of the Excimer Laser

The laser should be checked daily and between patients by a technician for proper homogeneous beam profile, alignment, and power output, according to the instructions of the manufacturer. The surgeon is also responsible for ensuring that the laser is functioning correctly before treating patients each day.

Preoperative Planning and Laser Programming

An important part of preoperative planning is programming the laser with the appropriate refraction. Often, the patient's manifest and cycloplegic refractions differ, or the amount and axis of astigmatism differ between the topographic evaluation and refractive examination. Thus, it may be unclear which refractive data to enter into the laser. The surgeon's decision about whether to use the manifest or the cycloplegic refraction is based on his or her individual nomogram and technique. The manifest refraction is more accurate than the cycloplegic refraction in determining cylinder axis and amount. If the refractive cylinder is confirmed to differ from the topographic cylinder, lenticular astigmatism or posterior corneal curvature is assumed to be the cause. In this case, the laser is still programmed with the axis and amount of cylinder noted on refraction. The surgeon should take particular care to check the axis on the refraction and topography with the value programmed into the laser because entering an incorrect value is a potential source of error, particularly when converting between plus and minus cylinder formats. Prior to all surgery, the surgeon and the technician should go over a checklist of information, confirming the patient's name, the refraction, and the eye on which surgery is to be performed.

In wavefront procedures, the treatment should correspond to the patient's refraction, and adjustments may be required to compensate for accommodation.

In many laser models, the surgeon also must enter the size of the optical zone and indicate whether a blend of the ablation zone should be performed. The *blend zone* is an area of peripheral asphericity designed to reduce the possible undesirable effects of an abrupt transition from the optical zone to the untreated cornea (see Fig 5-1B). A prolate blend zone reduces glare and halo following excimer laser photoablation.

Special considerations for wavefront-guided techniques

Wavefront mapping systems are unique to the specific wavefront-guided laser used. FDA-approved wavefront-guided excimer lasers include the Alcon CustomCornea, the VISX IR WaveScan, the Bausch & Lomb Zyoptix, and the WaveLight Allegretto WAVE systems. Calibration should be performed according to the manufacturer's specifications.

For wavefront-guided ablations, the wavefront maps are taken with the patient sitting up at an aberrometer under scotopic conditions and then applied to the cornea in the laser suite with the patient lying down under an operating microscope. Some systems require pupillary dilation to capture wavefront data, whereas others do not. The wavefront refraction indicated on wavefront analysis is then compared with the manifest refraction, and the difference should be no more than 0.75 D; if the difference exceeds 0.75 D, both the manifest refraction and the wavefront analysis may need to be repeated. The data are either electronically transferred to the laser or downloaded to a disk and then transferred to the laser. Unlike conventional or wavefront-optimized excimer laser treatment, where the manifest or cycloplegic refraction is used to program the laser, the wavefront-guided laser treatment uses programmed wavefront data to create a custom ablation pattern.

Preoperative Preparation of the Patient

Many surgeons use topical antibiotic prophylaxis preoperatively. The patient's skin is prepped with 5%–10% povidone-iodine or alcohol wipes before or after entering the laser suite, and 5% povidone-iodine solution is sometimes applied as drops to the ocular surface and then irrigated out for further antisepsis. There is no consensus about the utility of these measures. In addition, prior to laser treatment, patients should be instructed regarding the sounds and smells they will encounter during the laser treatment. They may receive an oral antianxiety medication such as diazepam.

If a large amount of astigmatism is being treated, some surgeons elect to mark the cornea at the horizontal or vertical axis while the patient is sitting up to ensure accurate alignment under the laser. This is done to compensate for the cyclotorsion that commonly occurs when the patient goes from a sitting to a lying position. A 15° offset in the axis of treatment can decrease the effective cylinder change by 35% and can result in a significant axis shift.

After the patient is positioned under the laser, a sterile drape may be placed over the skin and eyelashes according to the surgeon's preference. Topical anesthetic drops are placed in the eye; care should be taken to ensure that the drops are not instilled too early, as doing so may loosen the epithelium substantially. An eyelid speculum is placed in the operative eye and an opaque patch is placed over the fellow eye to avoid cross-fixation. A gauze pad may be taped over the temple between the operative eye and the ear to absorb any excess fluid. The patient is asked to fixate on the laser centration light while the surgeon reduces ambient illumination from the microscope, focuses on the cornea, and centers the laser. It is important for the plane of the eye to remain parallel to the plane of the laser, for the patient to maintain fixation, and for the surgeon to control centration even when using lasers with tracking systems. For most patients, voluntary fixation during photoablation produces more accurate centration than globe immobilization by the surgeon.

Preparation of the Bowman Layer or Stromal Bed for Excimer Ablation

The next surgical step for all excimer photoablation procedures is preparation of the cornea for ablation. With surface ablation procedures, such preparation consists of epithelial removal to expose the Bowman layer, while with LASIK, it involves the creation of a lamellar flap with either a mechanical microkeratome or a femtosecond laser to expose the central stroma.

Epithelial debridement techniques for surface ablation

The epithelium can be removed by (Fig 5-2)

- a sharp blade
- a blunt spatula
- a rotary corneal brush
- application of 20% absolute alcohol to the corneal surface for 20–45 seconds to loosen the epithelium
- a mechanical microkeratome with an epi-LASIK blade
- transepithelial ablation from the excimer laser itself

With both transepithelial ablation and epi-LASIK, the peripheral margin of the de-epithelialization is defined by the laser or epi-keratome itself. For other epithelial debridement techniques, the surgeon often defines the outer limit of de-epithelialization with an optical zone marker and then debrides from the periphery toward the center. An ophthalmic surgical cellulose sponge can be uniformly brushed over the surface of the cornea to remove any residual epithelium and provide a smooth surface. The epithelium should be removed efficiently and consistently to prevent hydration changes in the stroma, because excessive corneal stromal dehydration may increase the rate of excimer laser ablation and lead to overcorrection. The laser treatment zone must be free of epithelial cells, debris, and excess fluid before ablation.

Epithelial preservation techniques

LASEK In the LASEK variant of surface ablation, the goal is to preserve the patient's epithelium. Instead of debriding and discarding the epithelium or ablating the epithelium with the excimer laser, the surgeon loosens the epithelium with 20% alcohol for 20 seconds and folds back an intact sheet of epithelium.

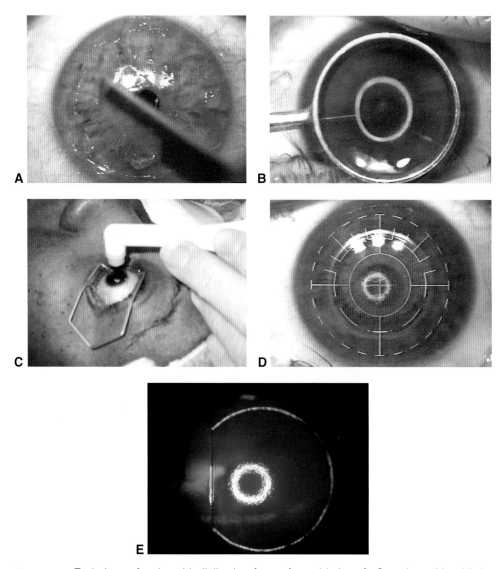

Figure 5-2 Techniques for de-epithelialization for surface ablation. **A,** Scraping with a blade. **B,** 20% dilution of absolute ethanol in an optical zone marker well. **C,** Rotary brush debridement. **D,** "Laser scrape," where a broad-beam laser exposes the entire treatment zone to ablation pulses that remove most of the epithelium that is fluorescing brightly, after which the basal epithelial layer is removed by scraping with a blade. **E,** Epi-LASIK with a mechanical microkeratome (the epithelial flap may be removed or retained). *(Parts A, B, and D courtesy of Roger F. Steinert, MD; part C courtesy of Steven C. Schallhorn, MD; part E courtesy of Eric D. Donnenfeld, MD.)*

Epi-LASIK Epi-LASIK, another technique that preserves the epithelium, has largely supplanted LASEK because there is no alcohol damage to the epithelium. In epi-LASIK, an epithelial flap is fashioned with a microkeratome fitted with a modified dull blade and a thin applanation plate that mechanically separates the epithelium. In this manner, epi-LASIK preserves more viable epithelial cells, may improve results compared with LASEK, and creates an epithelial flap that ideally will successfully adhere postoperatively. However, as the epithelial flap often does not adhere successfully, many surgeons use the epi-LASIK microkeratome to rapidly create a smooth corneal bed with regular epithelial borders and then discard the epithelial flap.

Although the goal of LASEK and epi-LASIK is to reduce postoperative pain, speed the recovery of visual acuity, and decrease postoperative haze formation compared to PRK, controlled studies have had mixed results. In addition, the epithelial flap may not remain viable but may slough off, actually delaying healing and visual recovery. To date, epi-LASIK and LASEK have not been proven to be advantageous over PRK in reducing corneal haze.

Ambrosio R Jr, Wilson S. LASIK vs LASEK vs PRK: advantages and indications. *Semin Ophthalmol.* 2003;18(1):2–10.

Matsumoto JC, Chu YS. Epi-LASIK update: overview of techniques and patient management. *Int Ophthalmol Clin.* 2006;46(3):105–115.

Flap creation for LASIK

Lamellar flap creation can be performed using either a mechanical microkeratome or a femtosecond laser. Many surgeons make asymmetric sterile ink marks in the corneal periphery, away from the intended flap hinge, just before placement of the suction ring. These marks can aid in alignment of the flap at the end of surgery and in proper orientation in the rare event of a free cap.

Microkeratome   The basic principles of the microkeratome and the role of the suction ring and cutting head are illustrated in Figure 5-3. The suction ring has 2 functions: to adhere to the globe, providing a stable platform for the microkeratome cutting head; and to raise the IOP to a high level, which stabilizes the cornea.

The dimensions of the suction ring determine the diameter of the flap and the size of the stabilizing hinge. The thicker the vertical dimension of the suction ring and the smaller the diameter of the ring opening, the less the cornea will protrude, and hence a smaller-diameter flap will be produced. The suction ring is connected to a vacuum pump, which typically is controlled by an on–off foot pedal.

The microkeratome cutting head has several key components. The highly sharpened disposable cutting blade is discarded after each patient, either after a single eye or after bilateral treatment. The applanation head, or plate, flattens the cornea in advance of the cutting blade. The length of the blade that extends beyond the applanation plate and the clearance between the blade and the applanation surface are the principal determinants of flap thickness. The motor, either electrical or gas-driven turbine, oscillates the blade rapidly, typically between 6000 and 15,000 cycles per minute. The same motor or a second motor is used to mechanically advance the cutting head, which is attached to the suction ring, across the cornea, although in some models the surgeon manually controls the advance of the cutting head. Smaller and thinner flap size and longer hinge cord length may be more important than hinge location in sparing the nerves and reducing the incidence and severity of dry eyes. Regardless of hinge type, patients generally recover corneal sensation to preoperative levels within 6–12 months after surgery.

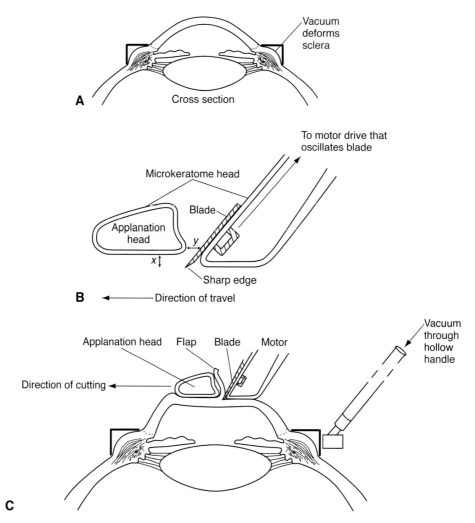

Figure 5-3 Schematic representation of the principles of a microkeratome. **A,** The suction ring serves as a platform for the microkeratome head, gripping the conjunctiva and sclera adjacent to the limbus. **B,** Simplified cross-section schematic of a typical microkeratome head. **C,** Creation of the flap. When the microkeratome head passes across the cornea, the applanating surface of the head flattens the cornea in advance of the blade. *(Illustration by Jeanne Koelling.)*

Once the ring is properly positioned, suction is activated (Fig 5-4). The IOP should be assessed at this point because low IOP can result in a poor-quality, thin, or incomplete flap. It is essential to have both excellent exposure of the eye, allowing free movement of the microkeratome, and proper suction ring fixation. Inadequate suction may result from blockage of the suction ports from eyelashes under the suction ring or from redundant or scarred conjunctiva. To avoid the possibility of pseudosuction (occlusion of the suction port with conjunctiva but not sclera), the surgeon can confirm the presence of true suction by observing that the eye moves when the suction ring is gently moved, the pupil is mildly dilated, and the patient can no longer see the fixation light. Methods used to assess whether the IOP is adequately elevated include use of a hand-held Barraquer plastic

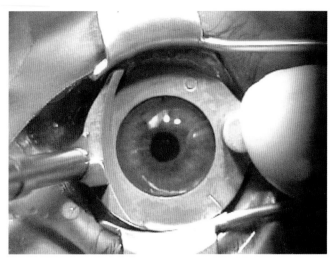

Figure 5-4 Placement of a suction ring. *(Courtesy of Roger F. Steinert, MD.)*

applanator or a pneumotonometer or palpation of the eye by the surgeon. Beginning surgeons are advised to use an objective rather than only a subjective method.

Prior to the lamellar cut, the surface of the cornea is moistened with proparacaine with glycerin or with nonpreserved artificial tears. Balanced salt solution should be avoided at this point because mineral deposits may develop within the microkeratome and interfere with its proper function. The surgeon places the microkeratome on the suction ring and checks that its path is free of obstacles such as the eyelid speculum, drape, or overhanging eyelid. The microkeratome is then activated, passed over the cornea (Fig 5-5) until halted by the hinge-creating stopper, and then reversed off the cornea.

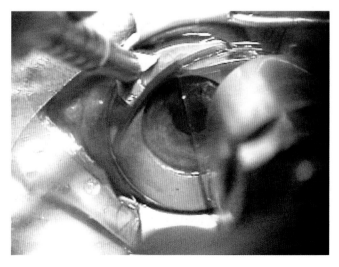

Figure 5-5 Movement of the microkeratome head across the cornea. *(Courtesy of Roger F. Steinert, MD.)*

Before surgery, the microkeratome and vacuum unit are assembled, carefully inspected, and tested to ensure proper function. The importance of meticulously maintaining the microkeratome and carefully following the manufacturer's recommendations cannot be overemphasized.

In addition, the surgeon should be aware that, regardless of the label describing the flap thickness of a specific device, the actual flap thickness varies with the type of microkeratome, patient age, preoperative corneal thickness, preoperative keratometry, preoperative astigmatism, corneal diameter, and translation speed of the microkeratome pass. It is important to maintain a steady translation speed to avoid creating irregularities in the stromal bed.

Barequet IS, Hirsh A, Levinger S. Effect of thin femtosecond LASIK flaps on corneal sensitivity and tear function. *J Refract Surg.* 2008;24(9):897–902.

Calvillo MP, McLaren JW, Hodge DO, Bourne WM. Corneal reinnervation after LASIK: prospective 3-year longitudinal study. *Invest Ophthalmol Vis Sci.* 2004;45(11):3991–3996.

Donnenfeld ED, Ehrenhaus M, Solomon R, Mazurek J, Rozell JC, Perry HD. Effect of hinge width on corneal sensation and dry eye after laser in situ keratomileusis. *J Cataract Refract Surg.* 2004;30(4):790–797.

Kumano Y, Matsui H, Zushi I, et al. Recovery of corneal sensation after myopic correction by laser in situ keratomileusis with a nasal or superior hinge. *J Cataract Refract Surg.* 2003;29(4):757–761.

Rosenfeld SI. Manual versus automated microkeratomes. In: Feder RS, Rapuano CJ, eds. *The LASIK Handbook: A Case-Based Approach.* Philadelphia: Lippincott Williams & Wilkins; 2007:pp 33–43.

Solomon KD, Donnenfeld E, Sandoval HP, et al; Flap Thickness Study Group. Flap thickness accuracy: comparison of 6 microkeratome models. *J Cataract Refract Surg.* 2004;30(5):964–977.

Femtosecond laser A femtosecond laser also creates flaps by performing a lamellar dissection within the stroma. Each laser pulse creates a discrete area of photodisruption of the collagen. The greater the number of laser spots and the more the spots overlap, the more easily the tissue will separate when lifted. The femtosecond laser allows adjustments for several variables involved in making the flap, including flap thickness, flap diameter, hinge location, hinge angle, bed energy, and spot separation. Although the goal is to try to minimize the total energy used in flap creation, a certain level of power is necessary to ensure complete photodisruption, and greater overlap of spots allows for easier flap lifting. With the computer programmed for flap diameter, depth, and hinge location and size, thousands of adjacent pulses are scanned across the cornea in a controlled pattern that results in a flap. Advocates cite the potential for obtaining better depth control, reducing or avoiding the occurrence of such complications as buttonhole perforations, and precisely controlling flap dimension and location. With a femtosecond laser, the side cut of the corneal flap can be modified in a manner that may reduce the incidence of epithelial ingrowth. One study of 208 eyes that underwent femtosecond laser flap creation showed that 1.9% had a loss of suction during femtosecond laser flap creation but that all had successful flap performance 5–45 minutes after reapplanation of the eye.

The use of a femtosecond laser generally takes more time than a mechanical microkeratome because it requires several extra steps. First, the suction ring is centered over the pupil and suction is applied. Proper centration of the suction ring is critical and is performed under a separate microscope, either the microscope from the adjacent excimer laser or an auxiliary microscope in the laser suite. The docking procedure is initiated under the femtosecond laser's microscope, while the patient's chin and forehead are kept level and the suction ring is kept parallel to the eye (Figs 5-6, 5-7). The applanation lens is then centered over the suction ring and lowered into place using the joystick, and the suction ring is unclipped to complete the attachment to the docking device (Fig 5-8). Complete applanation of the cornea must be achieved, or an incomplete flap or incomplete side cut may occur.

Once the laser's computer has confirmed centration, the surgeon administers the femtosecond laser treatment. The vacuum is then released, the suction ring is removed, and the patient is positioned under the excimer laser. A spatula with a semisharp edge

Figure 5-6 Intralase femtosecond laser with cone attached. *(Reproduced with permission from Feder RS, Rapuano CJ. The LASIK Handbook: A Case-Based Approach. Philadelphia: Lippincott Williams & Wilkins; 2007:45, fig 2.7. Photograph courtesy of Robert Feder, MD.)*

Figure 5-7 IntraLase suction ring. *(Reproduced with permission from Feder RS, Rapuano CJ. The LASIK Handbook: A Case-Based Approach. Philadelphia: Lippincott Williams & Wilkins; 2007:45, fig 2.8. Photograph courtesy of Robert Feder, MD.)*

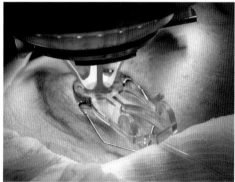

Figure 5-8 Docking of IntraLase cone with suction ring positioned on the eye. *(Reproduced with permission from Feder RS, Rapuano CJ. The LASIK Handbook: A Case-Based Approach. Philadelphia: Lippincott Williams & Wilkins; 2007:46, fig 2.9. Photograph courtesy of Robert Feder, MD.)*

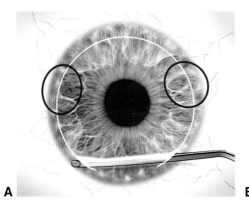

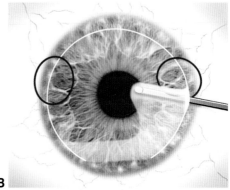

Figure 5-9 Flap lift technique following femtosecond laser application. **A,** After the flap edge is scored near the hinge on either side, a spatula is passed across the flap. **B,** The interface is separated by starting at the superior hinge and sweeping inferiorly. **C,** Dissecting one-third of the flap at a time reduces the risk of tearing the hinge. *(Reproduced with permission from Feder RS, Rapuano CJ. The LASIK Handbook: A Case-Based Approach. Philadelphia: Lippincott Williams & Wilkins; 2007:48, fig 2.12. Photograph courtesy of Robert Feder, MD.)*

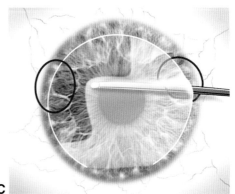

identifies and scores the flap edge near the hinge (Fig 5-9). The instrument is then passed across the flap along the base of the hinge, and the flap is lifted by sweeping inferiorly and separating the flap interface, dissecting one-third of the flap at a time and thus reducing the risk of tearing.

Several recent studies have compared the benefits of the mechanical microkeratome and femtosecond lasers for creating flaps (Table 5-2).

Davison JA, Johnson SC. Intraoperative complications of LASIK flaps using the IntraLase femtosecond laser in 3009 cases. *J Refract Surg.* 2010;26(11):851–857.

Durrie DS, Kezirian GM. Femtosecond laser versus mechanical keratome flaps in wavefront-guided laser in situ keratomileusis: prospective contralateral eye study. *J Cataract Refract Surg.* 2005;31(1):120–126.

Holzer MP, Rabsilber TM, Auffarth GU. Femtosecond laser–assisted corneal flap cuts: morphology, accuracy, and histopathology. *Invest Ophthalmol Vis Sci.* 2006;47(7):2828–2831.

Lim T, Yang S, Kim M, Tchah H. Comparison of the IntraLase femtosecond laser and mechanical microkeratome for laser in situ keratomileusis. *Am J Ophthalmol.* 2006;141(5):833–839.

Patel SV, Maguire LJ, McLaren JW, Hodge DO, Bourne WM. Femtosecond laser versus mechanical microkeratome for LASIK: a randomized controlled study. *Ophthalmology.* 2007; 114(8):1482–1490.

Slade SG, Durrie DS, Binder PS. A prospective, contralateral eye study comparing thin-flap LASIK (sub-Bowman keratomileusis) with photorefractive keratectomy. *Ophthalmology.* 2009;116(6):1075–1082.

Table 5-2 Advantages and Disadvantages of the Femtosecond Laser

Advantages	Disadvantages
Less increase in IOP required	Longer suction time
More control over flap diameter	More flap manipulation
Size and thickness of flap less dependent on corneal contour	Opaque bubble layer may interfere with excimer ablation
Centration easier to control	Bubbles in the anterior chamber may interfere with tracking and registration
Epithelial defects on flap are rare	
Less risk of free cap and buttonhole	Increased overall treatment time
More reliable flap thickness	Difficulty lifting flap >6 months
Hemorrhage from limbal vessels less likely	Increased risk of diffuse lamellar keratitis
	Increased cost
Ability to re-treat immediately if incomplete femtosecond laser ablation	Need to acquire new skills
	Delayed photosensitivity or good acuity plus photosensitivity (GAPP), which may require prolonged topical corticosteroid therapy

Modified with permission from Feder RS, Rapuano CJ. *The LASIK Handbook: A Case-Based Approach.* Philadelphia: Lippincott Williams & Wilkins; 2007.

Tran DB, Sarayba MA, Bor Z, et al. Randomized prospective clinical study comparing induced aberrations with IntraLase and Hansatome flap creation in fellow eyes: potential impact on wavefront-guided laser in situ keratomileusis. *J Cataract Refract Surg.* 2005;31(1):97–105.

Application of Laser Treatment

Tracking, centration, and ablation

For surface ablation, the exposed Bowman layer should be inspected and found to be smooth, uniformly dry, and free of debris. For LASIK, the flap must be lifted and reflected and the stromal bed uniformly dry prior to treatment. Fluid or blood accumulation on the stromal bed should be avoided, as it can lead to an irregular ablation.

Today, all excimer lasers employ tracking systems, which have improved clinical outcomes. The tracker used is an open-loop system, which employs video technology to monitor the location of an infrared image of the pupil and to shift the laser beam accordingly.

The laser is centered and focused according to the manufacturer's recommendations. Tracking systems, although effective, do not lessen the importance of keeping the reticule centered on the patient's entrance pupil. If the patient is unable to maintain fixation, the illumination of the operating microscope should be reduced. If decentration occurs and the ablation does not stop automatically, the surgeon should immediately stop the treatment until adequate refixation is achieved. It is still important for the surgeon to monitor for excessive eye movement, which can result in decentration despite the tracking device.

The change in illumination and in patient position (ie, lying down) can cause pupil centroid shift and cyclotorsion. In most patients, the pupil moves nasally and superiorly when it is restricted. *Registration* is a technique in which a fixed landmark is used at the time of aberrometry and treatment to apply the ablation to the correct area of the cornea; it does not rely on the pupil for laser centration (Fig 5-10). Once the patient confirms that the fixation light of the excimer laser is still visible and that he or she is looking directly

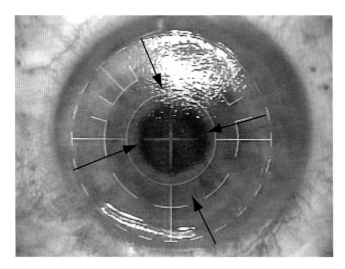

Figure 5-10 Excimer laser ablation of the stromal bed. Note the faint blue fluorescence of the stromal bed from the laser pulse *(arrows)*. The rectangular shape of the exposure by this broad-beam laser indicates that the laser is correcting the cylindrical portion of the treatment. (Photograph is enhanced to visualize fluorescence; the surgeon usually sees minimal or no fluorescence through the operating microscope.) *(Courtesy of Roger F. Steinert, MD.)*

at it, ablation begins. With or without a tracking device, the surgeon must monitor the patient to ensure that fixation is maintained throughout the treatment. Neither tracking nor iris registration is a substitute for accurate patient fixation. It is important to initiate stromal ablation promptly, before excessive stromal dehydration takes place. During larger-diameter ablations, a flap protector may be needed to shield the underside of the LASIK flap near the hinge from the laser pulses.

> Donnenfeld E. The pupil is a moving target: centration, repeatability, and registration. *J Refract Surg.* 2004;20(5):S593–S596.

Immediate Postablation Measures

Surface ablation

One of the major complications of surface ablation is corneal haze. To decrease the chance of post–surface ablation corneal haze, especially after prior corneal surgery such as previous PRK, LASIK, penetrating keratoplasty, or radial keratotomy, a soaked pledget of mitomycin C (usually 0.02% or 0.2 mg/mL) can be placed on the ablated surface for approximately 12 seconds to 2 minutes at the end of the laser exposure. The concentration and duration of mitomycin C application may vary by diagnosis and surgeon preference; however, most surgeons are tending toward shorter duration of mitomycin C exposure. Application of mitomycin C for 12 seconds appears to be as efficacious as prolonged delivery times. Many surgeons also employ mitomycin C in primary surface ablation for moderate to high treatments or deeper ablation depths. Some surgeons reduce the amount of treatment when applying mitomycin C in surface ablation due to reports of potential endothelial cell toxicity. The cornea is then copiously irrigated with balanced salt solution to remove excess mitomycin C. To avoid damage to limbal stem cells, care should be taken not to expose the limbus or conjunctiva to mitomycin C. Human confocal microscopy studies have shown a reduced keratocyte population and less haze in eyes that received mitomycin C.

Some surgeons apply sterile chilled balanced salt solution or a frozen cellulose sponge before and/or after the surface ablation procedure in the belief that cooling reduces pain and haze formation. However, the advantage of this practice has not been substantiated in a controlled study. Care should be taken to not expose the eye to tap water, as this may result in infectious contamination.

If the LASEK or epi-LASIK variant has been performed, the surgeon carefully floats and repositions the epithelial sheet back into position with balanced salt solution. Antibiotic, corticosteroid, and, sometimes, nonsteroidal anti-inflammatory drugs (NSAIDs) are then placed on the eye, followed by a bandage soft contact lens. Some NSAIDs can be placed directly on the corneal bed, while others should be placed only on the surface of the contact lens as they have been associated with poor corneal healing. If the patient cannot tolerate a bandage soft contact lens, a pressure patch may be used.

Lee DH, Chung HS, Jeon YC, Boo SD, Yoon YD, Kim JG. Photorefractive keratectomy with intraoperative mitomycin-C application. *J Cataract Refract Surg.* 2005;31(12):2293–2298.

Majmudar PA, Forstot SL, Dennis RF, et al. Topical mitomycin-C for subepithelial fibrosis after refractive corneal surgery. *Ophthalmology.* 2000;107(1):89–94.

Virasch VV, Majmudar PA, Epstein RJ, Vaidya NS, Dennis RF. Reduced application time for prophylactic mitomycin C in photorefractive keratectomy. *Ophthalmology.* 2010;117(5): 885–889.

LASIK

After the ablation is completed, the flap is replaced onto the stromal bed. The interface is irrigated until all interface debris is eliminated (which is better seen with oblique rather than coaxial illumination). The surface of the flap is gently stroked with a smooth instrument, such as an irrigation cannula or a moistened microsurgical spear sponge, from the hinge, or center, to the periphery to ensure that wrinkles are eliminated and that the flap settles back into its original position, as indicated by realignment of the corneal marks made earlier. The peripheral gutters should be symmetric and even. The physiologic dehydration of the stroma by the endothelial pump will begin to secure the flap in position within several minutes. If a significant epithelial defect or a large, loose sheet of epithelium is present, a bandage contact lens should be placed. Once the flap is adherent, the eyelid speculum is removed carefully so as not to disturb the flap. Most surgeons place varying combinations of antibiotic, NSAID, and corticosteroid drops on the eye at the conclusion of the procedure. The flap is usually rechecked at the slit lamp before the patient leaves to make sure it has remained in proper alignment. A clear shield or protective goggles are often placed to guard against accidental trauma that could displace the flap. Patients are instructed not to rub or squeeze their eyes.

Lui MM, Silas MA, Fugishima H. Complications of photorefractive keratectomy and laser in situ keratomileusis. *J Refract Surg.* 2003;19(2 suppl):S247–S249.

Price FW Jr. LASIK. *Focal Points: Clinical Modules for Ophthalmologists.* San Francisco: American Academy of Ophthalmology; 2000, module 3.

Schallhorn SC, Amesbury EC, Tanzer DJ. Avoidance, recognition, and management of LASIK complications. *Am J Ophthalmol.* 2006;141(4):733–739.

Postoperative Care

Surface ablation

After surface ablation, patients may experience variable amounts of pain, from minimal to severe, and some may need oral narcotic or neuropathic pain medications. Studies have shown that topical NSAID drops reduce postoperative pain, although they may also slow the rate of re-epithelialization and promote sterile infiltrates (see Chapter 6). Corneal melting and stromal scarring have been described after the use of some topical NSAIDs. For patients who are not healing normally following the surface ablation, any topical NSAID should be discontinued. Studies have also demonstrated a reduction in pain with the use of preserved and nonpreserved topical anesthetic drops. Patients must be carefully warned not to overuse topical anesthetic drops because, when used excessively over a prolonged period, the drops may cause severe corneal complications. Many patients benefit from oral NSAIDs preoperatively and postoperatively as well as from postoperative oral narcotics.

Patients should be followed closely until the epithelium is completely healed, which usually occurs within 3–4 days. As long as the bandage soft contact lens is in place, patients are treated with topical broad-spectrum antibiotics and corticosteroids, usually 4 times daily. Once the epithelium is healed, the bandage soft contact lens, antibiotic drops, and NSAID drops (if used) may be discontinued. Topical anesthetic drops, if used, should never be applied for more than a few days and should be confiscated after that.

The use of topical corticosteroids to modulate postoperative wound healing, reduce anterior stromal haze, and decrease regression of the refractive effect remains controversial. Although some studies have demonstrated that corticosteroids have no significant long-term effect on corneal haze or visual outcome after PRK, other studies have shown that corticosteroids are effective in limiting haze and myopic regression after PRK, particularly after higher myopic corrections. Some surgeons who advocate topical corticosteroids after the removal of the bandage soft contact lens restrict them to patients with higher levels of myopia (eg, myopia greater than –4.00 or –5.00 D). When used after removal of the bandage lens, corticosteroid drops are typically tapered over a 1- to 4-month period, depending on the patient's corneal haze and refractive outcome. Patients who received mitomycin C at the time of surgery have a reduced risk of haze formation and thus may have a shorter duration of corticosteroid use. Patients who had hyperopic PRK may experience prolonged epithelial healing because of the larger epithelial defect resulting from the larger ablation zone, as well as a temporary reduction in best-corrected distance visual acuity in the first week to month, which usually improves with time. Many hyperopic patients also experience a temporary myopic overcorrection, which regresses over several weeks to months. In the absence of complications, routine examinations are typically scheduled at approximately 2–4 weeks, 2–3 months, 6 months, and 12 months postoperatively and perhaps more frequently, depending on steroid taper used.

LASIK

Many surgeons instruct their patients to use topical antibiotics and corticosteroids postoperatively for 3–7 days. With femtosecond laser procedures, some surgeons prescribe more frequent applications of corticosteroid eye drops or a longer period of use. In addition, it is very important for the surface of the flap to be kept well lubricated in the early postoperative period. Patients may be told to use the protective shield for 1 day to 1 week when they shower or sleep and to avoid swimming and hot tubs for 2 weeks. Patients are examined 1 day after surgery to ensure that the flap has remained in proper alignment and that there is no evidence of infection or excessive inflammation. In the absence of complications, the next examinations are typically scheduled at approximately 1 week, 1 month, 3 months, 6 months, and 12 months postoperatively.

= ABx, steroid, lubrication 3-7 days

> Corbett MC, O'Brart DP, Marshall J. Do topical corticosteroids have a role following excimer laser photorefractive keratectomy? *J Refract Surg.* 1995;11(5):380–387.
>
> Solomon KD, Donnenfeld ED, Raizman M, et al. Safety and efficacy of ketorolac tromethamine 0.4% ophthalmic solution in post–photorefractive keratectomy patients. *J Cataract Refract Surg.* 2004;30(8):1653–1660.

Refractive Outcomes

As the early broad-beam excimer laser systems improved and surgeons gained experience, the results achieved with surface ablation and LASIK improved markedly. The ablation zone diameter was enlarged because it was found that small ablation zones, originally selected to limit depth of tissue removal, produced more haze and regression in surface ablation treatments and complaints of subjective glare and halos for both surface ablation and LASIK. The larger treatment diameters used today, including optical zones and gradual aspheric peripheral blend zones, improve optical quality and refractive stability in both myopic and hyperopic treatments. Central island elevations have become less common with improvements in beam quality, vacuums to remove the ablation plume, and the development of scanning and variable-spot-size excimer lasers.

> Solomon KD, Fernández de Castro LE, Sandoval HP, et al; Joint LASIK Study Task Force. LASIK world literature review: quality of life and patient satisfaction. *Ophthalmology.* 2009;116(4):691–701.

Outcomes for Myopia

Initial FDA clinical trials of conventional excimer laser treatments limited to low myopia (generally less than −6.00 D) revealed that 56%–86% of eyes treated with either PRK or LASIK achieved uncorrected visual acuity (UCVA) of at least 20/20, 88%–100% achieved UCVA of at least 20/40, and 82%–100% were within 1.00 D of emmetropia. Up to 2.1% of eyes lost ≥2 lines of best-corrected visual acuity (BCVA). Reports after 2000 have demonstrated significantly improved outcomes and safety profiles, with <0.6% of eyes losing 2 or more lines of BCVA.

> el Danasoury MA, el Maghraby A, Klyce SD, Mehrez K. Comparison of photorefractive keratectomy with excimer laser in situ keratomileusis in correcting low myopia (from −2.00 to −5.50 diopters): a randomized study. *Ophthalmology.* 1999;106(2):411–420.
>
> Fernandez AP, Jaramillo J, Jaramillo M. Comparison of photorefractive keratectomy and laser in situ keratomileusis for myopia of −6 D or less using the Nidek EC-5000 laser. *J Refract Surg.* 2000;16(6):711–715.

Sugar A, Rapuano CJ, Culbertson WW, et al. Laser in situ keratomileusis for myopia and astigmatism: safety and efficacy: a report by the American Academy of Ophthalmology. *Ophthalmology.* 2002;109(1):175–187.

Tole DM, McCarty DJ, Couper T, Taylor HR. Comparison of laser in situ keratomileusis and photorefractive keratectomy for the correction of myopia of –6.00 diopters or less. Melbourne Excimer Laser Group. *J Refract Surg.* 2001;17(1):46–54.

Watson SL, Bunce C, Alan BD. Improved safety in contemporary LASIK. *Ophthalmology.* 2005;112(8):1375–1380.

Outcomes for Hyperopia

In myopic ablations, the central cornea is flattened, whereas in hyperopic ablations, more tissue is removed from the midperiphery than from the central cornea, resulting in an effective steepening (see Fig 5-1B). To ensure that the size of the central hyperopic treatment zone is adequate, a large ablation area is required for hyperopic treatments. Most studies have employed hyperopic treatment zones with transition zones out to 9.0–9.5 mm. FDA clinical trials of hyperopic PRK and LASIK up to +6.00 D reported that 46%–59% of eyes had postoperative UCVA of 20/20 or better, 92%–96% had UCVA of 20/40 or better, and 84%–91% were within 1.00 D of emmetropia; while loss of >2 lines of BCVA occurred in 1%–3.5%. The VISX FDA clinical trial of hyperopic astigmatic PRK up to +6.00 D sphere and +4.00 D cylinder reported an approximate postoperative UCVA of 20/20 or better in 50% of eyes, UCVA of 20/40 or better in 97%, and 87% within ±1.00 D of emmetropia, with loss of >2 lines of BCVA in 1.5%. For the same amount of correction, the period from surgery to postoperative stabilization is longer for hyperopic than for myopic corrections. Overall, studies with larger ablation zones have demonstrated good results for refractive errors up to +4.00 for conventional treatments, but predictability and stability are markedly reduced with LASIK treatments for hyperopia above this level. Consequently, most refractive surgeons do not treat up to the highest levels of hyperopia that have been approved by the FDA for conventional treatments.

Davidorf JM, Eghbali F, Onclinx T, Maloney RK. Effect of varying the optical zone diameter on the results of hyperopic laser in situ keratomileusis. *Ophthalmology.* 2001;108(7):1261–1265.

Salz JJ, Stevens CA; LADARVision LASIK Hyperopia Study Group. LASIK correction of spherical hyperopia, hyperopic astigmatism, and mixed astigmatism with the LADARVision excimer laser system. *Ophthalmology.* 2002;109(9):1647–1656.

Tabbara KF, El-Sheikh HF, Islam SM. Laser in situ keratomileusis for the correction of hyperopia from +0.50 to +11.50 diopters with the Keracor 117C laser. *J Refract Surg.* 2001;17(2): 123–128.

Varley GA, Huang D, Rapuano CJ, Schallhorn S, Boxer Wachler BS, Sugar A. LASIK for hyperopia, hyperopic astigmatism, and mixed astigmatism: a report by the American Academy of Ophthalmology. *Ophthalmology.* 2004;111(8):1604–1617.

Wavefront-guided and wavefront-optimized treatment outcomes for myopia and hyperopia

Wavefront-guided or wavefront-optimized LASIK coupled with sophisticated eye-tracking systems have greatly improved the accuracy and reproducibility of results, allowing even higher percentages of patients to obtain UCVA of 20/20 and 20/40. In wavefront-guided LASIK for myopic astigmatism, for example, up to about –10.00 to –12.00 D, 79%–95% of patients obtained 20/20 UCVA, and 96%–100% obtained 20/40 UCVA. In wavefront-guided LASIK for hyperopic astigmatism up to +6.00 D, 55%–59% of patients obtained 20/20 UCVA, and 93%–97% obtained 20/40 UCVA. In wavefront-guided LASIK for mixed astigmatism with up to +5.00 D of cylinder, 56%–61% of patients obtained 20/20 UCVA, and 95% obtained 20/40 UCVA. A recent study found that the visual acuity results for the vast majority of patients were equivalent between wavefront-guided and wavefront-optimized LASIK.

Keir NJ, Simpson T, Jones LW, Fonn D. Wavefront-guided LASIK for myopia: effect on visual acuity, contrast sensitivity, and higher order aberrations. *J Refract Surg.* 2009;25(6):524–533.

Rajan MS, Jaycock P, O'Brart D, Nystrom HH, Marshall J. A long-term study of photorefractive keratectomy: 12-year follow-up. *Ophthalmology.* 2004;111(10):1813–1824.

Randleman JB, Perez-Straziota CE, Hu MH, White AJ, Loft ES, Stulting RD. Higher order aberrations after wavefront-optimized photorefractive keratectomy and laser in situ keratomileusis. *J Cataract Refract Surg.* 2009;35(2):260–264.

Schallhorn SC, Farjo AA, Huang D, et al. Wavefront-guided LASIK for the correction of primary myopia and astigmatism: a report by the American Academy of Ophthalmology. *Ophthalmology.* 2008;115(7):1249–1261.

Steinert RF, Hersh PS. Spherical and aspherical photorefractive keratectomy and laser in-situ keratomileusis for moderate to high myopia: two prospective, randomized clinical trials. Summit Technology PRK-LASIK Study Group. *Trans Am Ophthalmol Soc.* 1998;96:197–221.

Stonecipher KG, Kezirian GM. Wavefront-optimized versus wavefront-guided LASIK for myopic astigmatism with the ALLEGRETTO WAVE: three-month results of a prospective FDA trial. *J Refract Surg.* 2008;24(4):S424–S430.

Re-treatment (Enhancements)

Although excimer laser ablation reduces refractive error and improves UCVA in almost all cases, some patients have residual refractive errors and would benefit from re-treatment. The degree of refractive error that warrants re-treatment varies depending on the patient's lifestyle and expectations. Re-treatment rates also vary, depending on the degree of refractive error being treated, the laser and nomograms used, and the expectations of the patient population. One advantage of LASIK compared with surface ablation is that refractive stability generally occurs earlier, allowing earlier enhancements, typically within the first 3 months after LASIK; with surface ablation, the ongoing activation of keratocytes and the risk of haze after enhancement usually require a wait of up to 6 months before an enhancement surface ablation is undertaken. Typically, re-treatment rates are higher in hyperopia and in high astigmatism than for other indications.

Studies showed that rates of re-treatment are higher for higher initial correction, for residual astigmatism, and for patients older than 40 years. Re-treatment rates vary from 1% to 11%, based on surgeon experience, patient demands, and the other factors just described. Surface ablation re-treatment is nearly identical to primary surface ablation treatment, while LASIK re-treatment can be performed either by lifting the preexisting lamellar flap and applying additional ablation to the stromal bed or by performing surface ablation on the LASIK flap. In most cases, the flap can be lifted even several years after the original procedure, with reports of successfully lifted flaps 5–6 years after the *[handwritten margin notes: ↑ risk of haze on thinning (after PRK), do surface ablation; if 2-3 yrs post-LASIK, can do surface ablation (to avoid ↑ risk of epi ingrowth), but ↑ risk haze]*

initial procedure. However, because of the safety of surface ablation after LASIK and the increased risk of epithelial ingrowth with flap lifts, many surgeons now prefer to perform surface ablation re-treatment if the primary LASIK was performed more than 2–3 years earlier. Creating a new flap with a mechanical microkeratome is generally avoided because free slivers of tissue, irregular stromal beds, and irregular astigmatism may be produced. When possible, using the femtosecond laser to create a new side cut within the boundaries of the previous flap may facilitate flap-lift enhancements; however, it is important to have an adequate exposed diameter for ablation. When attempting to lift or manipulate a femtosecond flap, the surgeon must take care to avoid tearing it, because the femtosecond laser usually creates a thinner flap than traditional microkeratomes.

When a preexisting flap is lifted, it is important to minimize epithelial disruption. A jeweler's forceps, Sinskey hook, or 27-gauge needle can be used to localize the edge of the previous flap. Because the edge of the flap can be seen more easily at the slit lamp than with the diffuse illumination of the operating microscope of the laser, it may be easier to begin a flap lift at the slit lamp and then to complete it at the excimer laser. Alternatively, the surgeon can often visualize the edge of the flap under the diffuse illumination of the operating microscope by applying pressure with a small Sinskey hook or a similar device; the edge of the flap will dimple and disrupt the light reflex (Fig 5-11). A careful circumferential epithelial dissection is performed so that the flap can then be lifted without tearing the epithelial edges. Smooth forceps, iris spatulas, and several instruments specifically designed for dissecting the flap edge can be used to lift the original flap.

Once the ablation has been performed, the flap is repositioned and the interface is irrigated, as in the initial LASIK procedure. Special care must be taken to ensure that no loose epithelium is trapped beneath the edge of the flap that could lead to epithelial ingrowth; the risk of epithelial ingrowth is greater after re-treatment than after primary treatment.

Surface ablation may be considered to enhance a previous primary LASIK treatment. Surface ablation performed on a LASIK flap carries an increased risk of haze formation and irregular astigmatism, but it is an appealing alternative when the residual stromal bed is insufficient for further ablation; when the LASIK was performed by another surgeon

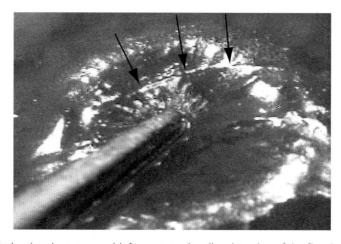

Figure 5-11   Indenting the cornea with forceps to visualize the edge of the flap *(arrows)* through an operating microscope prior to an enhancement procedure. *(Courtesy of Roger F. Steinert, MD.)*

and the flap thickness, or RSBT, is not known; or with conditions such as a buttonhole or incomplete flap. Care must be taken when removing the epithelium over a flap to avoid inadvertently lifting or dislocating the flap. Applying 20% ethanol for 20–30 seconds inside a corneal well will loosen the epithelium; this is followed by scraping motions extending from the hinge toward the periphery. A rotating brush should not be used to remove the epithelium from a LASIK flap. The risk of postoperative haze due to surface ablation over a previous LASIK flap may be avoided or reduced by topical corticosteroids and topical mitomycin C 0.02%.

The choice between conventional and wavefront-guided treatment for enhancing the vision of patients who have previously undergone conventional LASIK is not yet established. Some studies report better results in both safety and efficacy with conventional LASIK re-treatment. With wavefront-guided re-treatments, particularly in the setting of high spherical aberrations, the risk of overcorrection may be greater. Caution should be exercised in evaluating the degree of higher-order aberrations and the planned depth of the ablation when deciding between conventional and wavefront-guided treatments.

Carones F, Vigo L, Carones AV, Brancato R. Evaluation of photorefractive keratectomy retreatments after regressed myopic laser in situ keratomileusis. *Ophthalmology.* 2001;108(10): 1732–1737.

Davis EA, Hardten DR, Lindstrom M, Samuelson TW, Lindstrom RL. LASIK enhancements: a comparison of lifting to recutting the flap. *Ophthalmology.* 2002;109(12):2308–2313.

Hersh PS, Fry KL, Bishop DS. Incidence and associations of retreatment after LASIK. *Ophthalmology.* 2003;110(4):748–754.

Hiatt JA, Grant CN, Boxer Wachler BS. Complex wavefront-guided retreatments with the Alcon CustomCornea platform after prior LASIK. *J Refract Surg.* 2006;22(1):48–53.

Jin GJ, Merkley KH. Conventional and wavefront-guided myopic LASIK retreatment. *Am J Ophthalmol.* 2006;141(4):660–668.

Randleman JB, White AJ Jr, Lynn MJ, Hu MH, Stulting RD. Incidence, outcomes, and risk factors for retreatment after wavefront-optimized ablations with PRK and LASIK. *J Refract Surg.* 2009;25(3):273–276.

Weisenthal RW, Salz J, Sugar A, et al. Photorefractive keratectomy for treatment of flap complications in laser in situ keratomileusis. *Cornea.* 2003;22(5):399–404.

FDA Interest in LASIK

Recently, in response to feedback from experts and patient testimonials at a 2008 advisory panel regarding LASIK surgery, the FDA has developed additional measures to help facilitate reporting and increase education for patients and physicians. A collaborative study is being established with the National Eye Institute and the Department of Defense to examine the negative impact on quality of life after LASIK and the predictors of those problems. In addition, the FDA has issued letters to physicians providing information on the promotion of approved lasers used during LASIK. Furthermore, the American National Standards Institute has developed a new LASIK standard that creates national and international guidelines for device testing and performance. The FDA is continually evaluating these measures, along with several other initiatives, to ensure that the safety and effectiveness of LASIK are monitored and regulated. See Appendix 1.

CHAPTER 6

Photoablation: Complications and Side Effects

Surface ablation techniques, including photorefractive keratectomy (PRK), and LASIK are relatively safe and effective surgical procedures. As with all types of surgery, there are potential risks and complications. It is important to understand how to avoid, diagnose, and treat many of the complications seen in refractive surgery. Comprehensive ophthalmologists, as well as refractive surgeons, should be knowledgeable about these postoperative problems, given the popularity of refractive surgery in the general population.

Complications Common to Surface Ablation and LASIK

Overcorrection

Myopic or hyperopic surface ablation typically undergoes some degree of regression for at least 3–6 months. In general, patients with higher degrees of myopia and any degree of hyperopia require more time to attain refractive stability, which must be achieved before any decision is made regarding possible re-treatment of the overcorrection.

Overcorrection may occur if substantial stromal dehydration develops before the laser treatment is initiated, because more stromal tissue will be ablated per pulse. A long delay before beginning the ablation after removing the epithelium in surface ablation, or after lifting the flap in LASIK, allows excessive dehydration of the stroma and increases the risk of overcorrection. Controlling the humidity and temperature in the laser suite within the recommended guidelines should standardize the surgery and ideally improve refractive outcomes. Overcorrection tends to occur more often in older individuals because their wound-healing response is less vigorous and their corneas ablate more rapidly owing to their reduced hydration status. Studies reveal that older patients (ages 35–54) with moderate to high myopia have a greater response to the same amount of dioptric correction than younger patients do.

Various modalities are available for treating small amounts of overcorrection. Myopic regression can be induced after surface ablation by abrupt discontinuation of corticosteroids. Patients with consecutive hyperopia—that is, hyperopia that occurs when an originally myopic patient is overcorrected—and patients who are myopic due to overcorrection of hyperopia require less treatment to achieve emmetropia than previously untreated eyes, as they are considered to have overresponded to the initial treatment. When re-treating

93

— if fixing an overcorrection, ↓ ablation by 15-50% for the correction

such patients, the surgeon should take care not to overcorrect a second time. With conventional ablation, most surgeons will reduce the ablation by 15%–50% for consecutive treatments. For wavefront procedures, review of the depth of the ablation and the amount of higher-order aberration helps titrate the re-treatment.

Undercorrection

Undercorrection occurs much more commonly at higher degrees of ametropia because of decreased predictability due to the greater frequency and severity of regression. Patients with regression after treatment of their first eye have an increased likelihood of regression in their second eye. Sometimes the regression may be reversed with aggressive topical corticosteroids. The patient may undergo a re-treatment after the refraction has remained stable for at least 3 months postoperatively. A patient with significant corneal haze and regression after surface ablation is at higher risk after re-treatment for further regression, recurrence of visually significant corneal haze, and loss of best-corrected visual acuity (BCVA). Topical mitomycin C, administered at the time of re-treatment, can be used to modulate the response. It is recommended that the surgeon wait at least 6–12 months for the haze to improve spontaneously before repeating surface ablation. In patients with significant haze and regression, removal of haze with adjunctive use of mitomycin C should not be coupled with a refractive treatment, as the resolution of the haze will commonly improve the refractive outcome. Undercorrection after LASIK typically does not respond to any of the maneuvers just discussed.

Central Islands

A *central island* appears on computerized corneal topography as an area of central corneal steepening surrounded by an area of flattening that corresponds to the myopic treatment zone in the paracentral region (Fig 6-1). A central island is defined as a steepening of at least 1.00 D with a diameter of >1 mm compared with the paracentral flattened area. Central islands may be associated with decreased visual acuity, monocular diplopia and multiplopia, ghost images, and decreased contrast sensitivity.

The occurrence of central islands has been significantly reduced with the use of scanning and variable-spot-size lasers. Fortunately, most central islands resolve over time,

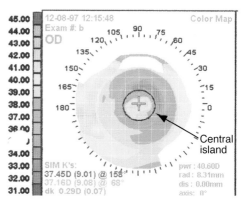

Figure 6-1 Corneal topography of a myopic ablation *(blue)* with a central island *(yellow)* in the visual axis. *(Courtesy of Roger F. Steinert, MD.)*

especially after surface ablation, although resolution may take 6–12 months. New treatment options such as topography-guided ablations may be helpful in treating persistent central islands.

Optical Aberrations

Some patients report optical aberrations after surface ablation and LASIK, including glare, ghost images, and halos. These symptoms are most prevalent after treatment with smaller ablation zones and after attempted higher spherical and cylindrical correction. These visual problems seem to be exacerbated in dim light conditions. Wavefront mapping can reveal higher-order aberrations associated with these subjective complaints. In general, a larger, more uniform, and well-centered optical zone provides a better quality of vision, especially at night.

Night-vision complaints are often caused by spherical aberration, although other higher-order aberrations also contribute. The cornea and lens have inherent spherical aberration. In addition, excimer laser ablation increases positive spherical aberration in the midperipheral cornea. Larger pupil size may correlate with frequency of complaints because spherical aberration increases when the midperipheral corneal optics contribute to the light energy passing to the retina. Customized wavefront-guided corneal treatment patterns are designed to reduce existing aberrations and to help prevent the creation of new aberrations, with the goal of achieving a better quality of vision after laser ablation.

Several studies have demonstrated that although the excimer laser photoablation causes the majority of change in lower-order and higher-order aberrations after LASIK surgery, the creation of the flap itself can also change lower-order and higher-order aberrations (Fig 6-2). Some studies have demonstrated that femtosecond lasers cause little or no change in higher-order aberrations, in contrast to mechanical microkeratomes. Pallikaris showed that LASIK flap creation alone, without lifting, caused no significant change in refractive error or visual acuity but did cause a significant increase in total higher-order wavefront aberrations.

Pallikaris IG, Kymionis GD, Panagopoulou SI, Siganos CS, Theodorakis MA, Pellikaris AI. Induced optical aberrations following formation of a laser in situ keratomileusis flap. *J Cataract Refract Surg*. 2002;28(10):1737–1741.

Porter J, MacRae S, Yoon G, Roberts C, Cox IG, Williams DR. Separate effects of the microkeratome incision and laser ablation on the eye's wave aberration. *Am J Ophthalmol*. 2003;136(2):327–337.

Tran DB, Sarayba MA, Bor Z, et al. Randomized prospective clinical study comparing induced aberrations with IntraLase and Hansatome flap creation in fellow eyes: potential impact on wavefront-guided laser in situ. *J Cataract Refract Surg*. 2005;31(1):97–105.

Waheed S, Chalita MR, Xu M, Krueger RR. Flap-induced and laser-induced ocular aberrations in a two step LASIK procedure. *J Refract Surg*. 2005;21(3):346–352.

Decentered Ablation

Accurate centration during the excimer laser procedure is important in optimizing the visual results. Centration is even more critical for hyperopic than myopic treatments. A decentered ablation may occur if the patient's eye slowly begins to drift and loses fixation

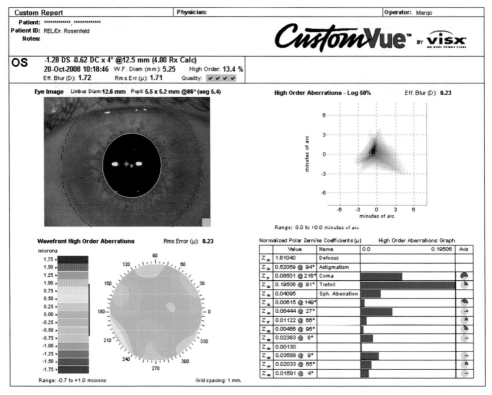

Figure 6-2 Wavefront analysis depicting higher-order aberrations after LASIK, including coma and trefoil. *(Courtesy of Steven I. Rosenfeld, MD.)*

or if the surgeon initially positions the patient's head improperly; if the patient's eye is not perpendicular to the laser treatment, parallax can result (Fig 6-3). In addition, centering the ablation on a pharmacologically miotic pupil may not be as accurate as centering it on a nonmiotic pupil. Miotics should not be used during photoablation because their use frequently leads to a pupillary shift nasally and sometimes superiorly. The incidence of decentration increases with surgeon inexperience and with higher refractive correction, probably because a longer ablation time requires longer patient cooperation with fixation. Larger decentrations may lead to complaints of glare, halos, and decreased visual acuity. Patients with larger pupils may experience such symptoms with smaller amounts of decentration because the edge of the decentered ablation is perceived more easily within the patient's pupillary opening. Decentration may be reduced by ensuring that the patient's head is in the correct plane—that is, perpendicular to the laser (parallel to the ground)—and that there is no head tilt. Treatment of decentration with wavefront- and topography-guided technology can be effective.

Corticosteroid-Induced Complications

The incidence of increased intraocular pressure (IOP) after surface ablation has been reported to range from 11% to 25%. Occasionally, the IOP may be quite high. In 1 study,

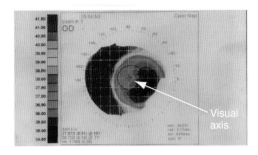

Figure 6-3 Corneal topography of a decen-tered ablation. *(Courtesy of Roger F. Steinert, MD.)*

2% of patients had IOP greater than 40 mm Hg. The majority of cases of elevated IOP are associated with prolonged topical corticosteroid therapy. Accordingly, postopera-tive steroid-associated IOP elevations are more likely to occur following surface ablation (after which steroid therapy can last 2–4 months to prevent postoperative corneal haze) or after complicated LASIK cases, such as with diffuse lamellar keratitis (DLK), in which long-term high-dose steroid therapy is indicated. Corticosteroid-induced elevated IOP occurs in 1.5%–3.0% of patients using fluorometholone but in up to 25% of patients using dexamethasone or stronger corticosteroids. The increase in IOP is usually controlled with topical IOP-lowering medications and typically normalizes after the corticosteroids are decreased or discontinued. Because of the changes in corneal curvature and/or corneal thickness, Goldmann tonometry readings after myopic surface ablation and LASIK are artifactually reduced (see the section Glaucoma After Refractive Surgery in Chapter 11). Measurement of IOP from the temporal rather than the central cornea may be more accurate, and pneumotonometry and Tono-Pen readings are also more reliable. Other corticosteroid-associated complications that have been reported after surface ablation are herpes simplex virus keratitis, ptosis, and cataracts.

Endothelial Effects

In most studies, no significant changes were found in central endothelial cell density after surface ablation or LASIK, unlike after radial keratotomy. In fact, the polymegathism as-sociated with contact lens use typically improves after laser refractive ablations, as dem-onstrated by the significant decrease in the peripheral coefficient of variation of cell size 2 years postoperatively.

Dry Eye and Corneal Sensation

Dry eye is one of the most frequent transient adverse effects of LASIK, but occasionally it may persist for months or years; it has been reported in 60%–70% of all patients, to varying degrees. Dry eye is generally less of a problem after surface ablation and usually resolves over 3–6 months (see the section Dry Eye in Chapter 10). The cornea is innervated by sen-sory nerve fibers from the ophthalmic division of the trigeminal nerve and sympathetic nerves. After entering the peripheral cornea, these nerve fibers run radially in the middle third of the stroma, divide to form a dense subepithelial plexus, and turn perpendicularly to penetrate the Bowman layer and supply the corneal epithelium. Corneal sensitivity decreases after LASIK because of the surgical amputation of nerves during flap formation and the destruction of superficial nerve fibers during the laser ablation. Compared to LASIK, surface ablation procedures are less likely to cause dry-eye syndrome because they avoid flap formation and ablate the more superficial nerve endings.

The surgeon must carefully monitor the patient postoperatively for signs of punctate keratitis or more severe manifestations of neurotrophic epitheliopathy following any form of laser vision correction surgery. As patients await the return of innervation, their treatment should include the use of nonpreserved artificial tears, gels, and ointments. To avoid the possibility of migration under the flap, however, ointments should not be used in the early postoperative period following LASIK. More severe or recalcitrant dry eyes may require topical cyclosporine, topical corticosteroids, oral tetracyclines, oral omega-3 fatty acids, and punctal occlusion.

Both the surgeon and the patient must remain aware that many patients seeking laser vision correction do so because of contact lens intolerance, and dry-eye syndrome is one of the most common reasons for such symptoms. This dryness will persist after the laser treatment and will be transiently worsened during the recovery period because of the corneal nerve damage described above. The patient may feel that long-term, persistent dryness has worsened and may blame the surface ablation or LASIK procedure. If the patient has known or suspected dry-eye syndrome before undergoing laser refractive surgery, intensive topical lubrication, topical cyclosporine, and systemic treatments, as outlined earlier, can be instituted preoperatively to try to improve the condition of the ocular surface. Some studies have reported better surgical and visual outcomes with such prophylactic maneuvers. Some dry-eye patients might also be better served with a surface ablation technique to reduce, but not eliminate, the risk of postoperative dry eye.

Salib GM, McDonald MB, Smolek M. Safety and efficacy of cyclosporine 0.05% drops versus unpreserved artificial tears in dry-eye patients having laser in situ keratomileusis. *J Cataract Refract Surg.* 2006;32(5):772–778.

Infectious Keratitis

Infectious keratitis may occur following surface ablation procedures or LASIK, as both surgeries involve disturbance of the ocular surface. The risk of infection varies depending on the specific technique. The most common etiologic agents for these infections are gram-positive organisms including *Staphylococcus aureus,* methicillin-resistant *Staphylococcus aureus* (MRSA), *Streptococcus pneumoniae,* and *Streptococcus viridans.* Although health-care workers and people exposed to hospitals and nursing homes may be at greatest risk for MRSA, it has been isolated in increasing numbers of cases without known risk factors. Atypical mycobacteria, *Nocardia asteroides,* and fungi have also been reported to cause infectious keratitis after surface ablation and LASIK (Fig 6-4).

PRK and other surface ablation techniques involve creation of an iatrogenic corneal epithelial defect that may take 3–5 days to heal. During this time, the risk of postoperative infectious keratitis is greatest due to the exposure of the stroma, use of a bandage contact lens, and topical steroid drops, all of which increase the opportunity for eyelid and conjunctival bacterial flora to gain access to the stroma. Management consists of sending the contact lens and corneal scrapings for culture and sensitivity and instituting appropriate

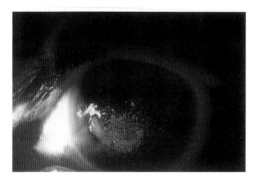

Figure 6-4 *Mycobacterium chelonae* interface infection presenting 3 weeks after LASIK; this infection was initially treated as diffuse lamellar keratitis with topical corticosteroids. *(Reproduced with permission from Feder RS, Rapuano CJ. The LASIK Handbook: A Case-Based Approach. Philadelphia: Lippincott Williams & Wilkins; 2007. Photograph courtesy of Christopher J. Rapuano, MD.)*

intensive topical antibiotic coverage for gram-positive organisms. Antibiotics may include fourth-generation fluoroquinolones, polymyxin B–trimethoprim, fortified vancomycin or cefazolin, and fortified tobramycin or gentamicin.

LASIK involves creation of a corneal flap, under which the eyelid and conjunctival flora may enter during or shortly after surgery and remain sequestered. The antimicrobial components in the tears and topically applied antibiotic drops have difficulty penetrating into the deep stroma to reach the organisms (Fig 6-5). When a post-LASIK infection is suspected, the flap should be lifted and the stromal bed scraped for cultures and sensitivities. Intensive topical antibiotic drops, as described previously, should be instituted pending culture results. If there is lack of clinical progress, additional scrapings may be obtained, the flap may be amputated, and the antibiotic regimen altered.

Karp CL, Tuli SS, Yoo SH, et al. Infectious keratitis after LASIK. *Ophthalmology.* 2003;110(3): 503–510.

Solomon R, Donnenfeld ED, Perry HD, et al. Methicillin-resistant *Staphylococcus aureus* infectious keratitis following refractive surgery. *Am J Ophthalmol.* 2007;143(4):629–634.

Wroblewski KJ, Pasternak JF, Bower KS, et al. Infectious keratitis after photorefractive keratectomy in the United States Army and Navy. *Ophthalmology.* 2006;113(4):520–525.

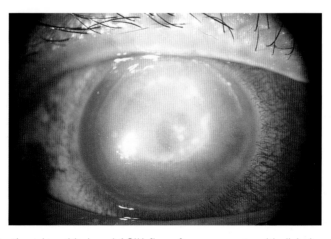

Figure 6-5 Infectious keratitis in a LASIK flap after recurrent epithelial abrasion. *(Courtesy of Jayne S. Weiss, MD.)*

Complications Unique to Surface Ablation

Persistent Epithelial Defects

Usually, the epithelial defect created during surface ablation heals within 3–4 days with the aid of a bandage soft contact lens or pressure patching. A frequent cause of delayed re-epithelialization is keratoconjunctivitis sicca, which may be treated with increased lubrication, cyclosporine, and/or temporary punctal occlusion. Patients who have undiagnosed autoimmune connective tissue disease or diabetes mellitus or who smoke may also have poor epithelial healing. Topical NSAIDs should be discontinued in patients with delayed re-epithelialization. Oral tetracycline-family antibiotics may be beneficial in persistent epithelial defects. Temporary discontinuation of other potentially toxic topical medications, such as glaucoma drops, may also help in re-epithelialization. The importance of closely monitoring patients until re-epithelialization occurs cannot be overemphasized, as a persistent epithelial defect increases the risk of corneal haze, irregular astigmatism, refractive instability, prolonged visual recovery, and infectious keratitis.

Sterile Infiltrates

The use of bandage contact lenses to aid in epithelial healing is associated with sterile infiltrates, especially in patients using topical NSAIDs for longer than 24 hours without concomitant topical corticosteroids. The infiltrates, which have been reported in approximately 1 in 300 cases, are secondary to an immune reaction (Fig 6-6). They are treated with institution of topical steroids, tapering and discontinuation of topical NSAIDs, and close follow-up. It must be kept in mind that any infiltrate may be infectious and should be managed appropriately. If infectious keratitis is suspected, the cornea should be scraped and cultured for suspected organisms.

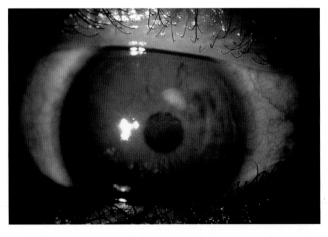

Figure 6-6 Stromal infiltrates seen with a bandage soft contact lens after PRK. *(Courtesy of Jayne S. Weiss, MD.)*

Corneal Haze

The manner of wound healing after surface ablation is important in determining postoperative topical corticosteroid management. Patients who have haze and are undercorrected may benefit from increased corticosteroid use. Patients who have clear corneas following surface ablation and are overcorrected may benefit from a reduction in topical corticosteroids, which may lead to regression of the overcorrection.

Subepithelial corneal haze typically appears several weeks after surface ablation, peaks in intensity at 1–2 months, and gradually diminishes or disappears over the following 6–12 months (Fig 6-7). *Late-onset corneal haze* may occur several months or even a year or more postoperatively after a period in which the patient had a relatively clear cornea. Histologic studies in animals with corneal haze after PRK demonstrate abnormal glycosaminoglycans and/or nonlamellar collagen deposited in the anterior stroma as a consequence of epithelial–stromal wound healing. Most histologic studies from animals and humans show an increase in the number and activity of stromal keratocytes, which suggests that increased keratocyte activity may be the source of the extracellular deposits.

Persistent severe haze is usually associated with greater amounts of correction or smaller ablation zones. Animal studies have demonstrated that ultraviolet (UV) B exposure after PRK prolongs the stromal healing process, with an increase in subepithelial haze. Clinical cases of haze after high UV exposure (such as at high altitude) corroborate these studies. Patients should be encouraged to wear UV-blocking sunglasses and brimmed hats for at least a year after surface ablation when they are in a sunny environment.

If clinically unacceptable haze persists, a superficial keratectomy or phototherapeutic keratectomy (PTK) may be performed. In addition, topical mitomycin C (0.02%) may be used to prevent recurrence of subepithelial fibrosis after debridement or PTK. Because haze is known to resolve spontaneously with normal wound remodeling, re-ablation should be delayed for at least 6–12 months. The clinician should be aware that in the presence of haze, refraction is often inaccurate, typically with an overestimation of the amount of myopia.

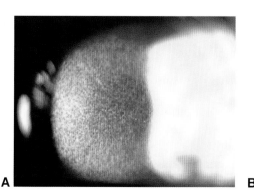
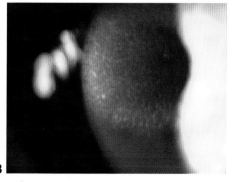

Figure 6-7 PRK haze. **A,** Severe haze 5 months after PRK. The reticular pattern is characteristic of PRK-induced haze. **B,** Haze has improved to moderate level by 13 months postoperatively. *(Courtesy of Roger F. Steinert, MD.)*

Conclusions: Surface Ablation Complications and Side Effects

PRK, LASEK, and epi-LASIK are reasonably safe, effective, and predictable techniques for correcting myopia, astigmatism, and hyperopia. The primary disadvantages of surface ablation are the degree of postoperative discomfort, the length of time required for visual recovery, and the increase in corneal haze with treatment of higher refractive errors. There is also an increased risk of infectious keratitis with surface ablation compared to LASIK due to the longer epithelial healing period. Wound-modulating agents such as mitomycin C are expanding the range of refractive errors that can be effectively treated. Surface ablation may be preferable to LASIK in patients with epithelial basement membrane disease and in patients with thin corneas. PRK, LASEK, and epi-LASIK avoid the increase in higher-order aberrations associated with creation of a LASIK flap. In addition, surface ablation removes the risk of flap complications such as incomplete flaps, buttonholes, and striae. Surface ablation also reduces the risk of ectasia and dry eye compared with LASIK. For these reasons, the use of surface ablation has increased over the last several years.

Carones F, Vigo L, Scandola E, Vacchini L. Evaluation of the prophylactic use of mitomycin-C to inhibit haze formation after photorefractive keratectomy. *J Cataract Refract Surg.* 2002; 28(12):2088–2095.

Corbett MC, Prydal JI, Verma S, Oliver KM, Pande M, Marshall J. An in vivo investigation of the structures responsible for corneal haze after photorefractive keratectomy and their effect on visual function. *Ophthalmology.* 1996;103(9):1366–1380.

Donnenfeld ED, O'Brien TP, Solomon R, Perry HD, Speaker MG, Wittpenn J. Infectious keratitis after photorefractive keratectomy. *Ophthalmology.* 2003;110(4):743–747.

Krueger RR, Saedy NF, McDonnell PJ. Clinical analysis of steep central islands after excimer laser photorefractive keratectomy. *Arch Ophthalmol.* 1996;114(4):377–381.

Matta CA, Piebenga LW, Deitz MR, Tauber J. Excimer retreatment for myopic photorefractive keratectomy failures. Six- to 18-month follow-up. *Ophthalmology.* 1996;103(3):444–451.

Complications Unique to LASIK

The complications associated with LASIK are primarily related to flap creation or postoperative flap positioning. The second-largest group of complications involves sequestration of material or microorganisms beneath the flap.

Microkeratome Complications

In the past, the more severe complications associated with LASIK were related to problems with the microkeratome, which caused the planned LASIK procedure to be abandoned in 0.6%–1.6% of cases. Today, advances in microkeratome technology have significantly reduced the incidence of severe, sight-threatening complications. However, it is still imperative that meticulous care be taken in the cleaning and assembly of the microkeratome to ensure a smooth, uninterrupted keratectomy.

Defects in the blade, poor suction, or uneven progression of the microkeratome across the cornea can produce an irregular, thin, or buttonhole flap (Fig 6-8), which can result in irregular astigmatism with loss of BCVA. Steep corneal curvature is a risk factor for the development of some intraoperative flap complications. If a thin or buttonhole flap

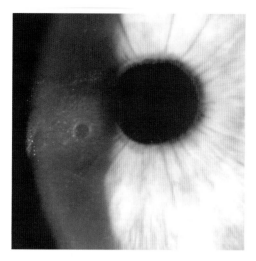

Figure 6-8 LASIK flap with buttonhole. *(Reproduced with permission from Feder RS, Rapuano CJ. The LASIK Handbook: A Case-Based Approach. Philadelphia: Lippincott Williams & Wilkins; 2007:95, fig 5.1. Photograph courtesy of Christopher J. Rapuano, MD.)*

is created, or if an incomplete flap does not provide a sufficiently large corneal stromal surface to perform the laser ablation, the flap should be replaced and the ablation should not be performed. Significant visual loss can be prevented if, under such circumstances, the ablation is not performed and the flap is allowed to heal before another refractive procedure is attempted months later. In such cases, a bandage soft contact lens is applied to stabilize the flap, typically for several days to a week. A new flap can usually be cut safely after at least 3 months of healing, preferably with a different microkeratome head, designed to produce a deeper cut, or with a femtosecond laser; and the ablation can be performed at that time. Alternatively, once the defective flap is judged to be healed, some surgeons prefer surface ablation.

Occasionally, a free cap is created instead of a hinged flap (Fig 6-9). In these cases, if the stromal bed is large enough to accommodate the laser treatment, the corneal cap is

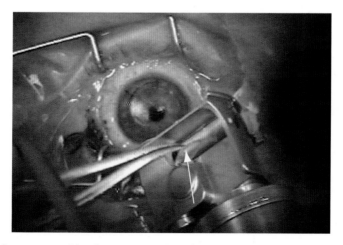

Figure 6-9 A free cap resulting from transection of the hinge. The cap is being lifted from the microkeratome with forceps *(arrow),* and care is being taken to maintain the orientation of the epithelial external layer to prevent accidental inversion of the cap when it is replaced. *(Courtesy of Roger F. Steinert, MD.)*

placed in a moist chamber while the ablation is performed. It is important to replace the cap with the epithelial side up and to position it properly using the previously placed radial marks. A temporary 10-0 nylon suture can be placed to create an artificial hinge, but the physiologic dehydration of the stroma by the endothelial pump will generally keep the cap secured in proper position. A bandage soft contact lens can help protect the cap. A flat corneal curvature (less than 40.00 D) is a risk factor for creating a free cap because the flap diameter is often smaller than average in flat corneas.

Corneal perforation is a rare but devastating intraoperative complication that can occur if the microkeratome is not properly assembled or if the depth plate in an older-model microkeratome is not properly placed. Before beginning the procedure, it is imperative for the surgeon to double-check that the microkeratome has been properly assembled. All microkeratomes made in the past 8–10 years are constructed with a prefixed depth plate, which eliminates this source of error. Corneal perforation can also occur when LASIK is performed on an excessively thin cornea. Corneal thickness must be measured with pachymetry prior to the LASIK procedure, especially in patients who are undergoing re-treatment. Intraoperative pachymetry should be considered, particularly during re-treatment of a patient who had LASIK performed by a different surgeon. In this situation, the surgeon may not have information about the prior flap thickness and thus may not know the thickness of the stromal bed after the flap is lifted. It is important to preoperatively counsel patients undergoing re-treatment that if intraoperative pachymetry reveals an unsafe residual stromal bed thickness (RSBT), the procedure may need to be aborted.

Jacobs JM, Taravella MJ. Incidence of intraoperative flap complications in laser in situ keratomileusis. *J Cataract Refract Surg.* 2002;28(1):23–28.

Lin RT, Maloney RK. Flap complications associated with lamellar refractive surgery. *Am J Ophthalmol.* 1999;127(2):129–136.

Epithelial Sloughing or Defects

The friction of microkeratome passage across the pressurized cornea may loosen a sheet of epithelium (*epithelial slough* or *slide*) or cause a frank epithelial defect. Although patients with epithelial basement membrane dystrophy are at particular risk, in which case surface ablation rather than LASIK is advisable, other patients show no preoperative abnormality. The risk of epithelial abnormality during LASIK correlates with older age. Also, in bilateral LASIK procedures, the second eye has a greater likelihood of sustaining an epithelial defect (57%) if the first eye developed an intraoperative epithelial defect. Techniques suggested to decrease the rate of epithelial defects include limiting toxic topical medications, using chilled proparacaine, minimizing use of topical anesthetic until just prior to the skin prep or to starting the procedure, having patients keep their eyes closed after topical anesthetic is administered, frequent use of corneal lubricating drops, meticulous microkeratome maintenance, and shutting off suction on the microkeratome reverse pass. The femtosecond laser is associated with a reduced incidence of epithelial defects because there is no microkeratome movement across the epithelium. In cases of significant epithelial defects, a bandage soft contact lens is often applied immediately postoperatively and retained until stable re-epithelialization occurs, with subsequent use of intensive lubricants and, occasionally, punctal occlusion. Persistent abnormal epithelium with recurrent erosions or loss of BCVA may require debridement and even superficial PTK using the technique employed for treatment of recurrent erosions (see BCSC Section 8, *External Disease and Cornea*). Epithelial defects are associated with an increased incidence of postoperative DLK, infectious keratitis, flap striae, and epithelial ingrowth, and surgeons should watch closely for these conditions.

Tekwani NH, Huang D. Risk factors for intraoperative epithelial defect in laser in-situ keratomileusis. *Am J Ophthalmol*. 2002;134(3):311–316.

Striae

Flap folds, or striae, are a major cause of decreased visual acuity after LASIK. Some 56% of flap folds are noted on the first postoperative day, and 95% are noted within the first week. Risk factors for development of folds include excessive irrigation under the flap during LASIK, thin flaps, and deep ablations with flap–bed mismatch. Recognition of visually significant folds is important because the success rate of treating folds falls dramatically over time. Early intervention is often critical in treating folds that cause loss of BCVA or visual distortion.

The first step in evaluating a patient with corneal folds is determining the BCVA. Folds are not treated if the BCVA and the subjective visual acuity are excellent. Visually significant folds often induce irregular astigmatism and may be associated with hyperopic astigmatic refractive errors.

Folds are examined with a slit lamp using direct illumination, retroillumination, and fluorescein staining. Circumferential folds may be associated with high myopia and typically resolve with time. Folds that are parallel and grouped in the same direction may indicate a flap slippage, which requires prompt intervention. Corneal topography is usually not helpful in diagnosing folds.

The challenge for the ophthalmologist is to determine which folds are visually significant and will not resolve with time. These folds should be treated promptly with flap massage at the slit lamp or by stretching the flap with sponges and forceps, with or without lifting. Folds that are visually insignificant cause minimal or no symptoms, are not associated with a loss of BCVA, demonstrate a normal fluorescein pattern and normal corneal topography, and may resolve with time (eg, circumferential folds after a large myopic ablation); they do not require intervention.

Folds are often divided into macrostriae and microstriae, although there is significant overlap (Table 6-1). *Macrostriae* represent full-thickness, undulating stromal folds. These folds invariably occur because of initial flap malposition or postoperative flap slippage (Fig 6-10A). Current approaches to smoothing the flap and avoiding striae at the end of the LASIK procedure vary widely. No matter which technique is used, however, the surgeon must carefully examine for the presence of striae once the flap is repositioned. Coaxial and oblique illumination should be used at the operating microscope for this purpose. Macrostriae may occur as patients attempt to squeeze their eyelids shut when the eyelid speculum is removed at the end of surgery. Checking the patient in the early postoperative period is important to detect flap slippage. A protective plastic shield is

Table 6-1 Differentiation of Macrostriae and Microstriae in LASIK Flaps

Characteristic		Macrostriae	Microstriae
Pathology		Large folds involving entire flap thickness	Fine folds, principally in the Bowman layer
Cause		Flap slippage	Mismatch of flap to new bed; contracture of flap
Slit-lamp appearance	Direct illumination	Broad undulations as parallel or radial converging lines; widened flap gutter may be seen	Fine folds, principally in the Bowman layer; gutter usually symmetric
	Retroillumination	Same as above	Folds more obvious on retroillumination
	Fluorescein	Same as above, with negative staining pattern	Often has normal fluorescein pattern
Analogy		Wrinkles in skewed carpet	Dried, cracked mud
Topography		Possible disruption over striae	Color map may be normal or slightly disrupted; Placido disk mires show fine irregularity
Vision		Decreased BCVA and/or multiplopia if central	Subtle decreased BCVA or multiplopia if clinically significant; microstriae masked by epithelium are universal and asymptomatic
Treatment options	Acute	Refloat/reposition flap immediately	Observe; support surface with aggressive lubrication
	Established	Refloat, de-epithelialize over striae, hydrate and stroke, apply traction, or suture Phototherapeutic keratectomy	If visually significant, refloat; try hydration, stroking, suturing Phototherapeutic keratectomy

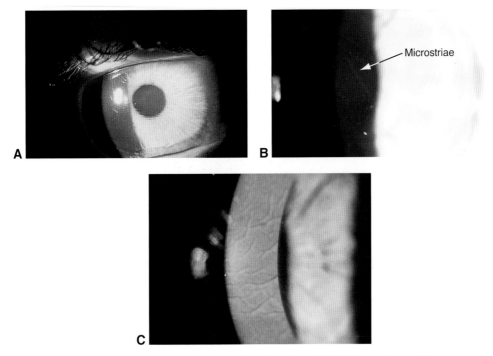

Figure 6-10   Post-LASIK striae. **A,** Retroillumination of multiple horizontal parallel macrostriae in the visual axis from mild flap dislocation. **B,** Diffuse illumination of visually insignificant microstriae in the visual axis after LASIK. **C,** Numerous randomly directed microstriae on fluorescein staining. These resemble multiple cracks in a piece of ice, are seen on the first postoperative day after LASIK, and usually resolve without intervention. *(Part A reprinted with permission from* External Disease and Cornea: A Multimedia Collection. *San Francisco: American Academy of Ophthalmology; 2000; part B courtesy of Jayne S. Weiss, MD; part C courtesy of Steven C. Schallhorn, MD.)*

often used for the first 24 hours to discourage the patient from touching the eyelids and inadvertently disrupting the flap.

Flap subluxation has been reported to occur in up to 1.4% of eyes. Careful examination should disclose a wider gutter on the side where the folds are most prominent. Flap slippage should be rectified as soon as it is recognized because the folds rapidly become fixed. Under the operating microscope or at the slit lamp, an eyelid speculum is placed, the flap is lifted and repositioned, copious irrigation with sterile balanced salt solution is used in the interface, and the flap is repeatedly stroked perpendicular to the fold until the striae resolve or improve. Using hypotonic saline or sterile distilled water as the interface irrigating solution swells the flap and may initially reduce the striae, but swelling also reduces the flap diameter, which widens the gutter, delays flap adhesion due to prolonged endothelial dehydration time, and may worsen the striae after the flap dehydrates. If the macrostriae have been present for more than 24 hours, reactive epithelial hyperplasia in the valleys and hypoplasia over the elevations of the macrostriae tend to fix the folds into position. In such a case, in addition to refloating the flap, the central 6 mm of the flap over the macrostriae may be de-epithelialized to remove this impediment to smoothing the wrinkles. A bandage soft contact lens should be used to stabilize the flap and to protect the surface until full re-epithelialization occurs. In cases of intractable macrostriae, a tight 360° anti-torque running suture or multiple interrupted sutures using 10-0 nylon may be placed for several weeks; but irregular astigmatism may still be present after suture removal.

Microstriae are fine, hairlike optical irregularities that are best seen on red reflex illumination or light reflected off the iris (Fig 6-10B, C). They are fine folds in the Bowman layer, and this anterior location accounts for the disruption of BCVA in some eyes. Computer topographic color maps do not usually show these fine irregularities. However, disruption of the surface contour may result in irregularity of the Placido disk image. In addition, application of dilute fluorescein often reveals so-called *negative staining*, where the elevated striae disrupt the tear film and fluorescence is lost over them.

If optically significant microstriae persist, the flap may be sutured in an attempt to reduce the striae by means of tension. As with macrostriae, however, suturing has the potential to induce new irregular astigmatism. An alternative procedure is PTK. Pulses from a broad-beam laser, set to a maximal diameter of 6.5 mm, are initially applied to penetrate the epithelium in about 200 pulses. The epithelium acts as a masking agent, exposing the elevated striae before the valleys between the striae. After the transepithelial ablation, additional pulses are applied, and a thin film of medium-viscosity artificial tears is administered every 5–10 pulses, up to a maximum of 100 additional pulses. If these guidelines are followed, little to no haze results, and an average hyperopic shift of less than +1.00 D occurs, due to the minimal tissue removal.

Ashrafzadeh A, Steinert RF. Results of phototherapeutic keratectomy in the management of flap striae after LASIK before and after developing a standardized protocol: long-term follow-up of an expanded patient population. *Ophthalmology.* 2007;114(6):1118–1123.

Jackson DW, Hamill MB, Koch DD. Laser in situ keratomileusis flap suturing to treat recalcitrant flap striae. *J Cataract Refract Surg.* 2003;29(2):264–269.

Traumatic Flap Dislocation

Flap subluxation has been reported to occur in up to 1.4% of eyes. Dislocation of the LASIK flap is not uncommon on the first postoperative day, when dryness and adhesion of the flap to the upper tarsal conjunctiva is sufficient to cause the flap to slip. After the first day, however, the re-epithelialization of the gutter begins the process of increasing flap stability. Within several weeks, keratocytes begin to lay down new collagen at the cut edge of the Bowman layer; and, eventually, a fine scar is established at the edge of the flap. Minimal healing occurs across the stromal interface for several years, however, allowing flap lifting for enhancement procedures. Late dislocation from blunt trauma has been reported many years after LASIK; this can also occur if the shearing force exceeds the strength of the peripheral Bowman layer–level healing. Flap dislocation requires urgent treatment to replace the flap in its proper anatomic position. The surgeon should make sure that there is no epithelium on the underside of the flap and covering the stromal bed, as this significantly increases the chances of epithelial ingrowth.

Diffuse Lamellar Keratitis

Diffuse lamellar keratitis (DLK) has been referred to as sterile interface inflammation, "sands of the Sahara" (SOS), and—perhaps most accurately—diffuse interface keratitis

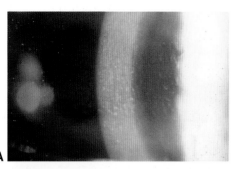

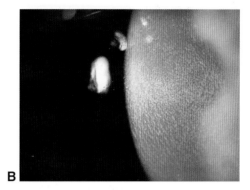

A

B

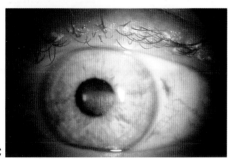

C

Figure 6-11 Diffuse lamellar keratitis (DLK). **A,** High magnification of stage 2 DLK (note accumulation of inflammatory cells in the fine ridges created by the oscillating microkeratome blade). **B,** Stage 3 DLK (dense accumulation of inflammatory cells centrally). **C,** Stage 4 DLK with central scar and folds. *(Parts A and B courtesy of Roger F. Steinert, MD; part C courtesy of Jayne S. Weiss, MD.)*

(Fig 6-11). This syndrome can range from asymptomatic interface haze near the edge of the flap to marked diffuse haze under the center of the flap with diminished BCVA. The condition appears to be a nonspecific sterile inflammatory response to a variety of mechanical and toxic insults. The interface under the flap is a potential space; any cause of anterior stromal inflammation may trigger the accumulation of white blood cells therein. DLK has been reported in association with epithelial defects that occur during primary LASIK or during enhancement, or even months after the LASIK procedure from corneal abrasions or infectious keratitis. Other reported inciting factors include foreign material on the surface of the microkeratome blade or motor, meibomian gland secretions, povidone-iodine solution (from the preoperative skin prep), marking ink, substances produced by laser ablation, contamination of the sterilizer with gram-negative endotoxin, and red blood cells in the interface. The inflammation generally resolves on its own without sequelae, but severe cases can lead to scarring or flap melting.

DLK is usually classified by the stages described in Table 6-2. Although stages 1 and 2 usually respond to frequent topical corticosteroid application, stages 3 and 4 usually

—usually self-limited, but can cause scarring or melt

Table 6-2 Staging of Diffuse Lamellar Keratitis

Stage	Findings
1	Peripheral faint white blood cells; granular appearance
2	Central scattered white blood cells; granular appearance
3	Central dense white blood cells in visual axis
4	Permanent scarring or stromal melting

—Stage 1+2: topical steroids

—Stage 3+4: lifting + irrigating flap vs adding po

require lifting the flap and irrigating, followed by intensive topical corticosteroid treatment. Systemic corticosteroids may be used adjunctively in severe cases. Some surgeons use topical and systemic corticosteroids in stage 3 DLK instead of lifting the flap. Recovery of vision in DLK is usually excellent if the condition is detected and treated promptly.

A surgeon should have a low threshold for lifting or irrigating underneath the flap in suspected cases of DLK. Lifting the flap allows removal of inflammatory mediators from the interface and direct placement of corticosteroids and NSAIDs to suppress inflammation and collagen necrosis. If there is any suspicion that the inflammation is due to infection, lifting the flap and obtaining samples for corneal cultures of the interface should be considered. Topical antibiotics can also be placed in the flap interface at the same time.

Haft P, Yoo SH, Kymionis GD, Ide T, O'Brien TP, Culbertson WW. Complications of LASIK flaps made by the IntraLase 15 and 30 kHz femtosecond lasers. *J Refract Surg.* 2009;25(11):979-984.

Hoffman RS, Fine IH, Packer M. Incidence and outcomes of LASIK with diffuse lamellar keratitis treated with topical and oral corticosteroids. *J Cataract Refract Surg.* 2003;29(3):451–456.

Holland SP, Mathias RG, Morck DW, Chiu J, Slade SG. Diffuse lamellar keratitis related to endotoxins released from sterilizer reservoir biofilms. *Ophthalmology.* 2000;107(7):1227–1233.

Linebarger EJ, Hardten DR, Lindstrom RL. Diffuse lamellar keratitis: diagnosis and management. *J Cataract Refract Surg.* 2000;26(7):1072–1077.

Differentiating infectious keratitis from DLK

It is important to differentiate sterile interface inflammation from potentially devastating infectious inflammation. Increased pain and decreased vision are the primary indicators of infection. However, postoperative eye pain is common, so it is difficult for patients to distinguish between normal and abnormal eye pain. Moreover, because corneal nerves are severed during flap creation, corneal sensation may be reduced, along with the subjective symptom of pain that usually accompanies infection. Infection following LASIK is usually associated with redness, photophobia, and decreased vision. Several distinct features can help distinguish between DLK and infectious keratitis (Table 6-3). DLK is usually visible within 24 hours of surgery and typically begins at the periphery of the flap. There is usually a gradient of inflammation, with the inflammation being most intense at the periphery and diminishing toward the center of the cornea. In general, the inflammatory

Table 6-3 Diffuse Lamellar Keratitis vs Infectious Keratitis

DLK	Infection
Usually seen within first 24 hours	Usual onset at least 2–3 days postoperatively
Typically begins at flap periphery	Can occur anywhere under flap
More intense inflammation at periphery decreasing toward center	
Inflammation primarily confined to interface	Inflammation extends above and below interface, and beyond flap edge
Diffuse inflammation	Focal inflammation around infection
Minimal to no anterior chamber reaction	Mild to moderate anterior chamber reaction
Flap melts can occur	Flap melts can occur

Modified with permission from Culbertson WW. Surface ablation and LASIK patients share similar infection potential. *Refractive Eyecare.* September 2006:12.

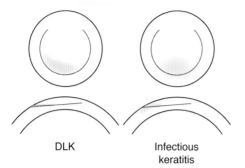

DLK Infectious
keratitis

Figure 6-12 Diffuse lamellar keratitis (DLK) is differentiated from infectious keratitis by the confinement of the infiltrate to the interface alone in DLK. *(Reproduced with permission from Culbertson WW. Surface ablation and LASIK patients share similar infection potential. Refractive Eyecare. September 2006:12.)*

reaction seen in DLK is diffusely distributed but localized and confined to the area of the flap interface; it does not extend far beyond the edge of the flap (Fig 6-12). In contrast, post-LASIK infectious keratitis usually begins 2–3 days after surgery and involves a more focal inflammatory reaction that is not confined to the lamellar interface. An anterior chamber reaction may further help to differentiate between an infectious and a sterile process. The inflammatory reaction can extend up into the flap, deeper into the stromal bed, and even beyond the confines of the flap.

Infection within the interface can lead to flap melting, severe irregular astigmatism, and corneal scarring that requires corneal transplantation. If infection is suspected, the flap should be lifted and the interface cultured and irrigated with antibiotics. The most common infections are from gram-positive organisms, followed in frequency by those caused by atypical mycobacteria. Mycobacteria can be diagnosed more rapidly by using acid-fast and fluorochrome stains rather than waiting for culture results (see Fig 6-4).

In general, the timing of the onset of symptoms provides a clue as to the etiology of the infection. Infections occurring within 10 days of surgery are typically bacterial, with the preponderance being from gram-positive organisms. Suggested empirical treatment may include fortified tobramycin (14 mg/mL) and vancomycin (25–50 mg/mL) or a fourth-generation fluoroquinolone and cefazolin (50 mg/mL). Infections presenting more than 10 days after surgery are more likely caused by atypical mycobacteria and fungi. Topical clarithromycin (10 mg/mL), oral clarithromycin (500 mg bid), and topical amikacin (8 mg/mL) are recommended for treatment of mycobacterial infections. If a filamentous fungus is identified, natamycin (50 mg/mL) is recommended; amphotericin (1.5 mg/mL) is recommended for yeast infections. Voriconazole (10 mg/mL) may be used for both yeasts and filamentous fungi and is often supplemented with voriconazole tablets (400 mg bid). If the infection does not respond to treatment, amputation of the flap may be necessary to improve antimicrobial penetration. The fourth-generation fluoroquinolones gatifloxacin and moxifloxacin have excellent efficacy against the more common bacteria that cause post-LASIK infections, including some atypical mycobacteria; however, monotherapy with these agents may not be sufficient. A LASIK flap infection may occur after a recurrent erosion (see Fig 6-5).

Freitas D, Alvarenga L, Sampaio J, et al. An outbreak of *Mycobacterium chelonae* infection after LASIK. *Ophthalmology.* 2003;110(2):276–285.

Karp CL, Tuli SS, Yoo SH, et al. Infectious keratitis after LASIK. *Ophthalmology.* 2003;110(3): 503–510.

Pressure-Induced Stromal Keratitis

Late-onset interface opacity similar to DLK, often with a visible fluid cleft in the interface, has been reported as a result of elevated IOP and has been termed *pressure-induced stromal keratitis (PISK)* (Fig 6-13). The surgeon must be aware of this unusual condition in order to properly diagnose and treat it. The pressure-induced interface fluid accumulation can appear very similar to DLK and is often associated with prolonged corticosteroid treatment. It is important to measure IOP both centrally and peripherally, possibly with a pneumotonometer or Tono-Pen, because applanation pressure may be falsely lowered centrally by fluid accumulation in the lamellar interface. Treatment for PISK involves rapid tapering or cessation of the corticosteroid drops and use of glaucoma medication to lower IOP. Severe glaucomatous visual loss has been reported in undiagnosed cases.

Hamilton DR, Manche EE, Rich LF, Maloney RK. Steroid-induced glaucoma after laser in situ keratomileusis associated with interface fluid. *Ophthalmology.* 2002;109(4):659–665.

Moya Calleja T, Iribarne Ferrer Y, Sanz Jorge A, Sedó Fernandez S. Steroid-induced interface fluid syndrome after LASIK. *J Refract Surg.* 2009;25(2):235–239.

Epithelial Ingrowth

Epithelial ingrowth occurs in less than 3% of eyes (Fig 6-14). Isolated nests of epithelial cells in the peripheral lamellar interface that are not advancing and are not affecting vision do not need to be treated. However, if the epithelium is advancing toward the visual axis, is associated with decreased vision from irregular astigmatism (Fig 6-15), or triggers overlying flap melting, it should be removed by lifting the flap, scraping the epithelium from both the underside of the flap and the stromal bed, and then repositioning the flap. After scraping the under-flap surface and stromal bed, some surgeons also remove epithelium from the peripheral cornea to allow for flap adherence before the epithelial edge advances to the flap edge. Recurrent epithelial ingrowth can be treated with repeated lifting and scraping, with or without flap suturing or using fibrin glue at the flap edge.

The incidence of epithelial ingrowth is greater in patients who develop an epithelial defect at the time of the procedure, who undergo a re-treatment with lifting of a preexisting flap, or who have traumatic flap dehiscence. In these cases, special care should be

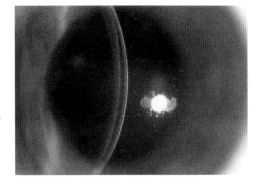

Figure 6-13 An optically clear fluid-filled space between the flap and stromal bed. This condition is hypothesized to be caused by transudation of fluid across the endothelium as a result of steroid-induced elevation of IOP. *(Reproduced with permission from Hamilton DR, Manche EE, Rich LF, Maloney RK. Steroid-induced glaucoma after laser in situ keratomileusis associated with interface fluid.* Ophthalmology. *2002;109(4):659–665.)*

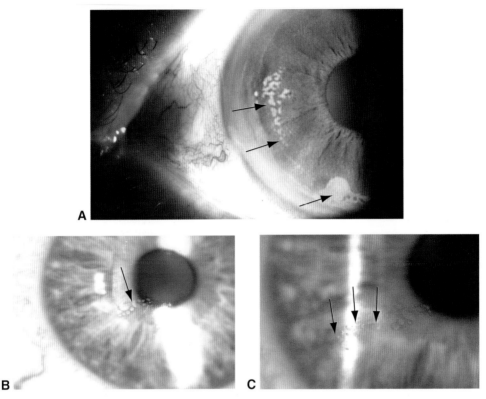

Figure 6-14 Epithelial ingrowth in the interface under a LASIK flap. **A,** Peripheral ingrowth of 1–2 mm *(arrows)* is common and inconsequential and does not require intervention unless it induces melting of the overlying flap. **B,** Central nests of epithelial cells *(arrow)* disrupt the patient's vision by elevating and distorting the flap. The flap must be lifted and the epithelium debrided. **C,** Inspection of the midperiphery shows the track followed by the invading epithelium from the periphery toward the center *(arrows). (Courtesy of Roger F. Steinert, MD.)*

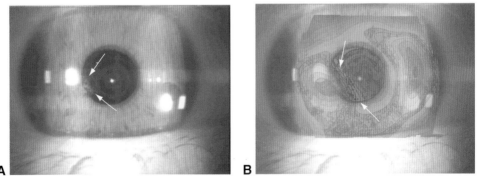

Figure 6-15 **A,** Epithelial ingrowth in visual axis *(arrows).* **B,** Corresponding topographic steepening and irregularity on Orbscan topography. *(Part B courtesy of Jayne S. Weiss, MD.)*

taken to ensure that no epithelium is caught under the edge of the flap when it is repositioned. Placement of a bandage contact lens at the conclusion of the procedure may also
decrease the incidence of epithelial ingrowth for patients at higher risk of developing this
complication.

Asano-Kato N, Toda I, Hori-Komai Y, Takano Y, Tsubota K. Epithelial ingrowth after laser in situ
keratomileusis: clinical features and possible mechanisms. *Am J Ophthalmol.* 2002;134(6):
801–807.

Interface Debris

Debris in the interface is occasionally seen postoperatively. The principal indication for
intervention, with flap lifting, irrigation, and manual removal of debris, is an inflammatory reaction elicited by the foreign material. Small amounts of lint, nondescript particles,
or tiny metal particles from stainless steel surgical instruments are usually well tolerated.
A small amount of blood that may have oozed into the interface from transected peripheral vessels may also be tolerated; however, a significant amount of blood usually elicits
an inflammatory cell response and should be irrigated from the interface at the time of
the LASIK procedure (Fig 6-16). Use of a topical vasoconstrictor such as epinephrine to
facilitate coagulation when the flap is being replaced helps to minimize this problem. The
surgeon should be aware that applying epinephrine prior to laser ablation can result in
pupillary dilation and treatment decentration. Blood remaining in the interface typically
resolves spontaneously with time.

Ectasia

The importance of an adequate residual stromal bed to prevent structural instability and
postoperative corneal ectasia is discussed in Chapter 2. Ectasia has been reported far more
frequently after LASIK than after surface ablation. This makes sense given that creation
of a LASIK flap allows for a deeper ablation and a thinner RSBT compared with surface

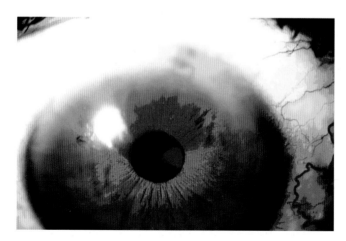

Figure 6-16   Blood in the LASIK interface. *(Courtesy of Jayne S. Weiss, MD.)*

ablation. Current standards recommend a minimum RSBT of at least 250 μm after completion of the LASIK ablation (see Chapter 2), although there are no controlled studies to confirm this clinical impression. Although keratectasia is usually associated with LASIK performed for higher myopic corrections, in thin corneas, or in patients who have had multiple laser ablations, some cases of ectasia have been reported with corrections as low as –4.00 D, where the RSBT was believed to be >250 μm. In many of these cases, later examination revealed that the microkeratome created a flap thicker than expected, leaving a thinner residual stromal bed. In other cases, preoperative forme fruste keratoconus, subtle keratoconus, pellucid marginal degeneration, or other ectasias may have been present. In a retrospective study of 10 eyes from 7 patients who developed corneal ectasia after LASIK, all patients had either preoperative undiagnosed forme fruste keratoconus (88%) or an RSBT of less than 250 μm (70%). Often, good vision can be restored with a rigid gas-permeable or hybrid contact lens. The implantation of symmetric or asymmetric intrastromal ring segments (eg, Intacs) to reduce the irregular astigmatism has been successful in selected cases. In extreme cases, corneal transplantation may be required.

In 2005, a joint statement was issued by the American Academy of Ophthalmology, the International Society for Refractive Surgery, and the American Society of Cataract and Refractive Surgery summarizing current knowledge of corneal ectatic disorders and ectasia after LASIK. Their 8 conclusions were

1. No specific test or measurement is diagnostic of a corneal ectatic disorder.
2. A decision to perform LASIK should take into account the entire clinical picture, not just the corneal topography.
3. Although some risk factors have been suggested for ectasia after LASIK, none are absolute predictors of its occurrence.
4. Because keratoconus may develop in the absence of refractive surgery, the occurrence of ectasia after LASIK does not necessarily mean that LASIK was a causative or contributing factor for its development.
5. Risk factors for ectasia after LASIK may not also predict ectasia after surface ablation.
6. Ectasia is a known risk of laser vision correction.
7. Forme fruste keratoconus is a topographic diagnosis rather than a clinical one. It is not a variant of keratoconus. Rather, forme fruste implies subclinical disease with the potential for progression to clinically evident keratoconus.
8. Although to date no formal guidelines exist and good scientific data for future guidelines are presently lacking, in order to reduce some of the risks of ectasia after LASIK, the groups recommended that surgeons review topography prior to surgery. Intraoperative pachymetry should be used to measure flap thickness and calculate the RST after ablation to ascertain if the RST is near the safe lower limits for the procedure, for that patient.

A recent study retrospectively analyzed the use of the Ectasia Risk Factor Score System and found it to have 91% sensitivity and 96% specificity. Numbers are assigned to 5 categories of risk factors: topography pattern, RSBT, patient age, preoperative corneal thickness, and preoperative spherical equivalent manifest refraction. The greater the number of points, the greater the risk for post-LASIK ectasia.

Binder PS, Lindstrom RL, Stulting RD, et al. Keratoconus and corneal ectasia after LASIK. *J Cataract Refract Surg.* 2005;31(11):2035–2038.

Ou RJ, Shaw EL, Glasgow BJ. Keratectasia after laser in situ keratomileusis (LASIK): evaluation of the calculated residual stromal bed thickness. *Am J Ophthalmol.* 2002;134(5):771–773.

Randleman JB, Russell B, Ward MA, Thompson KP, Stulting RD. Risk factors and prognosis for corneal ectasia after LASIK. *Ophthalmology.* 2003;110(2):267–275.

Randleman JB, Woodward M, Lynn MJ, Stulting RD. Risk assessment of ectasia after corneal refractive surgery. *Ophthalmology.* 2008;115(1):37–50.

Visual Disturbances Related to Femtosecond Laser LASIK Flaps

Good acuity, postoperative photophobia

Several weeks to months after LASIK with femtosecond laser flaps, some patients develop acute onset of pain, photophobia, and light sensitivity in an otherwise white and quiet eye with excellent UCVA. The cornea and flap interface appear normal. This rare entity has been termed *good acuity, postoperative photophobia (GAPP)*. It has been speculated that an acute onset of ocular inflammation or dry eyes is somehow related to the femtosecond laser. Treatment consists of frequent topical corticosteroids (eg, prednisolone acetate 1% every 2 hours) and topical cyclosporine A, titrated to the clinical condition. Almost all cases respond to treatment and resolve in weeks to months.

Rainbow glare

Rainbow glare, a new optical side effect of the femtosecond laser, is described as bands of color around white lights at night. This complication seems to be related to higher raster energy levels and length of time between service calls for the laser.

Rare Complications

Rare complications of LASIK include optic nerve ischemia, premacular subhyaloid hemorrhage, macular hemorrhage associated with preexisting lacquer cracks or choroidal neovascularization, choroidal infarcts, postoperative corneal edema associated with preoperative cornea guttata, and ring scotoma. Diplopia is another rare complication that may occur in patients whose refractive error has been corrected and who have iatrogenic monovision, improper control of accommodation (in patients with strabismus), or decompensated phorias.

Gimbel HV, Penno EE, van Westenbrugge JA, Ferensowicz M, Furlong MT. Incidence and management of intraoperative and early postoperative complications in 1000 consecutive laser in situ keratomileusis cases. *Ophthalmology.* 1998;105(10):1839–1848.

Kushner BJ, Kowal L. Diplopia after refractive surgery: occurrence and prevention. *Arch Ophthalmol.* 2003;121(3):315–321.

Stulting RD, Carr JD, Thompson KP, Waring GO III, Wiley WM, Walker JG. Complications of laser in situ keratomileusis for the correction of myopia. *Ophthalmology.* 1999;106(1):13–20.

Sugar A, Rapuano CJ, Culbertson WW, et al. Laser in situ keratomileusis for myopia and astigmatism: safety and efficacy: a report by the American Academy of Ophthalmology. *Ophthalmology*. 2002;109(1):175–187.

Conclusions: LASIK Complications and Side Effects

Although LASIK is the most popular refractive surgery procedure performed today, it has limitations. Many surgeons do not use LASIK to treat to the full extent allowed by FDA parameters, including higher levels of myopia (up to −14.00 D) and hyperopia (up to +6.00 D), because of poorer predictability and the increased possibility of complications.

Although LASIK has surpassed surface ablation in popularity for treating many refractive errors, visual results of the 2 procedures are actually very similar. The incidence of complications in LASIK decreases with surgeon experience; and, as with any surgical procedure, the surgeon should continuously work toward optimizing surgical technique to reduce complications. At the FDA hearing on LASIK in 2008, a major concern was dry eye. When recognized and properly treated, however, most complications will not result in loss of BCVA. For example, irregular astigmatism is a common cause of decreased BCVA; but often, epithelial hyperplasia and hypoplasia occur, smoothing the corneal surface over time, reducing the irregular astigmatism, and improving visual acuity. If significant symptoms persist, the patient may benefit from selective surface treatments.

Technological advances will continue to improve visual outcomes. Wavefront-guided laser ablation, also discussed in Chapter 1, offers the potential to improve visual quality. Treatment of highly irregular corneas with topography-guided ablations may allow clinicians to treat scars, keratoconus, and highly irregular corneas. Future advances in laser technology will undoubtedly further refine the safety and efficacy of excimer laser photoablation.

McColgin AZ, Steinert RF. LASIK. In: Tasman W, Jaeger EA, eds. *Duane's Clinical Ophthalmology*. Philadelphia: Lippincott Williams & Wilkins; 2001.

Netto MV, Dupps W Jr, Wilson SE. Wavefront-guided ablation: evidence for efficacy compared to traditional ablation. *Am J Ophthalmol*. 2006;141(2):360–368.

CHAPTER 7

Collagen Shrinkage and Crosslinking Procedures

Refractive surgical procedures aim to alter the refractive power of the cornea by changing its shape. Various methods are used to alter corneal curvature, including incising or removing corneal tissue or implanting artificial material into the eye. Procedures that change the character of the corneal collagen have also been developed. This chapter focuses on 2 such procedures: corneal collagen shrinkage and corneal collagen crosslinking.

Collagen Shrinkage

History

The idea of using heat to alter the shape of the cornea was first proposed by Lans, a Dutch medical student, in 1898. When Lans used electrocautery to heat the corneal stroma, he noticed astigmatic changes in the cornea. In 1900, Terrien reported the use of cautery to correct the severe astigmatism associated with Terrien marginal degeneration, and in 1928, Knapp used cautery to improve the visual acuity of patients with keratoconus.

In 1975, Gasset and Kaufman proposed a modified technique known as *thermokeratoplasty* to treat keratoconus. They theorized that the hot cautery used in prior reports caused collagen necrosis. Their goal was to apply heat to the cornea in a controlled fashion, in order to shrink collagen fibers without causing necrosis. It is now known that the optimal temperature for avoiding stromal necrosis while still obtaining corneal collagen shrinkage is approximately 58°–76°C. Human collagen fibrils can shrink by almost two-thirds when exposed to temperatures in this range, as the heat disrupts the hydrogen bonds in the supercoiled structure of collagen. In the cornea, the maximal shrinkage is approximately 7%. When higher temperatures are reached (>78°C), tissue necrosis occurs.

In 1984, Fyodorov introduced a technique of radial thermokeratoplasty that used a handheld heated Nichrome needle designed for deeper thermokeratoplasty. The handheld probe contained a retractable 34-gauge wire heated to 600°C. A motor advanced the wire to a preset depth of 95% of the corneal pachymetry for a duration of 0.3 second. Fyodorov used different patterns to treat hyperopia and astigmatism. However, excessive heating of the cornea resulted in necrosis and corneal remodeling, and regression of treatment and unpredictability limited the success of this technique.

Neumann AC, Fyodorov S, Sanders DR. Radial thermokeratoplasty for the correction of hyperopia. *Refract Corneal Surg.* 1990;6(6):404–412.

Laser Thermokeratoplasty

In the 1990s, multiple lasers were tested for use in laser thermokeratoplasty (LTK). Only the holmium:yttrium-aluminum-garnet (Ho:YAG) laser reached commercial production and FDA approval. The Ho:YAG laser produces light in the infrared region at a wavelength of 2100 nm and has corneal tissue penetration to approximately 480 to 530 μm. Two different delivery systems were investigated: a contact system and a noncontact version.

The noncontact Sunrise Hyperion system was approved by the FDA in 2000. This laser used a slit-lamp delivery system to apply 8 simultaneous spots at a wavelength of 2.1 μm at a frequency of 5 Hz and a pulse duration of 250 μsec. The system was approved for the temporary correction of 0.75 to 2.5 D of hyperopia with less than 1.0 D of astigmatism. Initial interest in LTK waned, primarily because of the significant refractive regression that frequently occurred. Few LTK units, if any, remain in clinical use.

Conductive Keratoplasty

In the past decade, radiofrequency has reemerged as a method of heating the cornea. In 2002, the FDA approved the ViewPoint CK system (Refractec, Bloomington, MN) for the temporary treatment of mild to moderate hyperopia with minimal astigmatism. In 2004, conductive keratoplasty (CK) received FDA approval for treatment of presbyopia in the nondominant eye of a presbyopic patient with an endpoint of −1.00 to −2.00 D. For both treatments, patients are typically 40 years of age or older and have had a stable refraction for at least 12 months.

CK is a nonablative, collagen-shrinking procedure based on the delivery of radiofrequency energy through a fine conducting tip that is inserted into the peripheral corneal stroma (Fig 7-1). As the current flows through the tissue surrounding the tip, resistance to the current creates localized heat. Collagen lamellae in the area surrounding the tip shrink in a controlled fashion and form a column of denatured collagen. The shortening of the collagen fibrils creates a band of tightening that increases the curvature of the central cornea.

For the treatment of hyperopia, the surgeon inserts the tip into the stroma in a ring pattern around the peripheral cornea. The number and location of spots determine the amount of refractive change, with an increasing number of spots and rings used for higher amounts of hyperopia. The CK procedure is performed under topical anesthesia and typically takes less than 5 minutes. The collagen shrinkage leads to visible striae between the treated spots, which fade with time (Fig 7-2).

Patient selection and results

The Refractec system is approved for the temporary reduction of spherical hyperopia in patients 40 years or older with a spherical equivalent of +0.75 to +3.25 D and ≤0.75 D of astigmatism. The clinical trial consisted of 12-month data in 401 eyes, with a mean cohort age of 55.3 years (range: 40.2–73.9 years). The mean cycloplegic spherical equivalent was

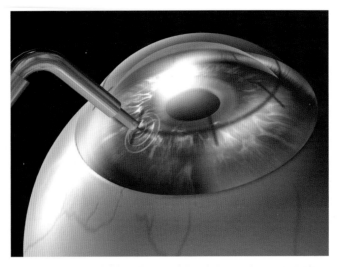

Figure 7-1 Conductive keratoplasty delivers radiofrequency energy to the cornea through a handheld probe that is inserted into the peripheral cornea. *(Courtesy of Refractec, Inc.)*

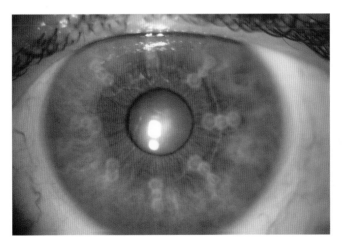

Figure 7-2 A month after a 24-spot CK treatment in a patient with +2.0 D hyperopia, the spots are beginning to fade. Three sets of 8 spots were applied at a 6.0-mm, 7.0-mm, and 8.0-mm optical zone. *(Courtesy of Refractec, Inc.)*

+1.86 ± 0.63 D. By 12 months postoperatively, 92% of study patients had achieved uncorrected visual acuity (UCVA) of 20/40 or better, 74% were 20/25 or better, and 54% were 20/20 or better. By 24 months postoperatively, 93% of study patients had achieved UCVA of 20/40 or better, 76% were 20/25 or better, and 52% were 20/20 or better. There was a slow continued drift toward increasing hyperopia, with regression of +0.21 D and +0.48 D at 12 and 24 months, respectively. Overall, there was a 20% loss of effect after 2 years. This "loss of effect" is probably a combination of true regression and the normal hyperopic drift that is seen as patients age. The results in the FDA CK trial for presbyopia were similar.

CK is not advised for use in patients who have undergone radial keratotomy, and it is not FDA approved for use in those with keratoconus, ectatic disorders, or significant irregular astigmatism. An upper limit of +1.50 D (spherical equivalent) appears to be the current treatment ceiling for this technology; multiple applications over time or more spots do not seem to enhance or increase that limit.

Hersh PS. Optics of conductive keratoplasty: implications for presbyopia management. *Trans Am Ophthalmol Soc.* 2005;103:412–456.

McDonald MB. Conductive keratoplasty: a radiofrequency-based technique for the correction of hyperopia. *Trans Am Ophthalmol Soc.* 2005;103:512–536.

Safety

Although the initial efficacy results for CK appear to be similar to those of LASIK and LTK, the safety variables are superior. In the principal FDA clinical trial, no patient was worse than 20/40 and no patient lost more than 2 lines of vision. One patient out of 391 had >2.0 D of induced cylinder, and no patient with a preoperative best-corrected visual acuity of ≥20/20 had <20/25 at 1 year. Although induced cylinder of >2.0 D is an FDA safety variable, smaller amounts of induced cylinder were apparent. At 1 year, 6% of patients had >1.0 D of induced cylinder. The magnitude of the induced cylinder decreases with time. No central corneal haze was noted at 12 months, and endothelial cell counts were similar before and after the study.

Despite initial reports of refractive stability, long-term follow-up has revealed regression and/or lack of adequate effect with CK. In a long-term (mean 73.1 months, range 44–90 months) follow-up of patients enrolled in the phase 3 multicenter trial of CK, Ehrlich and Manche found nearly complete regression of treatment effect in the 16 eyes (of the original 25 eyes) available for follow-up. Some surgeons have used CK in combination with collagen crosslinking in an attempt to correct the corneal curvature abnormalities in keratoconus.

Ehrlich JS, Manche EE. Regression of effect over long-term follow-up of conductive keratoplasty to correct mild to moderate hyperopia. *J Cataract Refract Surg.* 2009;35(9):1591–1596.

Kymionis GD, Kontadakis GA, Naoumidi TL, Kazakos DC, Giapitzakis I, Pallikaris IG. Conductive keratoplasty followed by collagen cross-linking with riboflavin-UV-A in patients with keratoconus. *Cornea.* 2010;29(2):239–243.

Other applications

A number of potential off-label uses also exist for CK. In overcorrected myopic LASIK and myopic PRK, CK can be used to correct hyperopia. In these cases, CK obviates the need to lift or cut another flap. In one report, CK was used to treat both keratoconus and post-LASIK ectasia. Although corneal irregularities improved immediately, with some visual improvement, some cases showed regression of effect at 1 month. Larger studies with additional follow-up are needed.

In postcataract or postkeratoplasty patients with astigmatism, CK can be used to steepen the flat axis, because each spot is individually placed. The overall effect is still a myopic shift, so CK is particularly useful when the spherical equivalent is hyperopic. In a study of 16 patients who had CK for hyperopia after cataract surgery, 1-year data showed that CK for low to moderate postcataract hyperopia was effective and safe.

CK appears to have advantages both in cost and in allowing flexible (off-label) treatment patterns because the tip can be placed anywhere on the cornea. More experience and long-term data will be required to determine how important CK will be in the refractive surgeon's armamentarium. Currently, however, its use remains fairly limited because of the high rate of refractive regression.

Alió JL, Ramzy MI, Galal A, Claramonte PJ. Conductive keratoplasty for the correction of residual hyperopia after LASIK. *J Refract Surg.* 2005;21(6):698–704.

Claramonte PJ, Alió JL, Ramzy MI. Conductive keratoplasty to correct residual hyperopia after cataract surgery. *J Cataract Refract Surg.* 2006;32(9):1445–1451.

Kolahdouz-Isfahani AH, McDonnell PJ. Thermal keratoplasty. In: Brightbill FS, ed. *Corneal Surgery: Theory, Technique, and Tissue.* 3rd ed. St Louis: CV Mosby; 1999.

Collagen Crosslinking

The corneal collagen crosslinking procedure combines riboflavin (vitamin B_2), which is a naturally occurring photosensitizer found in all human cells, and ultraviolet A (UVA) light to strengthen the biomechanical properties of the cornea. Although there may also be a slight flattening of the cornea, the most important effect of collagen crosslinking is that it appears to stabilize the corneal curvature and prevent further steepening and bulging of the corneal stroma. There is no significant change in the refractive index or the clarity of the cornea. The primary clinical application of collagen crosslinking is as a treatment to prevent the progression of keratoconus and ectasia following corneal refractive surgery.

Corneal collagen crosslinking was first described by Spörl and colleagues in 1997. In this procedure, riboflavin solution is continually applied to the eye for 30 minutes (in most studies) and the riboflavin is then activated by illumination with UVA light for 30 minutes, during which time application of the riboflavin solution continues concomitantly. The corneal epithelium is generally removed before application of the riboflavin so that its penetration is increased. Alternative riboflavin formulations and crosslinking techniques that avoid epithelial removal are being evaluated. Riboflavin alone has no crosslinking effect. Its function as a photosensitizer is to serve as a source for the generation of singlet oxygen and superoxide anion free radicals, which are split from its ring structure after excitation by the UV irradiation and which then lead to physical crosslinking of the corneal collagen fibers. In the presence of riboflavin, approximately 95% of the UVA light irradiance is absorbed superficially in the anterior 300 μm of the corneal stroma. Therefore, most studies require a minimal corneal thickness of 400 μm after epithelial removal in order to prevent corneal endothelial damage. Thinner corneas may be thickened temporarily with application of a hypotonic riboflavin formulation prior to UVA treatment.

Corneal collagen crosslinking is approved for use in many countries, though not currently in the United States. An FDA clinical trial evaluating collagen crosslinking for the treatment of keratoconus and corneal ectasia is ongoing. In one US clinical trial, patients had the corneal epithelium removed, which was followed by a 30-minute application of riboflavin (0.1% diluted in 20% dextran) every 2 minutes, followed by a 30-minute UVA treatment (370 nm; 3 mW/cm^2 irradiation), with concomitant administration of topical riboflavin as a photosensitizer (Fig 7-3). The results of these trials, thus far, are promising.

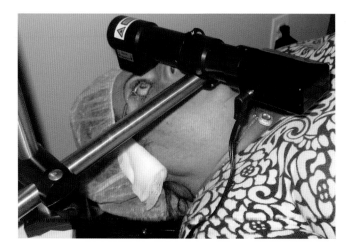

Figure 7-3 Ultraviolet light is applied to a patient undergoing collagen crosslinking. *(Courtesy of Eric D. Donnenfeld, MD.)*

Treated eyes initially show a slight steepening of the cornea, followed by corneal flattening of approximately 1 D, which peaks at 6 months after crosslinking. In addition, a reduction in corneal cylinder, a slight compaction of the cornea, and an increase in best-corrected visual acuity have been seen. There appears to be stabilization in most treated eyes. Some eyes may require re-treatment, however.

Complications of corneal collagen crosslinking vary by the technique used for the procedure and include delayed epithelial healing, corneal haze (may be visually significant), decreased corneal sensitivity, infectious keratitis, persistent corneal edema, and endothelial cell damage.

In some cases, corneal collagen crosslinking has been used successfully in combination with other treatment methods, such as intrastromal corneal ring segments, CK, and excimer laser photoablation.

Chan CCK, Sharma M, Boxer Wachler BS. The effect of inferior-segment Intacs with and without corneal collagen crosslinking with riboflavin (C3-R) on keratoconus. *J Cataract Refract Surg.* 2007;33(1):75–80.

Raiskup-Wolf F, Hoyer A, Spörl E, Pillunat LE. Collagen crosslinking with riboflavin and ultraviolet-A light in keratoconus: long-term results. *J Cataract Refract Surg.* 2008;34(5): 796–801.

Spörl E, Wollensak G, Dittert DD, Seiler T. Thermomechanical behavior of collagen-cross-linked porcine cornea. *Ophthalmologica.* 2004;218(2):136–140.

Spörl E, Wollensak G, Seiler T. Increased resistance of crosslinked cornea against enzymatic digestion. *Curr Eye Res.* 2004;29(1):35–40.

Stulting RD. Update on riboflavin-UV crosslinking. Paper presented at: ASCRS Symposium on Cataract, IOL and Refractive Surgery; April 6, 2009; San Francisco, CA.

Wittig-Silva C, Whiting M, Lamoureux E, Lindsay RG, Sullivan LJ, Snibson GR. A randomized controlled trial of corneal collagen cross-linking in progressive keratoconus: preliminary results. *J Refract Surg.* 2008;24(7):S720–S725.

Wollensak G, Spörl E, Seiler T. Riboflavin/ultraviolet-A-induced collagen crosslinking for the treatment of keratoconus. *Am J Ophthalmol.* 2003;135(5):620–627.

CHAPTER 8

Intraocular Surgery

In its first 2 decades, *refractive surgery* was synonymous with *corneal refractive (keratorefractive) surgery,* which compensates for refractive error by altering the contour of the anterior surface of the eye. Several factors have expanded the range of refractive surgery to include intraocular surgery. Ophthalmologists became accustomed to cataract patients not only expecting to see clearly after their operation but also becoming less dependent on glasses as a consequence of intraocular lens (IOL) surgery. Technology has helped to achieve this goal. Small-incision cataract surgery, with self-sealing, astigmatically neutral wounds, has all but eliminated the high postoperative astigmatism that was previously common. Improved biometry (eg, immersion A-scan and IOL Master [Carl Zeiss Meditec, Jena, Germany]), new IOL power calculation formulas, and new software have made IOL power selection more accurate. The surgeon's armamentarium now includes a wide variety of IOLs: foldable, multifocal, toric, accommodating, and phakic. These technological advances have led to a renewed interest in clear lens surgery.

Phakic IOLs (PIOLs) also expand the range of refractive surgery. The combination of corneal and intraocular refractive surgery, or *bioptics,* allows patients at the extremes of refractive error to achieve predictable outcomes by combining the advantages of the PIOL in treating large corrections with the adjustability of a keratorefractive technique. In addition, the optical quality may be improved by dividing the refractive correction between 2 different locations.

This chapter discusses the intraocular surgical techniques that are now, or are soon expected to be, within the reach of the refractive surgeon.

Phakic Intraocular Lenses

Background

The history of the PIOL to correct refractive error began in Europe in the 1950s, with Strampelli, Dannheim, and Barraquer each separately attempting to design a PIOL that would be well tolerated in the eye. The lack of modern IOL-manufacturing capabilities and microsurgical techniques resulted in an unacceptably high complication rate and an initial failure with this technology.

In the middle 1980s, interest in PIOLs was renewed. Improvements in IOL manufacturing, development of modern microsurgical techniques, increased viscoelastic and topical corticosteroid availability, and improved understanding of the function of the corneal endothelium and anterior segment structures led to greater success with PIOL surgery. Worst modified his aphakic, iris-fixated "claw" IOL to correct both myopia and hyperopia. Baikoff worked on variations of the open-loop, flexible anterior chamber IOL to correct myopia, and Fyodorov experimented with a plate-haptic IOL for use in the posterior chamber.

Refinements in IOL design have reduced the incidence of complications and, consequently, increased the popularity of these PIOLs outside the United States. Within the US, 2 PIOLs are currently approved by the FDA for myopia: the Visian and Verisyse lenses. The former is a posterior chamber PIOL distributed as the Visian ICL (Implantable Collamer Lens) by STAAR (Monrovia, CA); and the latter is an iris-fixated PIOL marketed as Verisyse by Abbott Medical Optics (AMO, Santa Ana, CA). The Verisyse PIOL is known outside the United States as the Artisan lens and is distributed by Ophtec (Groningen, the Netherlands). A toric version of the ICL is pending FDA approval. Representative lenses in each category (Table 8-1) are discussed in the following sections.

Huang D, Schallhorn SC, Sugar A, et al. Phakic intraocular lens implantation for the correction of myopia: a report by the American Academy of Ophthalmology. *Ophthalmology*. 2009;116(11):2244–2258.

Advantages

PIOLs have the advantage of treating a much larger range of myopic and hyperopic refractive errors than can be safely and effectively treated with corneal refractive surgery. The skills required for insertion are, with a few exceptions, similar to those used in cataract surgery. The equipment is significantly less expensive than an excimer laser and is similar to that used for cataract surgery. In addition, the PIOL is removable; therefore, the refractive effect should theoretically be reversible. However, any intervening damage caused by the PIOL would most likely be permanent. When compared with clear lens extraction, or refractive lens exchange (discussed later in this chapter), the PIOL has the advantage of preserving natural accommodation and may have a lower risk of postoperative retinal detachment because of the preservation of the crystalline lens and minimal vitreous destabilization.

Disadvantages

PIOL insertion is an intraocular procedure, with all the potential risks associated with intraocular surgery. In addition, each PIOL style has its own set of associated risks. In the case of PIOLs with polymethylmethacrylate (PMMA) optics, such as the Verisyse, insertion requires a larger wound, which may result in postoperative astigmatism. There is less flexibility than with LASIK for fine-tuning the refractive outcome. If a patient eventually develops a visually significant cataract, the PIOL will have to be explanted at the time of cataract surgery, possibly through a larger-than-usual wound. Although PIOLs for hyperopia are being investigated, there is less enthusiasm for these lenses because the anterior chamber tends to be shallower than in myopic patients, and progressive shallowing may occur with advancing age. This can be associated with pupil ovalization, angle closure, and increased endothelial cell loss.

Table 8-1 Phakic IOLS

Position	Model	Available Power	Optic Size/Effective Diameter	Length	Material	Manufacturer	FDA Approval
Angle-supported	ZSAL-4 Plus (myopia)	−6.00 to −20.00 D	5.5 mm/5.0 mm	12.0, 12.5, 13.0 mm	PMMA	Morcher (Stuttgart, Germany)	
	AcrySof Cachet (myopia)	−8.00 to −16.00 D	5.5 mm	12.5, 13.0, 13.5 mm	Acrylic	Alcon	
	Phakic 6 H2 (myopia) (hyperopia)	−4.00 to −20.00 D +2.00 to +10.00 D	5.5–6.0 mm	11.5–14.0 mm	PMMA	Ophthalmic Innovations International (O.I.I.; Ontario, CA)	
	Kelman Duet (myopia)	−6.00 to −20.00 D	6.3 mm/5.5 mm	12.0, 12.5, 13.0, 13.5 mm	Silicone optic PMMA haptics	Tekia (Irvine, CA)	
Iris-supported	Verisyse model* VRSM5US (myopia)	−5.00 to −20.00 D	5.0 mm	8.5 mm	PMMA	AMO	Approved
	Verisyse model* VRSM6US (myopia)	−5.00 to −15.00 D	6.0 mm	8.5 mm	PMMA	AMO	Approved
	Artisan model 203 (hyperopia)	+3.00 to +12.00 D	5.0 or 6.0 mm	8.5 mm	PMMA	Ophtec	
	Artisan toric IOL	Custom	5.0 or 6.0 mm	8.5 mm	PMMA	Ophtec	
	Artiflex/Veriflex (foldable) (myopia)	−3.00 to −23.50 D	5.0 or 6.0 mm	8.5 mm	Polysiloxane	Ophtec	
Sulcus-supported	Visian ICL (myopia)†	−3.00 to −20.00 D	4.9–5.8 mm	12.1, 12.6, 13.2, 13.7 mm	Collamer	STAAR	Approved
	Visian ICL (hyperopia)	+3.00 to +12.00 D		11.5–13.2 mm	Collamer	STAAR	
	Toric ICL	Up to +2.50 Custom to +4.00 D	4.75–5.50 mm	11.5–13.2 mm	Collamer	STAAR	
	Sticklens (myopia)	−7.00 to −25.00 D	6.5 mm	11.5 mm	Acrylic	IOLTech (La Rochelle, France)	
	Sticklens (hyperopia)	+4.00 to +7.00 D	6.5 mm	11.5 mm	Acrylic	IOLTech	

*The Artisan lens (Ophtec), marketed as the Verisyse lens (AMO), has been FDA approved for use in the lens power range of −5.00 to −20.00 D.
†The Visian ICL (STAAR) posterior chamber phakic IOL has received FDA approval to correct myopia in the range of −3.00 to −20.00 D.

Adapted in part from Lovisolo CF, Reinstein DZ. Phakic intraocular lenses. *Surv Ophthalmol.* 2005;50:549–587.

Patient Selection

Indications

Patients who are near or beyond the FDA-approved limits for laser vision correction may be candidates for a PIOL. Although the programmable upper limit of myopic excimer laser treatment is as high as –14.00 D, many surgeons have reduced the upper limit of LASIK and surface ablation in their refractive practices because of the decreased predictability, high rate of regression, large amount of stromal tissue removal, increased incidence of microstriae, and night-vision problems that can occur with treatment of a patient with high myopia. Similarly, LASIK and surface ablation for hyperopia above +4.00 D and astigmatism correction above 4.00 D of cylinder are less accurate than for lower corrections. If surgeons become comfortable with the use of PIOLs, they may also choose to implant them for refractive powers significantly lower than the programmable excimer laser limits.

Most PIOLs for myopia can correct up to –20.00 D (see Table 8-1). In the United States, for example, the 6-mm-optic Verisyse iris-fixated PIOL corrects up to –15.0 D, and the 5-mm-optic model corrects up to –20.0 D. PIOLs are available outside the United States for correcting hyperopia up to at least +10.00 D.

Because extremes of corneal curvature may lead to induced aberrations and degradation of optical quality, a predicted final corneal curvature flatter than 34.00 D in myopic corrections or steeper than 50.00 D in hyperopic corrections after laser refractive surgery may be a reason to consider intraocular refractive surgery. PIOLs may be considered off-label in eyes with irregular topographies from forme fruste keratoconus and even frank keratoconus.

Contraindications

PIOLs have specific contraindications. They should not be used if there is preexisting intraocular disease such as a compromised corneal endothelium, iritis, significant iris abnormality, rubeosis iridis, cataract, or glaucoma.

The anterior chamber diameter, anterior chamber depth, and pupil size must be appropriate for the specific PIOL being considered. (The anatomical requirements for the placement of each style of IOL are discussed in the next section.)

Patient evaluation

A thorough preoperative evaluation is necessary, as detailed in Chapter 2.

Informed consent

As with any refractive procedure, an informed consent specifically for this procedure should be obtained prior to surgery. The patient should be informed about both the potential short-term and long-term risks of the procedure and about other available alternatives. With newer technologies, long-term risks and results may not yet be known. The surgeon must also make sure that the patient has realistic expectations about the surgical outcome of the procedure.

Ancillary tests

Specular microscopy and corneal pachymetry are both helpful in evaluating the health of the corneal endothelium. In addition, anterior chamber depth should be carefully assessed because adequate depth is critical for the safe implantation of a PIOL. If the anterior chamber depth is <3.0 mm, the risk of endothelial and iris or angle trauma from the placement of an anterior chamber, iris-fixated, or posterior chamber PIOL is increased. Anterior chamber depth can be estimated at the slit lamp by using measured central corneal thickness as a reference. Anterior chamber depth can also be measured by ultrasound, anterior segment optical coherence tomography (OCT), slit-beam topography (eg, Orbscan [Bausch & Lomb, Rochester, NY]) or Scheimpflug imaging (eg, Pentacam [Oculus, Lynnwood, WA]; Galilei [Ziemer, Port, Switzerland]), if available.

Methods for IOL power selection are specific to each PIOL and manufacturer. Some manufacturers provide software for IOL power calculation.

Surgical Technique

Topical anesthesia with an intracameral supplement is appropriate if the patient can cooperate and the PIOL can be inserted through a small incision. If the patient cannot cooperate for topical anesthesia or if a large incision is required, peribulbar anesthesia is preferable. Retrobulbar anesthesia should be used with caution in patients with a high axial length because of the increased risk of globe perforation.

A peripheral iridotomy is recommended for all currently FDA-approved PIOLs to reduce the risk of pupillary block and angle closure. One or more laser iridotomies can be performed prior to the PIOL surgery, or an iridectomy can be performed as part of the implant procedure. Preoperative laser iridotomy is preferable when small-incision implant surgery is performed because surgical iridotomy or iridectomy is technically more difficult to perform through a beveled clear corneal incision. Viscoelastic should be meticulously removed at the conclusion of surgery to prevent postoperative elevation of IOP.

Angle-supported anterior chamber phakic intraocular lens (ACPIOL)

An ACPIOL can be inserted through a temporal clear corneal wound or a scleral pocket. The larger the incision, the greater the likelihood of induced astigmatism. The wound size depends on the diameter of the ACPIOL optic. No ACPIOL is currently FDA approved.

Iris-fixated PIOL

The iris-fixated PIOL is generally inserted through a superior limbal incision. The long axis of the PIOL is ultimately oriented perpendicular to the axis of the incision. A side port incision is made approximately 2 clock-hours on either side of the center of the incision; thus, a 12 o'clock incision requires side port incisions at 10 and 2 o'clock. The "claw" haptics are fixated to the iris in a process called *enclavation*. After the PIOL has been carefully centered over the pupil, it is stabilized with a forceps while a specially designed enclavation needle is introduced through one of the side port incisions and a knuckle of iris is brought up into the "claw" haptic. This is repeated on the other side. If adjustment of the PIOL position becomes necessary after fixation, the iris must be released before the PIOL is moved. Careful wound closure helps minimize surgically induced astigmatism.

The Verisyse (AMO) is currently FDA approved for myopia of –5.00 to –20.00 D, in patients 21 years of age and older, with a minimum anterior chamber depth of 3.2 mm with recommendations for minimal preoperative endothelial cell count dependent on age.

Sizing the iris-fixated PIOL Because this PIOL is fixated to the midperipheral iris, not the angle or sulcus, it has the advantage of having a "one-size-fits-all" length. It is 8.5 mm in length, with a 5.0- or 6.0-mm PMMA optic (Fig 8-1).

Posterior chamber phakic intraocular lens

The smaller incision used for foldable posterior chamber phakic intraocular lenses (PCPIOLs) offers the advantage of less induced astigmatism. The Implantable Collamer Lens, now called the Visian ICL (Fig 8-2), is made of a hydrophilic material known as collamer, which is a copolymer of HEMA (99%) and porcine collagen (1%). The optic of the PCPIOL is vaulted both to avoid contact with the crystalline lens and to allow aqueous to flow over the crystalline lens. This vaulting can be seen at the slit lamp as well as with ultrasound biomicroscopy or Scheimpflug photography (Fig 8-3). The lens manufacturers suggest that an acceptable amount of vaulting of the PCPIOL optic over the crystalline lens is 1.0 ± 0.5 corneal thicknesses. The Visian ICL is currently FDA approved for myopia of –3.00 to –20.00 D in adults 21–45 years old with a minimum anterior chamber depth of 3.0 mm.

For lens implantation, the pupil is dilated preoperatively. A 3.0- to 3.2-mm temporal clear corneal incision is then made, and a paracentesis is made superiorly and inferiorly to aid in positioning the PCPIOL. The PCPIOL is inserted using a cohesive viscoelastic; and, after the lens unfolds, the haptics are positioned under the iris (Fig 8-4). The surgeon should avoid contact with the central 6.0 mm of the ICL, as it might cause damage. Care should be taken to avoid touching the crystalline lens to minimize the risk of cataract. Positioning instruments should be inserted through the paracenteses and should be kept peripheral to this central area. The pupil is then constricted. It is critical to remove all viscoelastic at the conclusion of the case to reduce the risk of a postoperative IOP spike.

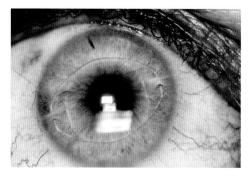

Figure 8-1 Verisyse, iris-fixated PIOL for myopic correction. *(Courtesy of AMO.)*

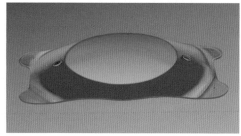

Figure 8-2 Side view of the Visian ICL PCPIOL. *(Courtesy of STAAR.)*

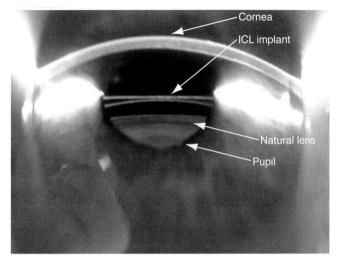

Figure 8-3 Visian ICL PCPIOL within the posterior chamber, as seen with Scheimpflug photography. *(Courtesy of STAAR.)*

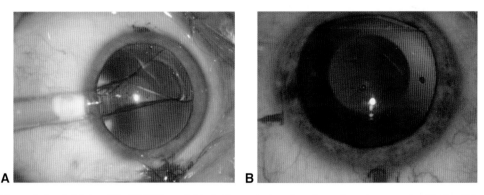

Figure 8-4 **A,** Visian ICL PCPIOL unfolds in the anterior chamber after placement with the IOL inserter. **B,** Visian ICL PCPIOL unfolded and in position in the posterior chamber anterior to the crystalline lens. *(Courtesy of STAAR.)*

Sizing the PCPIOL The correct IOL length is selected by using the white-to-white measurement between the 3 and 9 o'clock meridians. Alternative methods for sizing the IOL include high-frequency ultrasound, anterior segment OCT, slit-beam or Scheimpflug imaging, and laser interferometry. To date, no particular sizing technique has shown clear superiority over the others.

Outcomes

The outcomes and complications of surgery with the 2 FDA-approved PIOLs are shown in Tables 8-2 and 8-3. With better methods for determining PIOL power, outcomes have steadily improved. Significant postoperative gains in lines of BCVA over the preoperative

Table 8-2 Results With Phakic IOLs Update

Study	PIOL Model	Number of Eyes	Mean Preoperative Spherical Equivalent (Range)	Postoperative Result Within ±0.50 D of Emmetropia	Postoperative Result Within ±1.00 D of Emmetropia	Uncorrected Visual Acuity 20/40 or Better	Gain ±2 Lines Best-Corrected Visual Acuity	Loss ±2 Lines Best-Corrected Visual Acuity
Iris-fixated IOL								
Budo (2000)	Verisyse	249	−12.95 D ± 4.35 D	57.1%	78.8%	76.8%	63.3% in > −15.00 D group 23.5% in −5.00 to −15.00 D group	1.2%
FDA clinical trial (2004)	Verisyse	684	−12.6 ± 2.7 D (−5.00 to −20.00 D)	71.7% at 3 years	94.7% at 3 years	92% at 3 years		0.3% at 3 years n=591
PCPIOL								
FDA clinical trial (2005)	ICL	526	< −7 D, 21%; −7 to −10 D, 33%; −10 to −15 D, 36%; −15 to −20 D, 10% (−3.00 to −20.00 D)	70.0% at 3 years n=363	89.3% at 3 years n=363	94.7% at 3 years n=189		0.8%
Zaldivar (1998)	ICL	124	−13.38 D (−8.50 to −18.65 D)	44%	69%	68%	36%	0.8%
Arne (2000)	ICL	58	−13.85 D (−8.00 to −19.25 D)	Mean spherical equivalent −1.22 D	56.9%	Mean postoperative acuity 20/50	77.6% gained ≥1 line	3.4%
Vukich (2003)	ICL	258	−10.05 D (−3.00 to −20.00 D)	57.4% at 2 years	80.2% at 2 years	92.5% at 1 year	10.9%	1.2%
Davidorf (1998)	ICL (for hyperopia)	24	+6.51 D (+3.75 to +10.50 D)	58%	79%	63%	8%	4%

Table 8-3 Incidence of Complications With Phakic IOLs

Study	PIOL Model	Number of Eyes	Glare/Halos	Pupil Ovalization	Mean Endothelial Cell Loss	Cataract	Pigment Dispersion	IOP Elevation
FDA clinical trial (2004)	Verisyse	662	18.2% n=472	hyphema 0.2%	4.75% at 3 years n=353	5.2% (12/232)	Iritis 0.5%	None
FDA clinical trial (2005) (5-year specular microscopy data [2007])	ICL	526	3 years glare: worse 9.7%; better 12.0% halos: worse 11.4%; better 9.1%		Cumulative loss of 12.8% approaching stability at 5 years	Visually significant ASC 0.4%; NS 1.0%		0.4% No cases of visual field loss or nerve damage

levels are likely due to a reduction in the image minification that is present with spectacle correction of high myopia. A loss of BCVA is rare. Moreover, the loss of contrast sensitivity noted after LASIK for high myopia does not occur after PIOL surgery. In fact, contrast sensitivity increases in all spatial frequencies when compared with preoperative contrast sensitivity with best spectacle correction.

Boxer Wachler BS, Scruggs RT, Yuen LH, Jalali S. Comparison of the Visian ICL and Verisyse phakic intraocular lenses for myopia from 6.00 to 20.00 diopters. *J Refract Surg.* 2009;25(9):765–770.

Kamiya K, Shimizu K, Igarashi A, Hikita F, Komatsu M. Four-year follow-up of posterior chamber phakic intraocular lens implantation for moderate to high myopia. *Arch Ophthalmol.* 2009;127(7):845–850.

Kohnen T, Knorz MC, Cochener B, et al. AcrySof phakic angle-supported intraocular lens for the correction of moderate-to-high myopia: one-year results of a multicenter European study. *Ophthalmology.* 2009;116(7):1314–1321.

Lovisolo CF, Reinstein DZ. Phakic intraocular lenses. *Surv Ophthalmol.* 2005;50(6):549–587.

Sanders DR, Vukich JA, Doney K, Gaston M; Implantable Contact Lens in Treatment of Myopia Study Group. U.S. Food and Drug Administration clinical trial of the Implantable Contact Lens for moderate to high myopia. *Ophthalmology.* 2003;110(2):255–266.

Stulting RD, John ME, Maloney RK, Assil KK, Arrowsmith PN, Thompson VM; U.S. Verisyse Study Group. Three-year results of Artisan/Verisyse phakic intraocular lens implantation. Results of the United States Food and Drug Administration clinical trial. *Ophthalmology.* 2008;115(3):464–472.

United States Food and Drug Administration. Summary of Safety and Effectiveness Data. Artisan Phakic Lens. PMA: P030028. Date of approval: 9/10/04.

United States Food and Drug Administration. Summary of Safety and Effectiveness Data. STAAR Visian ICL (Implantable Collamer Lens). PMA: P030016. Date of approval: 2/22/05.

Complications

Most manufacturers continue to modify the design of their PIOLs to improve results and minimize complications. Older studies do not necessarily reflect the complication rate associated with more recently developed PIOLs. The major factor limiting the widespread use of these lenses is the potential for short-term and, especially, long-term sight-threatening complications. When experienced surgeons implant the currently approved PIOLs, the incidence of sight-threatening complications is quite low. However, because PIOLs are used in young, active individuals, long-term follow-up is needed to accurately determine their safety. Many of the most important potential complications of PIOLs, such as cataract, endothelial cell loss, and retinal detachment, may not manifest for many years. Both the patient and the surgeon need to recognize our current inability to accurately assess the incidence of long-term PIOL complications.

Angle-supported PIOLs

The complications reported most frequently for ACPIOLs are nighttime glare and halos, pupil ovalization, and endothelial cell loss. The risk of pupillary block is low now that iridotomies have become a standard part of the surgical protocol. Because complications such as endothelial cell loss and pupil ovalization may take years to develop, their true frequency can be assessed only after many years of follow-up.

Glare and halos, the most commonly reported symptoms following ACPIOL insertion, occur in 18.8%–20.0% of patients, but these symptoms appear to decrease by as much as 50% over a postoperative period of 7 years. Endothelial cell loss occurring 1–7 years after ACPIOL insertion ranges from 4.6% to 8.4%. Pupil ovalization can occur because of iris tuck during ACPIOL insertion, or it can occur over time due to chronic inflammation and fibrosis around the haptics within the anterior chamber angle. The incidence of pupil ovalization ranges from 5.9% to 27.5% and is directly related to the postoperative interval studied. Ovalization is more likely when the ACPIOL is too large. In contrast, endothelial damage and decentration are most often associated with movement of an ACPIOL that is too small.

Kohnen et al reported on the 1-year results of the AcrySof angle-supported ACPIOL in 190 eyes with moderate to high myopia. No eyes experienced pupillary block or pupil ovalization, while 3.2% required IOP-lowering treatment after the first month. The mean decrease in central endothelial cell density from preoperative status to 1 year postoperatively was 4.77%. However, 15.1% of eyes lost ≥10% central endothelial cell density.

Kohnen T, Knorz MC, Cochener B, et al. AcrySof phakic angle-supported intraocular lens for the correction of moderate-to-high myopia: one-year results of a multicenter European study. *Ophthalmology*. 2009;116(7):1314–1321.

Iris-fixated PIOLs

At 1-year follow-up in the FDA clinical trials of 662 patients who had the Verisyse (Artisan) iris-fixated PIOL implanted for myopia, 1 patient had a hyphema, 5 had IOL dislocations, and 3 had iritis. The change in glare, starbursts, and halos from the preoperative to postoperative state was assessed by questionnaire. The incidence of these symptoms developing after surgery was 13.5%, 11.8%, and 18.2%, respectively. However, improvement in these symptoms between the preoperative and postoperative status occurred in 12.9%, 9.7%, and 9.8%, respectively. In general, nighttime symptoms were worse in patients with larger pupil diameters.

Stulting et al reported a 3-year follow-up study on 232 eyes of the 662 eyes initially enrolled in the Verisyse FDA study. A total of 5 lenses had dislocated and required reattachment, and an additional 20 lenses required surgery due to insufficient lens fixation. No eyes required IOP-lowering medications after the first month. The mean decrease in endothelial cell density from baseline to 3 years was 4.8%. Six eyes required a retinal detachment repair (rate of 0.3% per year), and 3 eyes underwent cataract surgery.

Pop M, Payette Y. Initial results of endothelial cell counts after Artisan lens for phakic eyes: an evaluation of the United States Food and Drug Administration Ophtec Study. *Ophthalmology*. 2004;111(2):309–311.

Stulting RD, John ME, Maloney RK, Assil KK, Arrowsmith PN, Thompson VM; U.S. Verisyse Study Group. Three-year results of Artisan/Verisyse phakic intraocular lens implantation. Results of the United States Food and Drug Administration clinical trial. *Ophthalmology*. 2008;115(3):464–472.

Posterior chamber PIOLs

In addition to potential for nighttime glare and halos and endothelial cell damage seen with other types of PIOLs, the placement of a PCPIOL may increase the risk of cataract formation and pigmentary dispersion. If the PCPIOL is too small, the vaulting will decrease, but the risk of cataract may increase; if the PCPIOL is too large, iris chafing with pigmentary dispersion could result.

The incidence of nighttime visual symptoms was around 10% in the FDA clinical trial for the Visian ICL, but interestingly, a similar percentage had an improvement in these symptoms following surgery. The incidence of visually significant cataract in the FDA clinical trial as reported by Sanders and colleagues (2003) was 0.4% for anterior subcapsular cataracts and 1% for nuclear sclerotic cataracts.

Kamiya and colleagues reported 4-year follow-up on 56 eyes of 34 patients with Visian ICLs. No eyes developed pupillary block or a significant increase in IOP. The mean central endothelial cell loss from baseline to 4 years was 3.7%. Two eyes developed symptomatic cataracts requiring surgery, and 6 other eyes developed asymptomatic anterior subcapsular cataracts. Following more than 500 eyes for an average of 4.7 years, Sanders (2008) reported that 6%–7% of eyes developed anterior subcapsular opacities and 1%–2% developed visually significant cataracts.

The incidence of retinal detachment after PCPIOL insertion is very low. In a series of 16 eyes, surgical reattachment was achieved in 100%, with a mean follow-up of 35.25 months (range 12–67 months) and a mean postoperative best spectacle-corrected visual acuity of 20/28.

Huang D, Schallhorn SC, Sugar A, et al. Phakic intraocular lens implantation for the correction of myopia: a report by the American Academy of Ophthalmology. *Ophthalmology*. 2009;116(11):2244–2258.

Kamiya K, Shimizu K, Igarashi A, Hikita F, Komatsu M. Four-year follow-up of posterior chamber phakic intraocular lens implantation for moderate to high myopia. *Arch Ophthalmol*. 2009;127(7):845–850.

Kohnen T, Knorz MC, Cochener B, et al. AcrySof phakic angle-supported intraocular lens for the correction of moderate-to-high myopia: one-year results of a multicenter European study. *Ophthalmology*. 2009;116(7):1314–1321.

Martínez-Castillo V, Boixadera A, Verdugo A, Elíes D, Coret A, García-Arumí J. Rhegmatogenous retinal detachment in phakic eyes after posterior chamber phakic intraocular lens implantation for severe myopia. *Ophthalmology*. 2005;112(4):580–585.

Sanders DR. Anterior subcapsular opacities and cataracts 5 years after surgery in the Visian Implantable Collamer Lens FDA trial. *J Refract Surg*. 2008;24(6):566–570.

Sanders DR, Vukich JA, Doney K, Gaston M; Implantable Contact Lens in Treatment of Myopia Study Group. U.S. Food and Drug Administration clinical trial of the Implantable Contact Lens for moderate to high myopia. *Ophthalmology*. 2003;110(2):255–266.

STAAR Surgical Company. US Clinical Study. Specular Microscopy: 5-year Cumulative Data on Visian ICL. Submitted to FDA 2/7/07.

United States Food and Drug Administration. Summary of Safety and Effectiveness Data. STAAR Visian ICL (Implantable Collamer Lens). PMA: P030016. Date of approval: 2/22/05.

Bioptics

Bioptics is a term suggested by Zaldivar in the late 1990s to describe the combination of PCPIOL implantation followed at a later time by LASIK to treat patients with extreme myopia and/or residual astigmatism. Because of the limitations of the individual procedures, the concept of first inserting a PIOL to reduce the amount of myopia correction required and then refining the residual spherical and astigmatic correction with LASIK has gained appeal. LASIK is typically performed approximately 1 month after the PIOL surgery.

Another term, *adjustable refractive surgery (ARS)*, is also used to describe combined intraocular and corneal refractive surgery. Güell and colleagues have described ARS, which involves creating a corneal flap just prior to inserting an iris-fixated PIOL and then, at a later time, lifting the flap and performing the laser procedure. This 2-stage modification avoids the potential for endothelial trauma by an iris-fixated PIOL or an ACPIOL during the microkeratome pass. Microkeratomes were later shown to be safe in performing LASIK after implantation of iris-fixated PIOLs. The femtosecond laser also appears to be safe to use in bioptic procedures. The combination of bioptics with surface ablation is also a reasonable alternative, particularly for thinner corneas. As new treatment options are developed, the possibilities for other combinations of refractive surgery will likely increase.

The ability to successfully combine refractive procedures further expands the limits of refractive surgery. The predictability, stability, and safety of LASIK may increase if a smaller refractive error is treated with the corneal surgery. In addition, there is usually sufficient corneal tissue to maximize the treatment zone diameter without exceeding the limits of ablation depth. The LASIK procedure provides the feature of adjustability in the overall refractive operation. These benefits must be balanced against the combined risks of performing 2 surgeries rather than 1 surgery.

Outcomes

In the initial reports of bioptics and ARS, the range of treatment for myopia was −18.75 to −35.00 D and −16.00 to −23.00 D, respectively. If the long-term results of PIOLs prove acceptable, the use of bioptics may expand to the treatment of smaller refractive errors because of the advantages of superior optical performance and greater accuracy of refractive correction.

Güell JL, Vázquez M, Gris O. Adjustable refractive surgery: 6-mm Artisan lens plus laser in situ keratomileusis for the correction of high myopia. *Ophthalmology*. 2001;108(5):945–952.

Leccisotti A. Bioptics: where do things stand? *Curr Opin Ophthalmol*. 2006;17(4):399–405.

Zaldivar R, Davidorf JM, Oscherow S, Ricur G, Piezzi V. Combined posterior chamber phakic intraocular lens and laser in situ keratomileusis: bioptics for extreme myopia. *J Refract Surg*. 1999;15(3):299–308.

Refractive Lens Exchange (Clear Lens Extraction)

Patient Selection

Indications

The indications for refractive lens exchange—that is, clear lens extraction with IOL implantation—are evolving. Refractive lens exchange is usually considered only if alternative refractive procedures are not feasible and there is a strong reason why spectacles or contact lenses are unacceptable alternatives. If the cornea is too thin, too flat, or too steep, or if the refractive error exceeds the limit for corneal refractive surgery, clear lens extraction and IOL implantation are options. Refractive lens exchange may be preferable to a PIOL in the presence of a lens opacity that is presently visually insignificant but that may soon progress and cause visual loss. Clear lens extraction for refractive correction is generally not considered medically necessary and is usually not covered by the patient's insurance.

Informed consent

Potential candidates must be capable of understanding the short-term and long-term risks of refractive lens exchange. They must understand that performing the surgery on both eyes sequentially rather than simultaneously is recommended to decrease the potential of a devastating complication such as bilateral endophthalmitis. Patients must understand that unless they are left with a degree of myopia or a multifocal or accommodating IOL is implanted, they will incur the loss of uncorrected near vision. A consent form should be given to the patient prior to surgery to allow ample time for review and signature. A sample consent form for refractive lens exchange for the correction of hyperopia and myopia is available from the Ophthalmic Mutual Insurance Company (OMIC) at www.omic.com.

Myopia

In addition to all the risks associated with cataract surgery, the surgeon must specifically inform the patient about the substantial risk of retinal detachment associated with removal of the crystalline lens. Myopia is already a significant risk factor for retinal detachment in the absence of lens surgery, and this risk rises with increased axial length. The risk of retinal detachment in eyes with up to 3.00 D of myopia may be as much as 4 times greater than it is in emmetropic eyes, while in eyes with >3.00 D of myopia, the risk may be as high as 10 times that in emmetropia. In the absence of trauma, more than 50% of retinal detachments occur in myopic eyes.

Arevalo JF. Posterior segment complications after laser-assisted in situ keratomileusis. *Curr Opin Ophthalmol.* 2008;19(3):177–184.

Law RW, Li RT, Ng JS, Tang H, Yan Y, Lam DS. Refractive lensectomy in extreme myopia. *J Cataract Refract Surg.* 2001;27(12):1899–1900.

Nachiketa N, Munshi V. Refractive lensectomy in extreme myopia. *J Cataract Refract Surg.* 2001;27(12):1900–1901.

Preferred Practice Patterns Committee, Retina Panel. *Posterior Vitreous Detachment, Retinal Breaks, and Lattice Degeneration.* San Francisco: American Academy of Ophthalmology; 2008.

Hyperopia

As patients approach presbyopic age, moderate and high hyperopia become increasingly bothersome. The perceived accelerated onset of presbyopia occurs because some accommodation is expended in an effort to clarify distance vision. Many hyperopic patients have significant chronic accommodative spasm.

If the amount of hyperopia is beyond the range of alternative refractive procedures, refractive lens exchange might be the only available surgical option. As with myopic correction, the patient must be informed about the risks of intraocular surgery. A patient with a shallow anterior chamber from a thickened crystalline lens or small anterior segment would not be a candidate for a PIOL and could benefit from a reduced risk of angle-closure glaucoma after clear lens extraction. The hyperopic patient has a lower risk of retinal detachment than the myopic patient.

Fink AM, Gore C, Rosen ES. Refractive lensectomy for hyperopia. *Ophthalmology.* 2000; 107(8):1540–1548.

Surgical Planning and Technique

Although refractive lens exchange is similar to cataract surgery, there are some special considerations for planning and performing the procedure. It is important to determine whether the source of myopia is a steep cornea or an increased axial length. If the cornea is quite steep, corneal topography should be performed to rule out an ectatic corneal condition. Keratoconus and pellucid marginal degeneration induce irregular astigmatism, which can affect the immediate visual outcome and can have long-term implications. When astigmatism is present in the refraction, keratometry and corneal topography will help the surgeon determine whether the astigmatism is lenticular or corneal in origin. Only the corneal component of astigmatism will remain postoperatively. The patient should be informed if substantial astigmatism is expected to be present after surgery, and to optimize the visual outcome, a plan should be devised to correct it. Small amounts of corneal astigmatism (<1.00 D) may be reduced if the incision is placed in the steep meridian.

Limbal relaxing incisions may be used to correct larger amounts of corneal astigmatism (see Chapter 3). Toric IOLs are another option. Supplemental surface ablation or LASIK could also be considered (see the preceding discussion of bioptics). Although glasses or contact lenses are an alternative for managing residual astigmatism, refractive surgery patients may reject this option.

All patients should have a dilated fundus examination prior to surgery; in addition, patients with high axial myopia should also have a detailed evaluation of the peripheral retina because of the increased risk of retinal detachment. If relevant pathology is discovered, appropriate treatment or referral to a retina specialist is warranted. In patients with high axial myopia, retrobulbar injections should be performed with caution because of the risk of perforating the globe. Peribulbar, sub-Tenon, topical, and intracameral anesthesia are alternative options.

An excessively deep anterior chamber may develop during surgery in a patient with high axial myopia. A deep anterior chamber can impair surgical visualization and instrument manipulation. The patient may complain of pain, particularly when the eye is anesthetized with topical and intracameral anesthetic only. In hyperopic patients, a small cornea may be more prone to surgical trauma, the lens may be located more anteriorly, and the crowded anterior chamber may make surgical maneuvers more difficult. In a highly hyperopic eye with an axial length of less than 18 mm, the diagnosis of nanophthalmos should be considered. These eyes are prone to uveal effusion syndrome and postoperative choroidal detachment (see BCSC Section 11, *Lens and Cataract*).

Many surgeons believe that an IOL should always be used after clear lens extraction in a patient with high myopia, even when little or no optical power correction is required. Plano power IOLs are available if indicated. The IOL acts as a barrier to anterior prolapse of the vitreous, maintaining the integrity of the aqueous–vitreous barrier, in the event that Nd:YAG laser posterior capsulotomy is required. Some IOL models also reduce the rate of posterior capsule opacification.

IOL Calculations in Refractive Lens Exchange

High patient expectations for excellent UCVA make accurate IOL power determination critical. However, IOL power formulas are less accurate at higher levels of myopia and hyperopia. In addition, in high myopia, a posterior staphyloma can make the axial length measurements less reliable. Careful fundus examination and B-scan ultrasound can identify the position and extent of staphylomas. The SRK/T formula is generally considered to be the most accurate for use in moderate and highly myopic patients, whereas the Hoffer Q formula is more accurate for moderate and highly hyperopic eyes. The Haigis formula can be used in patients with short or long eyes but requires a large surgeon-specific patient base with varied axial lengths for optimal utility. The Holladay formula is excellent for short eyes. Software programs now available can give the surgeon IOL predictions calculated by several formulas. The subject of IOL power determination is covered in greater detail in BCSC Section 11, *Lens and Cataract.*

In the case of a patient with high hyperopia, biometry may suggest an IOL power beyond what is commercially available. The upper limit of available IOL power is now +40.00 D. A special-order IOL of a higher power may be available or may be designed, but acquiring or designing such a lens usually requires the approval of the institutional review board at the hospital or surgical center, which delays the surgery. Another option is a "piggyback" IOL system, in which 2 posterior chamber IOLs are inserted. One IOL is placed in the capsular bag, and the other is placed in the ciliary sulcus. The Holladay 2, Hoffer Q, and Haigis formulas can be used to calculate piggyback IOL power. When piggyback IOLs are used, the combined power may need to be increased +1.50 to +2.00 D to compensate for the posterior shift of the posterior IOL. One serious complication of piggyback IOLs is the potential for developing an interlenticular opaque membrane. These membranes cannot be mechanically removed or cleared with the Nd:YAG laser; the IOLs must be removed. Interlenticular membranes have occurred most commonly between 2 acrylic IOLs, especially when both IOLs are placed in the capsular bag. When piggyback lenses are used, they should be of different materials and the fixation should be split between the bag and the sulcus. Piggyback IOLs may also shallow the anterior chamber and increase the risk of iris chafing.

Hill WE. http://doctor-hill.com.

Hill WE, Byrne SF. Complex axial length measurements and unusual IOL power calculations. *Focal Points: Clinical Modules for Ophthalmologists.* San Francisco: American Academy of Ophthalmology; 2004, module 9.

Complications

The incidence of retinal detachment in 49 refractive lens exchange patients with greater than –12.00 D of myopia was reported to be 2% at 4 years, increasing to 8.1% at 7 years. It is not known if the risk continues to increase with even longer follow-up. In this study population, 61% of patients required Nd:YAG laser posterior capsulotomy. Laser capsulotomy increased the risk of detached retina from 5.3% to 10% over a 7-year period. Retinal detachment was also significantly more common in males than in females. The effectiveness of prophylactic laser treatment to the retina to prevent detachment is unproven. Limiting the incision size with small-incision techniques may help to reduce complications in refractive lens exchange.

Colin J, Robinet A, Cochener B. Retinal detachment after clear lens extraction for high myopia: seven-year follow-up. *Ophthalmology.* 1999;106(12):2281–2285.

Advantages

Refractive lens exchange has the advantage of greatly expanding the range of refractive surgery beyond what can be achieved with other available methods. The procedure retains the normal contour of the cornea, which may enhance the quality of vision, and it may treat presbyopia as well as refractive error with the use of multifocal and/or accommodating IOLs.

Disadvantages

The disadvantages of refractive lens exchange include the risks associated with any intraocular surgery, including endophthalmitis and choroidal hemorrhage. Although retinal detachment is a significant concern in myopic eyes, it is less of a risk in hyperopic eyes. Patient expectations for excellent UCVA are much higher in this surgery than in cataract surgery, which increases the need for thorough preoperative discussion, close attention to detail preoperatively and intraoperatively, and postoperative treatment of residual refractive error.

Toric Intraocular Lenses

Corneal astigmatism of ≥1.50 D is present in 15%–29% of cataract patients. Corrective surgical techniques include arcuate keratotomy or limbal relaxing incisions during or after cataract surgery; excimer laser ablation by either LASIK or surface ablation after adequate healing of the incision; or, for small amounts of cylinder, placement of the incision in the axis of plus cylinder. Alternatively, a toric IOL can incorporate the astigmatic correction into the spherical IOL power. Toric IOL placement after clear lens extraction has not been well studied.

Instrumentation

The STAAR toric IOL (Fig 8-5) is an FDA-approved, single-piece, plate-haptic, foldable silicone IOL designed to be placed in the capsular bag using an injector through a 3-mm incision. Once in the eye, it must be oriented with its long axis precisely in the steep meridian. The 6-mm optic is biconvex with a spherocylindrical anterior surface and a spherical posterior surface. The optic has a mark at either end to indicate the axis of plus cylinder. The IOL is available in a length of 10.8 mm or 11.2 mm. A 1.15-mm fenestration located at the end of each haptic is designed to maximize capsular fixation. The IOLs are available in the range of +9.5 to +28.5 D spherical powers, with a choice of cylindrical powers of 2.00 D and 3.50 D. The toric surface corrects less astigmatism when measured at the corneal plane; STAAR states that the 2.00 D IOL corrects 1.50 D of corneal astigmatism and the 3.50 D IOL corrects 2.25 D.

The Alcon AcrySof IQ Toric IOL (Fig 8-6), more recently approved by the FDA, is built on the same platform as the standard AcrySof posterior chamber lens implant. The toric version has a 6.0-mm biconvex acrylic toric optic, available in the range of +6.0 to +30.0 D. The lens is available in the following 3 astigmatism powers: +1.50 D, +2.25 D, and +3.00 D, which correct +1.03 D, +1.55 D, and +2.06 D, respectively, at the spectacle plane. The axis of plus cylinder is marked on the lens optic.

Patient Selection

A toric IOL is appropriate for cataract patients with moderate regular corneal astigmatism. Patients with astigmatism in amounts exceeding the upper correction limits of these lenses require additional measures to obtain full correction. In addition to understanding the risks associated with intraocular surgery, a patient must be capable of understanding

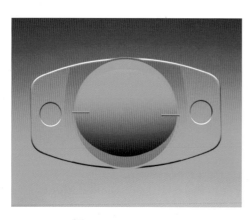

Figure 8-5 STAAR toric IOL. Note the 2 horizontal marks; these should be aligned with the axis of plus cylinder in the cornea. *(Courtesy of STAAR.)*

Figure 8-6 AcrySof IQ toric IOL. Note the 2 sets of 3 dots; these are aligned with the axis of plus cylinder in the cornea. *(Courtesy of Alcon.)*

the limitations of this IOL. The patient should be informed that implantation of a toric IOL will not eliminate the need for reading glasses (unless monovision is planned). The patient also needs to be informed that the IOL may rotate in the capsular bag shortly after surgery and that a secondary intraocular surgery may be required to reposition it. Because the STAAR toric IOL is available only in silicone, it would not be appropriate for patients who may require silicone oil for retinal detachment repair in the future. The acrylic AcrySof IQ toric IOL would be a more appropriate choice in these patients.

Planning and Surgical Technique

The amount and axis of the astigmatism should be measured accurately with a keratometer and confirmed if possible with corneal topography. The axis of astigmatism from the refraction should not be used because it is in part due to lenticular astigmatism, which will be eliminated with cataract surgery.

The manufacturers of these toric IOLs have online applications to aid in surgical planning. After the surgeon enters data such as keratometry measurements, axes, IOL spherical power generated by A-scan, average surgeon-induced astigmatism, and axis of astigmatism, the programs will generate the correct power and model lens as well as orientation of the lens alignment markers.

The vertical and horizontal meridians should be marked on the cornea with the patient in an upright position; in this way, any misalignment resulting from the torsional globe rotation that sometimes occurs with movement to a supine position is avoided. Cataract surgery with a wound that is astigmatism-predictable is necessary to achieve the intended benefit of a toric lens.

After the IOL is injected into the capsular bag, the viscoelastic material behind the IOL is aspirated and the IOL is rotated into position on the steep meridian. If the IOL is too short for the capsular bag diameter, it may rotate when balanced salt solution is used to re-form the anterior chamber. Some surgeons choose to insert the STAAR toric IOL with the spherocylindrical surface facing the posterior capsule in an effort to minimize the risk of postoperative lens rotation. According to data available from the FDA on the safety of the AcrySof toric IOL, the incidence of postoperative surgical intervention for IOL rotation was only 0.4% (1/244).

When a plate-haptic toric IOL is used, the surgeon should take care when performing Nd:YAG capsulotomy. If the capsulotomy is too large, a plate-haptic IOL may prolapse posteriorly. Capsular fixation around the fenestrations helps to stabilize this IOL. This is not an issue with the AcrySof IQ toric IOL.

Outcomes

In clinical trials with the STAAR toric IOL, 48%–84% of patients achieved UCVA of ≥20/40. Data provided by the FDA report UCVA of ≥20/40 in 93.8% of 198 patients implanted with Alcon AcrySof toric IOLs (all sizes combined). Postoperative astigmatism was <0.50 D in 48% of patients and <1.00 D in 75%–81% of patients with the plate-haptic IOLs and 61.6% and 87.7%, respectively, for the AcrySof toric IOL.

In cases of corneal astigmatism greater than that correctable by toric IOLs, surgeons may opt to simultaneously or sequentially correct residual astigmatism with incisional procedures such as astigmatic keratotomy or limbal relaxing incisions.

Complications

The major disadvantage of toric IOLs is the possibility of IOL rotation resulting in a misalignment of the astigmatic correction. Full correction is not achieved unless the IOL is properly aligned in the axis of astigmatism. According to STAAR, a 10° off-axis rotation of the lens reduces the correction by approximately one-third, a 20° off-axis rotation reduces the correction by two-thirds, and an off-axis correction of greater than 30° can actually increase the cylindrical refractive error. In the FDA clinical trials, 76% of patients were reportedly within 10° of preoperative alignment, and 95% were within 30°. Till and colleagues found that 14% of 100 consecutive STAAR toric IOLs inserted had rotated postoperatively by more than 15°. According to data on the AcrySof toric IOL available from the FDA, the degree of postoperative rotation in 242 implanted eyes was 5° or less in 81.1% and 10° or less in 97.1%. None of the eyes exhibited postoperative rotation greater than 15°.

Typically, a misaligned IOL is recognized within days of the surgery; it should be repositioned before permanent fibrosis occurs within the capsular bag. However, waiting 1 week for some capsule contraction to occur may ultimately help stabilize this IOL.

Lane SS, Ernest P, Miller KM, Hileman KS, Harris B, Waycaster CR. Comparison of clinical and patient-reported outcomes with bilateral AcrySof toric or spherical control intraocular lenses. *J Refract Surg.* 2009;25(10):899–901.

Ruhswurm I, Scholz U, Zehetmayer M, Hanselmayer G, Vass C, Skorpik C. Astigmatism correction with a foldable toric intraocular lens in cataract patients. *J Cataract Refract Surg.* 2000;26(7):1022–1027.

Sun XY, Vicary D, Montgomery P, Griffiths M. Toric intraocular lenses for correcting astigmatism in 130 eyes. *Ophthalmology.* 2000;107(9):1776–1781.

Till JS, Yoder PR Jr, Wilcox TK, Spielman JL. Toric intraocular lens implantation: 100 consecutive cases. *J Cataract Refract Surg.* 2002;28(2):295–301.

Multifocal Intraocular Lenses

Multifocal IOLs have the advantage of providing patients with functional vision at near, intermediate, and far distances. Careful patient selection and counseling, along with preoperative measurement, are critically important for achieving patient satisfaction postoperatively. Three multifocal lenses are currently FDA approved for use after cataract extraction: the ReZoom lens (AMO), the AcrySof ReSTOR (Alcon, Fort Worth, TX), and the Tecnis (AMO) multifocal IOL. These lenses are sometimes also used off-label in refractive lens exchange. These types of lenses and their outcomes are discussed in detail in Chapter 9, in the section Multifocal IOL Implants.

Patient Selection

Patients likely to be successful with a multifocal IOL after lens surgery are adaptable, relatively easygoing people who place a high value on reducing dependence on glasses or contact lenses. They should have good potential vision. They generally have less than 1.00 D of preexisting corneal astigmatism unless there is a plan to treat this surgically. Patients generally adapt to the multifocal effect more quickly after lens surgery on both eyes.

Surgical Technique

The surgical technique for multifocal IOL insertion is the same as that used in standard small-incision cataract surgery with a foldable acrylic IOL. Optimal refractive effects depend on good IOL centration. If the posterior capsule is not intact, IOL decentration is more likely to occur, and an accommodating IOL should not be used; adequate fixation for a multifocal IOL should be evaluated. If adequate centration is not assured, a multifocal lens should not be used either, and a monofocal IOL should be placed instead.

Outcomes

Patients are most likely to achieve independence from glasses following implantation of multifocal IOLs bilaterally. A reduction in contrast sensitivity may occur with multifocal IOLs. Also, best spectacle-corrected visual acuity may rarely be reduced.

As patients age, the pupillary diameter may decrease. When the pupillary diameter falls below 2.0 mm, unaided reading ability may diminish. Gentle dilation with topical mydriatic agents or laser photomydriasis may restore near acuity. Photomydriasis may be performed with an argon or dye photocoagulator, by placing green laser burns circumferentially outside the iris sphincter, or with a Nd:YAG photodisruptor, by creating approximately 4 partial sphincterotomies.

Side Effects and Complications

A patient with a multifocal IOL is likely to have significantly more glare, halos, and ghosting than a patient with a monofocal IOL or an accommodating IOL. The complaints of halos tend to subside over several months, perhaps from the patient's neural adaptation. Because of a reduction in contrast sensitivity, the subjective quality of vision after multifocal IOL insertion may not be as good as after a monofocal IOL implantation. The trade-off of decreased quality of vision in return for reduced dependence on glasses must be fully discussed with the patient preoperatively. Intermediate vision may be weaker with multifocal IOLs than with an accommodating IOL. Some surgeons adjust the IOL power for the nondominant eye to ensure a full range of visual function; others use different models of IOLs in the 2 eyes to maximize the range of visual function.

Cillino S, Casuccio A, Di Pace F, et al. One-year outcomes with new-generation multifocal intraocular lenses. *Ophthalmology.* 2008;115(9):1508–1516.

Cionni RJ, Osher RH, Snyder ME, Nordlund ML. Visual outcome comparison of unilateral versus bilateral implantation of apodized diffractive multifocal intraocular lenses after cataract extraction: prospective 6-month study. *J Cataract Refract Surg.* 2009;35(6):1033–1039.

Packer M, Chu YR, Waltz KL, et al. Evaluation of the aspheric Tecnis multifocal intraocular lens: one-year results from the first cohort of the Food and Drug Administration clinical trial. *Am J Ophthalmol.* 2010;149(4):577–584.

Wallace RB III. Multifocal and accommodating lens implementation. *Focal Points: Clinical Modules for Ophthalmologists.* San Francisco: American Academy of Ophthalmology; 2004, module 11.

Accommodating Intraocular Lenses

As with multifocal IOLs discussed earlier, accommodating lenses are sometimes used off-label in refractive lens exchange. Currently, the Crystalens (Bausch & Lomb Surgical, Aliso Viejo, CA) is the only accommodating IOL approved by the FDA for improvement of near, intermediate, and distance vision, although other accommodating IOLs are being investigated. Examples of single-optic IOLs in development include BioComFold Type 43E (Morcher, Stuttgart, Germany), 1 CU (HumanOptics, Erlangen, Germany), and TetraFlex (Lenstec, St Petersburg, FL). Development is also currently under way for dual-optic IOLs (eg, the Synchrony IOL [Visiogen, Irvine, CA]) and deformable IOLs (eg, the SmartIOL [Medennium, Irvine, CA]). These investigational IOLs are discussed in Chapter 9.

Hoffman RS, Fine IH, Packer M. Accommodating IOLs: current technology, limitations, and future designs. *Current Insight.* San Francisco: American Academy of Ophthalmology. Available at http://one.aao.org/CE/News/CurrentInsight/Detail.aspx?cid=97507d43-9b16-4a8d-b4f5-6ac6fff7eafe.

Wallace BR III. Multifocal and accommodating lens implantation. *Focal Points: Clinical Modules for Ophthalmologists.* San Francisco: American Academy of Ophthalmology; 2004, module 11.

Light-Adjustable Intraocular Lenses

The Light-Adjustable Lens, or LAL (Calhoun Vision, Pasadena, CA), currently under investigation, is a 3-piece silicone-optic PCIOL in which the silicone matrix has been embedded with silicone subunits called *macromers.* When the IOL is irradiated with ultraviolet light through a slit-lamp delivery system, the macromers polymerize and are depleted. Macromers from the nonirradiated part of the IOL optic are in higher concentration and, because of the induced osmotic gradient, diffuse toward the area of irradiation, causing the IOL to swell in this region. The light is thus able to induce a change in the shape of the IOL (Fig 8-7). For myopia, irradiation of the IOL periphery causes a reduction in the central thickness of the IOL. For hyperopia, irradiation of the center of the IOL causes it to swell. Correction of astigmatism can be achieved through a toric exposure pattern. Nomograms have been developed that reportedly can correct hyperopia, myopia, and astigmatism over a 5.00 D range. Once the desired power has been achieved, the IOL optic is diffusely irradiated in a subsequent session within 1–2 weeks postoperatively. This

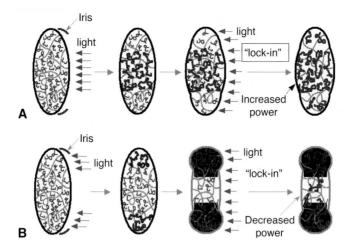

Figure 8-7 Light-adjustable IOL. **A,** When the IOL is treated with light in the center, polymerization occurs and macromers move to the center, increasing the IOL power. **B,** When the IOL is treated with light in the periphery, macromers move to the periphery, decreasing the IOL power. *(Courtesy of Calhoun Vision.)*

causes all remaining macromers to polymerize in their current location, stopping further diffusion and "locking in" the IOL shape. After that step, the power change becomes irreversible and is no longer adjustable.

Theoretically, the effect of the initial irradiation is reversible to a limited degree. If, for example, an overcorrection of residual myopia occurred and the patient became hyperopic, the previously untouched IOL center could be irradiated in a second procedure prior to the final locking-in step.

This system could hypothetically be used to induce a reversible monovision state that could be adjusted if the patient failed to adapt to it in the first week after surgery. In laboratory studies, multifocal patterns have been placed in the IOL optic and could possibly be designed for specific pupil diameters. In principle, it may be possible to induce a wavefront correction on the IOL that could correct higher-order aberrations.

This IOL is foldable and is reportedly biocompatible in the rabbit model. The system has accurately induced intended power changes at specific irradiation levels in vitro. At the time of this writing, it is approved for use in the European Union and clinical trials are ongoing in the United States.

One disadvantage of this IOL system is the need to protect the IOL from sunlight exposure between implantation and the locking-in treatment. Further, it seems possible that an error in the irradiation treatment related to centration or improper data entry could cause irreversible changes in the IOL's visual properties and require IOL exchange surgery. See also Chapter 9.

Schwartz DM, Jethmalani J, Sandstedt C, et al. Adjustable IOLs. In: Durrie DS, O'Brien TP, eds. Refractive surgery: back to the future. *Subspecialty Day Program 2002.* San Francisco: American Academy of Ophthalmology; 2002.

Accommodative and Nonaccommodative Treatment of Presbyopia

Introduction

Presbyopia, the normal progressive loss of accommodation, affects all individuals beginning in middle age, regardless of any underlying refractive error. This relentless loss of near vision and dependency on glasses may be particularly distressing for emmetropic individuals who have previously enjoyed excellent uncorrected vision. The possibility of "curing" or reducing the effects of presbyopia remains the "Holy Grail" of refractive surgery.

A number of procedures intended to increase the amplitude of accommodation are being investigated. Some of these techniques rely on various types of so-called *scleral expansion*. Others involve intraocular lenses (IOLs) capable of anteroposterior movement, with a subsequent change in effective lens power. Still others involve the creation of a multifocal cornea or use of a multifocal IOL. Some procedures were initially based, in part, on the rejection of the long-accepted Helmholtz theory of accommodation. Because several proposed types of surgery for presbyopia are based on new theories of accommodation, we begin by examining the different theories of accommodation.

Theories of Accommodation

We do not yet have a complete understanding of the relationship between the effect of ciliary muscle contraction and zonular tension on the equatorial lens. In addition, a few markedly different anatomical relationships have been described between the origin of the zonular fibers and the insertion of these fibers into the lens.

The *Helmholtz hypothesis,* or *capsular theory,* of accommodation states that during distance vision, the ciliary muscle is relaxed and the zonular fibers that cross the circumlental space between the ciliary body and the lens equator are at a "resting" tension. With accommodative effort, circumferential ciliary muscle contraction releases this tension on the zonules. An anterior movement of the ciliary muscle annular ring also occurs during accommodation. The reduced zonular tension allows the elastic capsule of the lens to contract, causing a decrease in equatorial lens diameter and an increase in the curvatures of the anterior and posterior lens surfaces. This "rounding up" of the lens yields a corresponding increase in its dioptric power, as necessary for near vision (Fig 9-1). When the accommodative effort ceases, the ciliary muscle relaxes and the zonular tension on the lens equator rises to its resting state. This increased tension on the lens equator causes a flattening of the lens, a decrease in the curvature of the anterior and posterior lens surfaces, and a decrease in the dioptric power of the unaccommodated eye.

In the Helmholtz theory, the equatorial edge of the lens moves away from the sclera during accommodation and toward the sclera when accommodation ends. In this theory, all zonular fibers are relaxed during accommodation and all are under tension when the accommodative effort ends. According to Helmholtz, presbyopia results from the loss of lens elasticity with age. When the zonules are relaxed, the lens does not change its shape to the same degree as the young lens; therefore, presbyopia is an aging process that can be reversed only by changing the elasticity of the lens or its capsule.

Southall JPC, ed. *Helmholtz's Treatise on Physiological Optics.* Translated from the 3rd German ed. New York: Dover Publications; 1962.

Diametrically opposed to Helmholtz is the *Schachar theory* of accommodation. Schachar suggests that during accommodation, ciliary muscle contraction leads to a selective increase in equatorial zonular tension—rather than to the uniform decrease (anterior, equatorial, and posterior) proposed by the Helmholtz theory—with a subsequent pulling of the equatorial lens outward toward the sclera (Fig 9-2). Schachar postulates

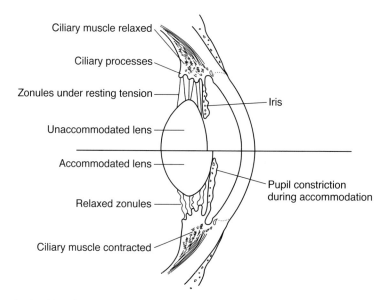

Figure 9-1 In the Helmholtz theory of accommodation, contraction of the ciliary muscle leads to a relaxation of the zonular fibers. The reduced zonular tension allows the elastic capsule of the lens to contract, causing an increase in the anterior and posterior lens curvature. *(Illustration by Jeanne Koelling.)*

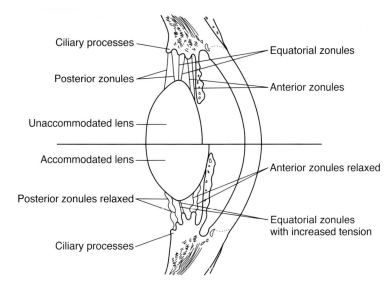

Figure 9-2 The Schachar theory proposes that only the equatorial zonules are under tension during accommodation and that the anterior and posterior zonular fibers serve solely as passive support structures for the lens. *(Illustration by Jeanne Koelling.)*

that accommodation occurs through the direct effect of zonular tension (as opposed to the passive effect proposed by Helmholtz), causing an increase in lens curvature. In this theory, the loss of accommodation with age is a result of the continued growth of the lens, with increasing lens diameter, and a decrease in the lens–ciliary body distance, which results in a loss of zonular tension. Anything that increases resting zonular tension (eg, scleral expansion) should restore accommodation.

Schachar proposes that the mechanism for functional lens shape change is equatorial stretching by the zonules; this decreases the peripheral lens volume and increases the central volume, thus producing the central steepening of the anterior central lens capsule (Fig 9-3). During accommodation and ciliary muscle contraction, tension on the equatorial zonular fibers increases, whereas tension on the anterior and posterior zonules is reduced. These actions allow the lens to maintain a stable position at all times, even as it undergoes changes in shape. Schachar suggests that the anterior and posterior zonules serve as passive support structures for the lens, whereas the equatorial zonules are the active components in determining the optical power of the lens.

Schachar RA. Cause and treatment of presbyopia with a method for increasing the amplitude of accommodation. *Ann Ophthalmol.* 1992;24(12):445–447, 452.

Evidence from recent studies on both human and nonhuman primates disputes Schachar's theories on accommodation and presbyopia. Investigations in human tissues and with scanning electron microscopy reveal no zonular insertions (equatorial or otherwise) at the iris root or anterior ciliary muscle. Various imaging techniques consistently indicate that the diameter of the crystalline lens *decreases* with accommodation. In vitro laser scanning imaging shows that the crystalline lens does not change focal length when increasing and decreasing radial stretching forces are applied. This runs contrary to

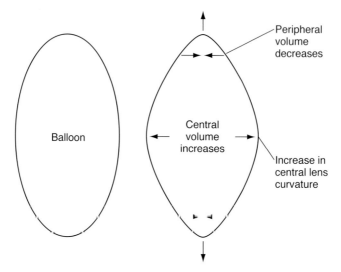

Figure 9-3 The Schachar theory proposes that the increase in equatorial zonular tension causes a decrease in peripheral lens volume and, thus, an increase in central lens volume and central lens curvature. *(Illustration by Jeanne Koelling.)*

Schachar's proposal that the lens remains pliable with age and that presbyopia is due solely to lens growth and crowding that prevents optimum ciliary muscle action.

Glasser A, Kaufman PL. The mechanism of accommodation in primates. *Ophthalmology.* 1999;106(5):863–872.

Strenk SA, Strenk LM, Koretz JF. The mechanism of presbyopia. *Prog Retin Eye Res.* 2005;24(3): 379–393.

Nonaccommodative Treatment of Presbyopia

Monovision

Currently in the United States, monovision is the technique used most frequently for modifying presbyopia in phakic individuals. In this approach, the refractive power of 1 eye is adjusted to improve near vision. Monovision may be achieved with contact lenses, LASIK, surface ablation, conductive keratoplasty, or even lens surgery. The process involves intentionally undercorrecting a myopic patient, overcorrecting a hyperopic patient, or inducing mild myopia in an emmetropic individual. Historically, the term *monovision* was typically applied to patients who wore a distance contact lens in 1 eye and a near contact lens in the other. Often, the power difference between the 2 eyes was significant (1.25 to 2.50 D) because the patient had the option of replacing the near lens with a distance lens when the activity demanded. Obviously, this is not possible with refractive surgery, so many refractive surgeons routinely target mild myopia (−0.50 to −1.50 D) for the near eye in the presbyopic and peripresbyopic population. The term *modified monovision* is probably more appropriate for this lower level of myopia for the near-vision eye. Although not affecting accommodative amplitude, this level of myopia is associated with only a mild decrease in distance vision, retention of good stereopsis, and a significant increase in the intermediate zone of functional vision. The intermediate zone is where many activities of daily life occur (eg, looking at a computer screen, store shelves, or a car dashboard). Patients retain good distance vision in their distance eye and experience an increase in near and intermediate vision in their near eye. For many patients, this compromise between good distance vision in both eyes and a loss of near vision versus good distance vision in 1 eye and an increase in near visual function is an attractive alternative to constantly reaching for a pair of reading glasses. Selected patients who want better near vision may prefer higher amounts of monovision correction (–1.50 to –2.50 D) despite the accompanying decrease in distance vision and stereopsis.

Patient selection

Appropriate patient selection is important in determining the overall success of monovision treatment. Although the monovision correction can be demonstrated with trial lenses in the examination room, a contact lens trial at home is often more useful. Patients who are not presbyopic nor approaching presbyopia are typically not good candidates for modified monovision. A 25-year-old myopic patient will not appreciate the long-term benefit of mild myopia in 1 eye. Young myopic individuals are usually looking for the best possible distance vision in both eyes.

The best candidates for modified monovision are myopic patients over the age of 40 who, because of their refractive error, retain some useful near vision. These patients understand the importance of near vision, and they have always experienced adequate near vision simply by removing their glasses. Patients who do not have useful uncorrected near vision (myopia worse than –4.50 D, high astigmatism, hyperopia, or contact lens wearers) may be more accepting of the need for reading glasses when their refractive error is treated. In addition, for most patients, a minimum of 20/25 or better uncorrected distance visual acuity (UCVA) is required to function without spectacles. Individuals whose correction is high have a decreased likelihood of achieving that level of UCVA. It is typically better to attempt distance correction in both eyes in order to increase the chance of obtaining adequate distance vision. For most other patients, many refractive surgeons routinely aim for mild myopia (–0.50 to –0.75 D, occasionally up to –1.50 D) in the non-dominant eye. Other surgeons may demonstrate monovision with trial lenses or give the patient a trial with contact lenses to ascertain patient acceptance and the exact degree of near vision desired.

Conductive Keratoplasty

As discussed earlier (see Chapter 7), conductive keratoplasty (CK) is a nonablative, collagen-shrinking procedure approved for the correction of low levels of hyperopia (+0.75 to +3.25 D). In CK, radiofrequency (RF) energy is delivered through a fine conducting tip inserted into the peripheral corneal stroma in a circular pattern. The application of RF energy shrinks the collagen in the periphery, which steepens the central cornea and induces a myopic shift (see Chapter 1, Fig 1-19). The number and placement of the spots is dictated by the amount of myopic shift desired and is determined by a nomogram provided by the manufacturing company, Refractec (Bloomington, MN). The procedure is now FDA approved for the treatment of presbyopia in hyperopic and emmetropic individuals. The treatment does not restore accommodation but, rather, induces mild myopia (modified monovision) in 1 eye. The decrease in distance vision is relatively mild compared to the degree of improvement in near vision. Data collected 12 months postoperatively showed that 98% of patients could read newspaper print (J5), and 87% had both 20/20 uncorrected distance acuity and J3 uncorrected near acuity binocularly. The gain in near vision appears to be greater than expected for the amount of myopia induced and may result from the multifocal nature of the post-CK cornea. CK is a relatively simple, minimally invasive procedure that spares the central corneal visual axis and has an excellent safety profile. Although it does not increase accommodative amplitude, CK for presbyopia is capable of increasing the range of functional vision in the presbyopic population. Nevertheless, the effectiveness of the procedure may lessen over time in some patients, either through regression of CK or decrease in accommodation from natural aging.

Multifocal IOL Implants

The IOL options for patients undergoing cataract surgery have increased in recent years. Patients can have a traditional monofocal IOL with a refractive target of emmetropia, mild myopia, or monovision (1 eye distance, 1 eye near); or they can choose a multifocal or an accommodating IOL for greater range of focus.

The Array (Advanced Medical Optics, later Abbott Medical Optics [AMO], Santa Ana, CA) multifocal silicone PCIOL was the first multifocal IOL to be granted FDA approval in the United States. It has since been replaced by the ReZoom lens (AMO), approved in 2005, which was based on the Array design. The ReZoom lens is a flexible, 3-piece, acrylic, distance-dominant zonal refractive IOL that can be inserted through a 2.8-mm clear corneal incision. The lens has 5 expanded refractive zones within the 6.0-mm optic and produces 2.80 D of near power (Fig 9-4). The pupil must be at least 2.0 mm to achieve the near effect.

Figure 9-4 ReZoom multifocal IOL showing the 5 concentric refractive zones. *(Courtesy of Abbott Medical Optics.)*

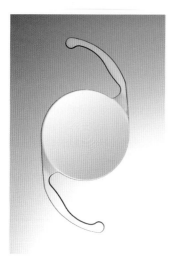

Figure 9-5 ReSTOR multifocal IOL. Note the apodized diffractive changes on the lens optic. *(Courtesy of Alcon.)*

Another multifocal IOL, the AcrySof ReSTOR lens (Alcon Laboratories, Fort Worth, TX) was also approved by the FDA in 2005 (Fig 9-5). ReSTOR is available either as a 1- or 3-piece acrylic aspheric foldable diffractive lens that, similar to the other multifocal lenses, simultaneously focuses light from both distance and near targets. The lens, however, is apodized and gradually tapers its diffractive step heights to allow an even distribution of light, which theoretically makes for a smoother transition among images from distance, intermediate, and near targets. The ReSTOR IOL gradually reduces and blends the step heights of its 3.6-mm diffractive area from 1.3 μm centrally to 0.2 μm peripherally. The peripheral lens area outside the central 3.6-mm diffractive zone is used mainly for distance vision, whereas the central area of the lens is mainly for near work. Depending on pupil size, there is a loss of 6%–19% of light, which can adversely affect contrast sensitivity, especially in patients with smaller pupils.

The ReSTOR IOL is manufactured with a +4.00 D or +3.00 D add at the IOL plane. In the FDA study of the +4.00 add IOL, 84% of patients achieved an uncorrected distance acuity of 20/25 and near acuity of J2 or better. Complete spectacle freedom occurred in 80%, and patient satisfaction was at 94%. In some instances, however, patients who received the +4.00 add IOL expressed dissatisfaction with the near focal point being too close. Thus, the company developed the +3.00 D add IOL, which was approved by the FDA in December 2008. Studies showed that the percentage of patients who achieved 20/20 or better uncorrected acuity at distance, intermediate, and near with +3.00 D add was almost fourfold that of patients with the +4.00 D version. Moreover, the patient satisfaction rate was 95%.

In January 2009, the FDA approved the Tecnis multifocal IOL (AMO), a foldable, hydrophobic, diffractive aspheric acrylic lens. The diffractive steps are on the posterior aspect of the lens and extend fully to the periphery. In bilaterally implanted patients in the FDA study, more than 94% achieved simultaneous 20/25 or better distance visual acuity and 20/32 or better near visual acuity at 4–6 months. Spectacle independence was achieved in 93.8%, and the rate of patient satisfaction was 94.6%.

Complications

Capsular opacification is of greater concern with multifocal IOLs because minimal changes in the capsule can cause early deterioration in vision. Nd:YAG capsulotomy may be required earlier or more frequently in patients with multifocal IOLs to achieve optimal vision. However, other possible causes of visual disturbance (eg, irregular astigmatism, cystoid macular edema, or an epiretinal membrane) should be excluded prior to Nd:YAG capsulotomy, which would make IOL exchange more complicated. Multifocal IOLs cause an increased incidence of glare and halos around lights at night, although the newer multifocal IOLs incorporate technology that significantly reduces these optical phenomena. In addition, most of these symptoms decrease over time, and they can be further reduced through the use of nighttime driving glasses or instillation of topical brimonidine drops to reduce scotopic pupil size. Nevertheless, careful selection of motivated, well-informed patients is prudent.

Custom or Multifocal Ablations

The approach used in the treatment of presbyopia with the excimer laser is to create a multifocal cornea rather than to restore accommodation. The potential for improving near vision without significantly compromising distance vision was investigated after ophthalmologists noted that, following myopic and hyperopic surface ablation or LASIK, the uncorrected near vision of many patients improved more than expected. Hyperopic ablations induce central steepening in a relatively small optical zone and have a large peripheral blend zone (Fig 9-6).

Attempts to correct both distance and near vision use a variation of this multifocal approach. A number of ablation patterns are being evaluated and include the following:

- a small central steep zone, where the central portion of the cornea is used for near and the midperiphery is used for distance
- an inferior near-zone ablation pattern
- an inferiorly decentered hyperopic ablation
- a central distance ablation with an intermediate/near midperipheral ablation

Some of these patterns rely on simultaneous vision (similar to patterns used by some bifocal contact lenses or the ReZoom IOL); others use the pupillary constriction that occurs with the near reflex (accommodative convergence) to concentrate light rays through the steeper central ablation.

The safety and efficacy of multifocal ablations is being evaluated in a Canadian multicenter trial at the University of Ottawa Eye Institute. Thus far, the study has found that multifocal correction for presbyopia has not compromised the accuracy of distance correction. According to preliminary results, at 12 months, uncorrected distance vision was 20/20 or better in 57% and 20/40 or better in 98%, while near vision was J1 in 67% and J5 in 97%, of the 75 eyes of 47 patients studied. Contrast sensitivity was initially reduced postoperatively but returned to baseline in the 50- to 75-year age group.

Some investigators approach multifocal ablation for presbyopia by correcting the central optical zone for distance and the successive concentric zones for intermediate and

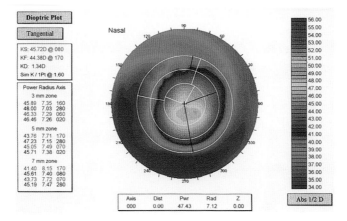

Figure 9-6 Multifocal ablation. Corneal topographic map showing a multifocal pattern after hyperopic LASIK in a 62-year-old with preoperative hyperopia of +4.00. Postoperatively, the UCVA at distance is 20/25^{-2} and the UCVA at near is J1. Manifest refraction of –0.25 +0.75 × 20 yields 20/20. Corneal topography demonstrates central hyperopic ablation *(green)* with relative steepening in the lower portion of the pupillary axis *(orange)*, which provides the near add for reading vision. *(Courtesy of Jayne S. Weiss, MD.)*

near. These ablations use a 10-mm optical zone under a very large flap but supposedly result in a final overall aspheric curvature to the cornea.

Although the data are limited, the excimer laser offers some potential advantages over other methods for managing presbyopia. The procedure is less invasive than scleral expansion or an accommodating IOL, although more invasive than a corneal inlay, which can be removed. It can concomitantly correct the near and distance refractive error. Continued refinements of the multifocal pattern, using computer modeling that considers a patient's pupil size, treatment diameter, and corneal shape, along with data from long-term studies, may further improve this treatment.

Corneal Inlays

Presbyopia can also be surgically corrected by placing a biocompatible polymer lens in the central cornea either beneath a LASIK flap or via a stromal tunnel. These inlays create near vision through different methods (eg, change in corneal curvature, multifocality, pinhole effect). See Chapter 4 for more details.

Accommodative Treatment of Presbyopia

Scleral Surgery

A number of scleral surgical procedures have been evaluated for the reduction of presbyopia. They all share the objective of attempting to increase zonular tension by weakening or altering the sclera over the ciliary body to allow for its passive expansion. Thornton first proposed weakening the sclera by creating 8 or more scleral incisions over the ciliary body (anterior ciliary sclerotomy, or ACS). Results were mixed and any positive effect appeared short-lived, but numerous studies to advance the technique and understand its effect continue. A prospective study of ACS using a 4-incision technique was discontinued because of significant adverse events, including anterior segment ischemia. In 2001, the American Academy of Ophthalmology stated that ACS was ineffective and a potentially dangerous treatment for presbyopia.

Another method involves the placement of scleral expansion bands. Although scleral expansion bands have had mixed results with regard to safety, efficacy, and patient satisfaction, clinical trials are ongoing for these devices (Fig 9-7). The bands act as stents, pulling on the sclera and actively expanding the space between the ciliary body and the lens equator. This procedure has been shown to temporarily improve near vision in some patients, and its safety profile is better than that of previous scleral expansion techniques.

Despite some encouraging results in recent FDA trials, it remains unclear whether any of these expansion procedures produce real and lasting results with an acceptable safety profile. It has not been proved that the temporary improvement in near vision results from restoration of true accommodation of the lens. However, although the theoretical basis for these procedures may be dubious, it does not necessarily follow that the surgery is ineffective. Indeed, some type of pseudoaccommodation may be responsible. Multiple alternative theories have been suggested for the improvement in near acuity. One of these,

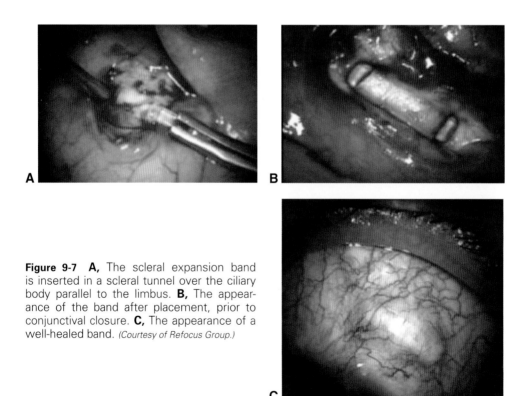

Figure 9-7 **A,** The scleral expansion band is inserted in a scleral tunnel over the ciliary body parallel to the limbus. **B,** The appearance of the band after placement, prior to conjunctival closure. **C,** The appearance of a well-healed band. *(Courtesy of Refocus Group.)*

for example, is that scleral expansion surgery may produce anterior displacement of the crystalline lens with myopic shift and, as a result, improve near vision.

Hamilton DR, Davidorf JM, Maloney RK. Anterior ciliary sclerotomy for treatment of presbyopia: a prospective controlled study. *Ophthalmology.* 2002;109(11):1970–1977.

Kleinmann G, Kim HJ, Yee RW. Scleral expansion procedure for the correction of presbyopia. *Int Ophthalmol Clin.* 2006;46(3):1–12.

Mathews S. Scleral expansion surgery does not restore accommodation in human presbyopia. *Ophthalmology.* 1999;106(5):873–877.

Accommodating IOLs

Although scleral expansion surgery is designed for phakic patients, accommodating IOLs attempt to restore a significant amount of true accommodation to patients with surgically induced pseudophakia. Accommodating IOLs were designed after it was observed that some patients who received a silicone-plate IOL reported a return of their near vision beyond what would be expected from their refractive result. Investigations revealed that, during ciliary muscle contraction, forward displacement of the IOL led to an increase in the IOL's effective power and thus an improvement in near vision. (Anterior chamber IOLs have lower *A* constants than posterior chamber IOLs for the same reason.) However, some studies have questioned the amplitude of true accommodation that can be expected based solely on anterior displacement of the IOL optic. Other factors, such as pupil size, with-the-rule astigmatism, and mild myopia, may also contribute to unaided near visual acuity.

An IOL that uses this accommodative approach is the Crystalens (Bausch & Lomb Surgical, Aliso Viejo, CA). The Crystalens (Fig 9-8) is a modified silicone, plate-haptic lens. The lens has a biconvex optic and hinged haptics, which potentially allow anterior movement of the lens during accommodation. Another theory is that ciliary body contraction causes a steepening of the anterior optic surface, allowing for better near vision.

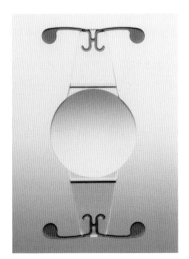

Figure 9-8 The Crystalens has a flexible hinge in the haptic at the proximal end and a polyamide footplate at the distal end. The footplate functions to maximize contact with the capsule and ciliary body, and the hinge transfers the horizontal force into an anteroposterior movement of the optic. *(Courtesy of Eyeonics.)*

Although the exact cause of the movement is unclear, it appears to be a combination of posterior chamber pressure on the back surface of the IOL and ciliary body pressure on the IOL haptics that vaults the optic forward. As the ciliary body contracts, increased pressure is transmitted via the vitreous body to the polyamide haptics. The compression between the haptics causes the IOL to bow forward. The exaggerated anterior displacement is postulated to result in an effective increase in optical power and near vision. Yet another theory postulates that accommodative "arching" of the lens results in enhanced depth of focus. In the FDA study of the Crystalens at 1 year, 100% of patients were reading J3 or better, and 50.4% of patients were reading J1 or better. At 3 years, the number of patients reading J1 increased to 67.7%, and the number reading J3 was stable. Most patients had excellent uncorrected distance and intermediate vision at 1 and 3 years. In addition, 98.4% of cataract patients implanted with Crystalens in both eyes could pass a driver's test without glasses, and 98.4% of Crystalens cataract surgery patients could see well enough to read the newspaper and the phone book without glasses. First approved in 2003, the Crystalens has gone through several modifications changing both the size and design of the optic and haptics to enhance lens stability, visual quality, and reading ability.

Findl O, Kiss B, Petternel V, et al. Intraocular lens movement caused by ciliary muscle contraction. *J Cataract Refract Surg.* 2003;29(4):669–676.

Langenbucher A, Huber S, Nguyen NX, Seitz B, Gusek-Schneider GC, Küchle M. Measurement of accommodation after implantation of an accommodating posterior chamber intraocular lens. *J Cataract Refract Surg.* 2003;29(4):677–685.

Other IOL Innovations on the Horizon

The Crystalens is thought to work via lens effectivity secondary to a change in the position of the optic in the eye. Thus, its accommodative range is limited. A number of other lenses are undergoing clinical investigation. The Synchrony (Visiogen, Irvine, CA) is a dual-optic accommodating IOL that has already been approved for use in Europe and has entered phase 3 trials in the United States. The 2 silicone optics are connected by a system of springlike struts that push the lenses apart. A +34.0 D anterior lens is paired with an appropriate minus-powered posterior lens, yielding a suitable net effective power for a specific patient. During accommodation, the lens system confined within the capsular bag undergoes an adjustment in the separation of the 2 optics, resulting in an increase in effective lens power. The lens can be injected into the eye through a 3.5-mm incision.

The SmartLens (Medennium, Irvine, CA) is made from a thermoplastic acrylic gel that can be customized to any size, shape, or power specified by the physician. The hydrophobic acrylic material is chemically bonded to wax, which melts inside the eye at body temperature and allows the predetermined shape and power of the material to emerge. Theoretically, compression of this pliable lens by the capsular bag would allow adjustment of its effective power in a manner similar to the way the crystalline lens adjusts. Other examples of deformable IOLs that are also in the preliminary stages of development are FlexOptic (AMO), FluidVision IOL (PowerVision, Belmont, CA), and NuLens (NuLens, Herzliya Pituach, Israel).

In addition, flexible polymers are being designed for injection into a nearly intact capsular bag, after extraction of the crystalline lens through a tiny, laterally placed capsulorrhexis. Other lenses being developed appear to have much greater accommodative capacity. One such lens is the NuLens Accommodating IOL (NuLens, Herzliya Pituach, Israel). The NuLens changes its power rather than changing its position in the eye. It incorporates a small chamber of silicone gel and a posterior piston with an aperture.

The Light Adjustable Lens (LAL; Calhoun Vision, Pasadena, CA) is made from a macromer silicone matrix with smaller, embedded photosensitive molecules that will allow for postoperative customization of the power via tunable ultraviolet light treatment (see Chapter 8 for more detail).

The future appears bright, with many emerging possibilities for counteracting the inevitable process of presbyopia, but only time will tell which of these innovations will be successful in clinical practice.

CHAPTER 10

Refractive Surgery in Ocular and Systemic Disease

Introduction

Although many ophthalmologists viewed the field of refractive surgery with skepticism only a few decades ago, it has since achieved wide acceptance. As refractive surgery has evolved from controversial to routine, the spectrum of indications has grown, and an increasing proportion of patients who seek refractive surgery have other known ocular or systemic diseases.

During this period, refractive surgeons have discovered that many of the patients excluded from the original FDA clinical trials can be successfully treated with refractive surgery, and some former absolute contraindications have changed to relative contraindications. In other cases, it may not be clear whether refractive surgery poses an unacceptable risk.

The surgeon must always remember that refractive surgery is elective and involves risks. Refractive surgery is typically contraindicated in the monocular patient; the adverse effect of even small risks is markedly magnified in such a patient because any postoperative visual loss could prove devastating.

However, the envelope is constantly being pushed, and refractive surgery is now being performed successfully in patients previously considered poor candidates. With increased experience, LASIK and surface ablation have been performed safely and effectively in many patients with ocular or systemic diseases. Nevertheless, it is considered off-label use when these procedures are performed on patients whose conditions would have excluded them from participation in the original FDA protocols.

As with other surgeries, ophthalmologists should never go beyond their comfort zone when performing refractive surgery. The surgeon may want to obtain a second opinion for a difficult case or refer certain patients to more experienced colleagues. In the higher-risk patient, unilateral surgery may offer the advantage of providing assurance that 1 eye is doing well before surgery is performed on the second eye. In addition, when deciding whether a patient with connective tissue disease or immunosuppression is an appropriate candidate for refractive surgery, the surgeon may find that consultation with the patient's primary physician provides important information about the patient's systemic health. The process of consent should be altered not only to inform the patient but also to document the patient's understanding of the additional risks and limitations of postoperative results associated with any coexisting ocular or systemic diseases. The refractive surgeon may choose to supplement the standard written consent with additional points to highlight specific concerns. The ophthalmologist should assiduously avoid the high-risk refractive surgery patient who volunteers to sign any preoperative consent because "I know these complications won't happen to me." This patient has not heard or understood the informed consent.

> Preferred Practice Patterns Committee, Refractive Errors Panel. *Refractive Errors and Refractive Surgery*. Preferred Practice Pattern. San Francisco: American Academy of Ophthalmology; 2007.

Ocular Conditions

Dry Eye

Dry-eye symptoms after LASIK are the most common side effects of refractive surgery. Corneal nerves are severed when the flap is made, and the cornea overlying the flap is significantly anesthetic for 3–6 months. As a result, most patients experience a decrease in tear production. Patients who had dry eyes before surgery or whose eyes were marginally compensated before surgery will have the most severe symptoms. In addition, most patients with dry eyes after LASIK or surface ablation will experience tear film and ocular surface disruption and will often complain of fluctuating vision between blinks and at different times of the day. In a review of 109 patients following LASIK surgery, Levinson and colleagues found that dry-eye symptoms and blepharitis were the most common diagnoses leading to patient dissatisfaction with the procedure, even in the setting of relatively good postoperative visual outcomes. Among patients with dry eye or blepharitis, 42% had postoperative uncorrected visual acuity (UCVA) of 20/15–20/20, and 53% had UCVA of 20/25–20/40. Those patients with persistent dry eye were among the most unhappy in this series. Fortunately, in the great majority of these patients, symptoms resolve 3–6 months after surgery. To optimize outcomes, it is imperative for dry-eye disease to be diagnosed and treated before surgery.

Several steps may be taken to reduce the incidence and severity of dry-eye symptoms after refractive surgery. One of the most important is to screen patients carefully for dry eye and tear-film abnormalities before surgery. Many patients seeking refractive surgery are actually dry-eye patients who are intolerant of contact lens wear. Because their preexisting dry-eye syndrome causes them to be uncomfortable wearing contact lenses, these patients often turn to refractive surgery for visual rehabilitation. Any mention of contact lens intolerance during the course of the patient history should suggest the possibility of underlying dry eye.

Refractive surgery may be problematic in dry-eye patients because a normal tear-film layer is important to the healing of the corneal stroma and epithelium. Epidermal growth factor, vitamin A, and IgA in the tears help to prevent postoperative infection and to potentiate wound healing. Consequently, severe dry-eye syndrome was previously thought to be a relative contraindication to refractive surgery. However, a series of 543 eyes of 290 patients after LASIK showed no significant differences in UCVA or best-corrected visual acuity (BCVA) among eyes with or without preoperative dry eye; and there was no increased incidence of epithelial defects in the patients with preoperative dry eye. Nevertheless, the dry-eye group demonstrated a slower recovery of corneal sensation, more vital dye staining of the ocular surface, lower tear production, and more severe dry-eye symptoms until 1 year after LASIK.

Any refractive surgery candidate with signs or symptoms of dry eyes should be thoroughly evaluated. Patient history should include questions about collagen-vascular diseases and conjunctival cicatrizing disorders; these conditions are relative contraindications to refractive procedures and should be addressed prior to any surgical consideration (see Chapter 2).

External examination should include evaluation of eyelid closure for such conditions as incomplete blink, lagophthalmos, entropion, ectropion, or eyelid notching. On slit-lamp examination, notation should be made of blepharitis, meibomitis, and tear-film quantity and quality. Ancillary testing for dry eyes, such as Schirmer testing, tear break-up time, fluorescein corneal staining, and lissamine green or rose bengal conjunctival staining, can be performed.

If collagen-vascular diseases or cicatrizing diseases are suspected, appropriate referral or laboratory testing should be performed to rule out these conditions before refractive surgery is considered. Preexisting abnormalities should be treated, and topical tear replacement and/or punctal occlusion can be performed. If appropriate, a preoperative course of topical anti-inflammatory agents such as corticosteroids or cyclosporine may be given (see BCSC Section 8, *External Disease and Cornea*). As in many non–refractive surgery patients, topical cyclosporine has been shown to improve dry eye and refractive outcomes in dry-eye patients undergoing LASIK and surface ablation. Blepharitis or meibomitis should be treated. Flaxseed and fish oils work synergistically to reduce dry eye in some patients as well.

Although excimer laser ablation may be performed in selected patients with dry eye, these patients must be cautioned about the increased risk of their dry-eye condition becoming worse postoperatively, which may result in additional discomfort or visual decrease and may be permanent.

Levinson BA, Rapuano CJ, Cohen EJ, Hammersmith KM, Ayres BC, Laibson PR. Referrals to the Wills Eye Institute Cornea Service after laser in situ keratomileusis: reasons for patient dissatisfaction. *J Cataract Refract Surg.* 2008;34(1):32–39.

Preferred Practice Patterns Committee, Cornea/External Disease Panel. *Dry Eye Syndrome.* Preferred Practice Pattern. San Francisco: American Academy of Ophthalmology; 2008.

Salib GM, McDonald MB, Smolek M. Safety and efficacy of cyclosporine 0.05% drops versus unpreserved artificial tears in dry-eye patients having laser in situ keratomileusis. *J Cataract Refract Surg.* 2006;32(5):772–778.

Smith RJ, Maloney RK. Laser in situ keratomileusis in patients with autoimmune diseases. *J Cataract Refract Surg.* 2006;32(8):1292–1295.

Toda I, Asano-Kato N, Hori-Komai Y, Tsubota K. Laser-assisted in situ keratomileusis for patients with dry eye. *Arch Ophthalmol.* 2002;120(8):1024–1028.

Toda I, Yagi Y, Hata S, Itoh S, Tsubota K. Excimer laser photorefractive keratectomy for patients with contact lens intolerance caused by dry eye. *Br J Ophthalmol.* 1996;80(7):604–609.

Herpesvirus

Many surgeons avoid laser vision correction in patients with a history of herpes simplex virus (HSV) keratitis because of concern that the ultraviolet light exposure from the excimer laser may increase viral shedding and recurrence. Although current evidence is insufficient to determine conclusively whether surface ablation or LASIK increases the risk of recurrence in a patient with prior HSV keratitis, many such cases have been reported in the literature. Because recurrences have taken place months after excimer laser treatment, some authors have concluded that the recurrence simply reflects the natural course of the disease and not reactivation due to excimer laser ablation. Others, however, have postulated that trauma from the lamellar dissection or exposure to the excimer laser reactivates the virus and causes recurrent keratitis. Several case reports have also been published on patients with a history of oral HSV infection without preexisting corneal disease who developed HSV keratitis after excimer ablation, including 1 case that occurred on the first postoperative day, suggesting that caution should also be exercised in individuals with a history of systemic HSV infection.

The role of excimer laser ablation in inciting recurrence of HSV keratitis has been investigated in the laboratory. Rabbits infected with HSV type 1 had viral reactivation after exposure of the corneal stroma to 193-nm ultraviolet radiation during PRK and after LASIK. Pretreatment with systemic valacyclovir before laser treatment decreased the rate of recurrence in the rabbit model. Another rabbit latency model study demonstrated that systemic valacyclovir reduced ocular shedding of HSV after LASIK.

Reactivation of HSV keratitis has been reported in humans after radial keratotomy (RK), phototherapeutic keratectomy (PTK), PRK, and LASIK. Fagerholm and colleagues reported a 25% incidence of postoperative HSV keratitis in the 17 months after PTK for surface irregularities from prior HSV infections, compared with an 18% recurrence rate in the same time period prior to PTK. They concluded that the procedure does not seem to significantly increase the incidence of recurrences.

A retrospective review of 13,200 PRK-treated eyes with no history of corneal HSV revealed a 0.14% incidence of HSV keratitis. Of these cases, 16.5% occurred within 10 days of the procedure, which the authors postulated could indicate a direct effect of the excimer ultraviolet laser. In 78%, HSV keratitis occurred within 15 weeks, which could be related to the corticosteroid therapy.

Corneal perforation after LASIK has been reported in a patient who had a prior penetrating keratoplasty for herpetic disease with resultant high myopia and astigmatism. The HSV keratitis recurred 10 days after the LASIK, with corneal thinning and subsequent perforation.

Reactivation of herpes zoster ophthalmicus has also been reported after LASIK, associated with vesiculoulcerative lesions on the tip of the nose in 1 case. These few cases responded to topical and oral antiviral treatment with excellent recovery of vision. There are anecdotal reports of flap interface inflammation, resembling diffuse lamellar keratitis, after LASIK in the setting of herpes simplex or zoster keratitis. In these cases, topical corticosteroids may also be required.

Because of the potential for visual loss from herpetic recurrence, some refractive surgeons consider prior herpetic keratitis a contraindication to refractive surgery. Caution should be exercised in making the decision to perform surface ablation, PTK, or LASIK in a patient with a history of prior ocular herpetic infection. The HEDS Study showed only a 50% reduction in the risk of recurrence with a prophylactic dose of oral acyclovir over the course of a year in patients with latent HSV and no inciting factors such as an excimer laser. Patients with pronounced corneal hypoesthesia or anesthesia, vascularization, thinning and scarring, or recent herpetic attacks should not be considered candidates for refractive surgery.

Some surgeons will consider LASIK in a patient with a history of HSV keratitis who has not had any recent recurrences and who has good corneal sensation, minimal or no corneal vascularization or scarring, and normal BCVA. Preoperative and postoperative prophylaxis with systemic antiviral agents should be strongly considered. Any patient with a history of herpes simplex or zoster keratitis must be counseled about the continued risk of recurrence and its concomitant potential for visual loss after excimer laser vision correction.

Asbell PA. Valacyclovir for the prevention of recurrent herpes simplex virus eye disease after excimer laser photokeratectomy. *Trans Am Ophthalmol Soc.* 2000;98:285–303.

Dhalliwal DK, Romanowski EG, Yates KA, et al. Valacyclovir inhibition of recovery of ocular herpes simplex virus type 1 after experimental reactivation by laser in situ keratomileusis. *J Cataract Refract Surg.* 2001;27(8):1288–1293.

Fagerholm P, Ohman L, Orndahl M. Phototherapeutic keratectomy in herpes simplex keratitis: clinical results in 20 patients. *Acta Ophthalmol.* 1994;72(4):457–460.

Nagy ZZ, Keleman E, Kovacs A. Herpes simplex keratitis after photorefractive keratectomy. *J Cataract Refract Surg.* 2003;29(1):222–223.

Keratoconus

Keratoconus is generally considered a contraindication to LASIK and surface ablation. Weakening of the cornea as a result of the loss of structural integrity involved in creating the LASIK flap and removal of tissue significantly increases the risk of progressive ectasia, even if the keratoconus was stable prior to treatment. Although different stages of keratoconus can be diagnosed by slit-lamp examination, more sensitive analyses using corneal topography and corneal pachymetry can reveal findings ranging from clearly normal to clearly pathologic. No specific agreed-upon test or measurement is diagnostic of a corneal ectatic disorder, but both of these diagnostic tests should be part of the evaluation because subtle corneal thinning or curvature changes can be overlooked on slit-lamp evaluation. Newer testing modalities such as the evaluation of central epithelial thickness and corneal hysteresis measurements are potential additions to preoperative testing, but their value has yet to be proven.

The existing literature on ectasia and longitudinal studies of the fellow eye of unilateral keratoconus patients indicate that asymmetric inferior corneal steepening or asymmetric bow-tie topographic patterns with skewed steep radial axes above and below the horizontal meridian (Fig 10-1) are risk factors for progression to keratoconus and post-LASIK ectasia. LASIK should not be considered in such patients using current technology. Patients with an inferior "crab-claw" pattern accompanied by central flattening are at risk of developing pellucid marginal degeneration or a "low sagging cone" variety of

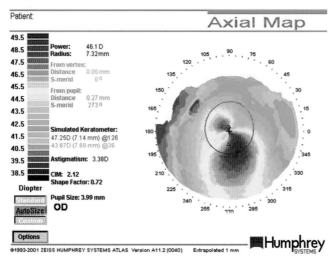

Figure 10-1 Forme fruste keratoconus with asymmetric irregular steepening. *(Courtesy of Eric D. Donnenfeld, MD.)*

keratoconus, even in the absence of clinical signs (Fig 10-2). This pattern may be designated "pellucid suspect," and LASIK should be avoided in eyes exhibiting this topographic pattern. Global pachymetry measurements may be important in helping to rule out forme fruste keratoconus. Posterior curvature evaluation with new corneal imaging technology may also prove to be of significant importance (Fig 10-3). Often, the refractive surgeon is the first physician to inform a refractive surgery candidate that she or he has forme fruste keratoconus. The patient may have excellent vision with glasses or contact lenses and may be seeking the convenience of a more permanent correction through LASIK. It is important that the ophthalmologist clearly convey that although the presence of forme fruste keratoconus does not necessarily indicate the presence of a progressive disease, refractive surgery should not be performed because of the potential for unpredictable results and loss of vision.

Intrastromal corneal ring segments (eg, Intacs) are FDA approved for keratoconus (see Chapter 4). Corneal collagen crosslinking with riboflavin and ultraviolet A exposure shows promising early results and may prove to be effective in preventing and treating corneal ectasia (see Chapter 7 and also BCSC Section 8, *External Disease and Cornea*). Although some early case reports have suggested that combining collagen crosslinking treatments with PRK may offer some benefit to keratoconus patients, the clinical experience remains very preliminary.

Binder PS, Lindstrom RL, Stulting RD, et al. Keratoconus and corneal ectasia after LASIK. *J Cataract Refract Surg.* 2005;31(11):2035–2038.

Chan CC, Sharma M, Wachler BS. Effect of inferior segment Intacs with and without corneal C3-R on keratoconus. *J Cataract Refract Surg.* 2007;33(1):75–80.

Kirkness CM, Ficker LA, Steele AD, Rice NS. Refractive surgery for graft-induced astigmatism after penetrating keratoplasty for keratoconus. *Ophthalmology.* 1991;98(12):1786–1792.

Randleman JB, Russell B, Ward MA, Thompson KP, Stulting RD. Risk factors and prognosis for corneal ectasia after LASIK. *Ophthalmology.* 2003;110(2):267–275.

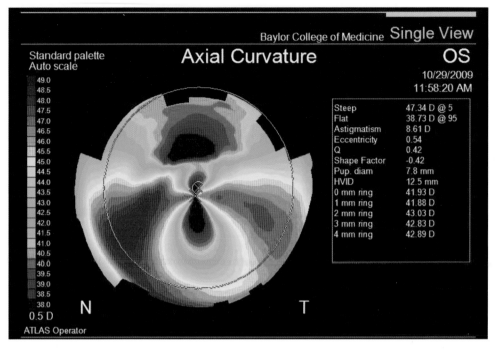

Figure 10-2 Topography of pellucid marginal degeneration showing the "crab-claw" appearance. *(Courtesy of M. Bowes Hamill, MD.)*

Post–Penetrating Keratoplasty

Refractive unpredictability following penetrating keratoplasty (PKP) is extremely common owing to the inherent imprecision of the operation, with most series documenting mean cylinders of 4.0–5.0 D and significant anisometropia. In many cases, these refractive errors are not amenable to spectacle correction, and between 10% and 30% of patients require contact lens correction to achieve good vision after PKP. However, contact lens fitting may not be successful in this patient population due to either the abnormal corneal curvature or the patient's inability to tolerate or manipulate a contact lens.

Surgical alternatives for the correction of post-PKP astigmatism include corneal relaxing incisions, compression sutures, and wedge resections. In a series of 201 corneal transplants for keratoconus, 18% of patients required refractive surgery for the correction of astigmatism. These procedures can significantly decrease corneal cylinder and are highly effective. However, they have minimal effect on spherical equivalent. In addition, they can be unpredictable and may destabilize the graft–host wound.

Pseudophakic patients with significant anisometropia may be candidates for an intraocular lens (IOL) exchange or a piggyback IOL; new options include toric IOLs (see Chapter 8). This alternative requires another intraocular procedure, which increases the risk of endothelial decompensation, glaucoma, and cystoid macular edema and may incite a graft rejection.

Given the success of the excimer laser in treating myopia and astigmatism, PRK has been studied and used to treat post-PKP refractive errors. PRK has the disadvantages associated with epithelial removal in a corneal transplant and may result in corneal haze

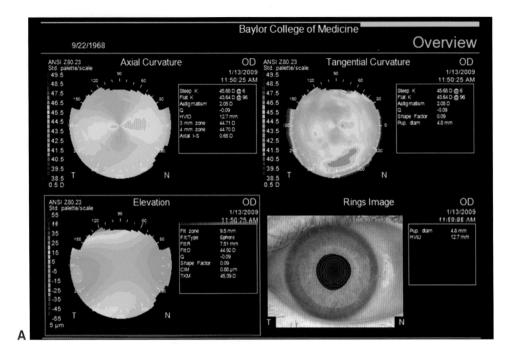

Case 1: OD—Galilei keratoconus report

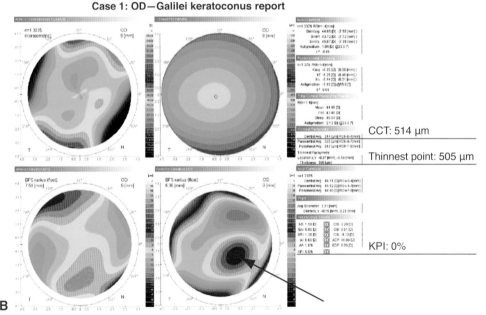

CCT: 514 μm

Thinnest point: 505 μm

KPI: 0%

Figure 10-3 A 40-year-old man wishes to correct his myopia and high astigmatism. He does not wear contact lenses. His manifest refraction is –4.00 +3.00 × 4 OD and –3.75 +3.00 × 168 OS; BSCVA is 20/20 OU. Both eyes appeared normal on slit-lamp examination. **A,** Although the topography appears normal on first glance, there is subtle inferior steepening that requires close inspection to appreciate. **B,** A clearly abnormal "hot spot" *(arrow)* is apparent on the Galilei dual Scheimpflug analyzer posterior elevation map, which may indicate forme fruste keratoconus. Technologies that evaluate corneal thickness as well as anterior curvature may improve the identification of early keratoconus patients. *(Courtesy of Douglas D. Koch, MD.)*

when high refractive errors are treated. With increased use of prophylactic mitomycin C, PRK has become a more common treatment option for refractive errors following PKP. Although the refractive results are often fairly good, PRK in post-PKP patients is generally less predictable and less effective than it is for naturally occurring astigmatism and myopia.

LASIK following PKP is subject to the same patient selection constraints as conventional LASIK. Without extenuating circumstances, monocular patients or patients with limited visual potential in the fellow eye are not candidates. In addition, patients with wound-healing disorders, significant dry-eye syndrome, or a collagen-vascular disease should be offered other options. Finally, patients should have realistic expectations for their rehabilitation after post-PKP LASIK. The goal of LASIK following PKP is to return the patient to spectacle-corrected binocularity or to enable the patient to wear contact lenses successfully, as accuracy of the procedure is less predictable than that of conventional LASIK. It is also important to note that there are no FDA-approved procedures to treat irregular astigmatism. Preoperative evaluation of the post-PKP patient who is considering refractive surgery should include the indications for the PKP. Herpetic keratitis is a relative contraindication for refractive surgery, as is connective tissue disease. Patients with low endothelial cell counts may be at an increased risk of flap dislocation due to the impairment of the endothelial cell pump function.

The timing of refractive surgery after PKP is controversial. All sutures should be removed, and refraction should be stable. To avoid wound dehiscence, many surgeons wait at least 1 year after PKP and an additional 4 months after all sutures are removed. An interval of at least 18–24 months after PKP provides sufficient wound healing in most cases. No matter how long after the PKP surgery, the graft–host wound should be carefully inspected to make sure it appears strong enough to undergo a LASIK procedure, as there is a small but real risk of keratoplasty wound dehiscence during application of the vacuum ring used to create the LASIK flap.

Rigid gas-permeable contact lenses should be discontinued for at least 1 month prior to the final refraction. Refraction and corneal topography should be stable, as documented by 2 consecutive readings on separate visits at least 1 month apart. Areas of suspected ectasia should be confirmed with pachymetry to avoid perforation. Refractive surgery should be avoided if the corneal graft shows evidence of inflammation, diffuse vascularization, ectasia, inadequate healing of the graft–host interface, refractive instability, or signs of rejection or decompensation.

Because eye alignment under the laser is critical to accurate treatment of astigmatism, some surgeons mark the vertical or horizontal axis of the cornea at the slit lamp prior to placing the patient under the laser. Suction time should be minimized to decrease stress on the corneal wound and to lessen the potentially devastating complication of wound dehiscence. If the corneal curvature is very steep, cutting a thicker flap during the microkeratome pass may decrease the risk of buttonhole formation. PRK should also be considered in steep corneas to avoid flap complications, although late-developing corneal haze has been reported.

The creation of a lamellar flap may itself cause a change in the amount and axis of the astigmatism, and some surgeons perform LASIK in 2 stages. First, the flap is cut and laid back down. One or more weeks later, after the curvature has stabilized, the flap is lifted and laser ablation is performed. Other authors have reported minimal refractive changes following flap creation; and some surgeons prefer to perform LASIK in 1 step to avoid increasing the potential complications associated with performing 2 separate procedures, including infection, graft rejection, and epithelial ingrowth. Flap retraction and necrosis have been reported in patients undergoing LASIK after keratoplasty.

The mean percentage reduction of astigmatism after LASIK following PKP ranges from 54.0% to 87.9%. Although most series report an improvement in UCVA, up to 42.9% of patients require enhancement due to cylindrical undercorrection. In addition, up to 35% of patients are reported to lose 1 line of BCVA. Corneal graft rejection has been described after PRK; thus, higher and more prolonged dosing with topical corticosteroids should be prescribed in post-PKP refractive surgery patients to decrease this risk.

Alió JL, Javaloy J, Osman AA, Galvis B, Tello A, Haroun HE. Laser in situ keratomileusis to correct post-keratoplasty astigmatism: 1-step vs 2-step procedure. *J Cataract Refract Surg.* 2004;30(11):2303–2310.

Busin MB, Arffa RC, Zambianchi L, Lamberti G, Sebastiani A. Effect of hinged lamellar keratotomy on postkeratoplasty eyes. *Ophthalmology.* 2001;108(2):1845–1850.

Hardten DR, Chittcharus A, Lindstrom RL. Long term analysis for the correction of refractive errors after penetrating keratoplasty. *Cornea.* 2004;23(5):479–489.

Kollias AN, Schaumberger MM, Kreutzer TC, Ulbig MW, Lackerbauer CA. Two-step LASIK after penetrating keratoplasty. *Clin Ophthalmol.* 2009;3:581–586.

Lam DS, Leung AT, Wu JT, Tham CC, Fan DS. How long should one wait to perform LASIK after PKP? *J Cataract Refract Surg.* 1998;24(1):6–7.

Sharma N, Sinha R, Vajpayee RB. Corneal lamellar flap retraction after LASIK following penetrating keratoplasty. *Cornea.* 2006;25(4):496.

Ocular Hypertension and Glaucoma

Glaucoma is 2–3 times more prevalent among patients with myopia. Between 9% and 28% of myopic patients have primary open-angle glaucoma (POAG). Consequently, it is likely that some patients with glaucoma will request refractive surgery.

Of particular concern in patients with ocular hypertension or POAG is the effect of the acute rise in intraocular pressure (IOP) to more than 65 mm Hg when suction is applied to cut the stromal flap for LASIK or the epithelial flap for epi-LASIK. Although the normal optic nerve seems to tolerate this degree of IOP elevation, we do not yet fully know the resultant effect on the compromised optic nerve. There have been a few reports of new visual field defects immediately after LASIK attributed to mechanical compression or ischemia of the optic nerve head from the temporary increase in IOP.

Evaluation of the patient with ocular hypertension or POAG includes a complete history and ocular examination with peripheral visual field testing and corneal pachymetry. A history of poor IOP control, noncompliance with treatment, maximal medical therapy, or prior surgical interventions may suggest progressive disease, which may contraindicate refractive surgery. As part of the complete examination, the surgeon should note the status of the angle, the presence and amount of optic nerve cupping, and the degree of visual field loss.

Several studies have confirmed that central corneal thickness affects the Goldmann applanation tonometry (GAT) measurement of IOP (see the section Glaucoma After Refractive Surgery in Chapter 11). The principle of applanation tonometry assumes a corneal thickness of 520 μm. Studies have demonstrated that thinner-than-normal corneas give falsely lower IOP readings, whereas thicker corneas give falsely higher readings. For example, IOP is underestimated by approximately 5.2 mm Hg in a cornea with a central thickness of 450 μm. Although all reports agree that central corneal thickness affects GAT IOP measurement, there is no consensus on a specific formula to compensate for this effect in clinical practice.

When treating myopia, LASIK and surface ablation procedures remove tissue to reduce the steepness of the cornea; this sculpting process creates thinner central corneas, which will cause artifactually low IOP measurements postoperatively. Such inaccurately low central applanation tonometry measurements have been reported to hinder the diagnosis of corticosteroid-induced glaucoma after keratorefractive procedures, resulting in optic nerve cupping, visual field loss, and decreased visual acuity (Fig 10-4). Because of

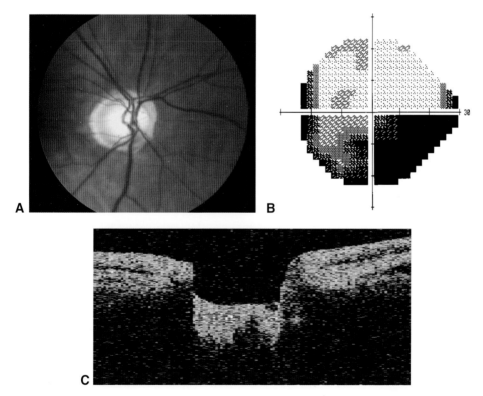

Figure 10-4 Glaucomatous optic nerve atrophy in a patient with "normal IOP" after LASIK. **A,** Increased cup–disc ratio in a patient diagnosed with glaucoma 1 year after LASIK. Patient had decreased vision, with BCVA of 20/40 and IOP of 21 mm Hg. **B,** Humphrey 24-2 visual field with extensive inferior arcuate visual field loss corresponding to thinning of the superior optic nerve rim. **C,** Optical coherence tomography demonstrates marked optic nerve cupping. *(Parts A and B courtesy of Jayne S. Weiss, MD; part C courtesy of Steven I. Rosenfeld, MD.)*

the difficulty that PRK and LASIK cause in the accurate measurement of IOP, these refractive procedures should not be considered for a patient whose IOP is poorly controlled. Furthermore, patients should be advised of the effect of refractive surgery on their IOP measurements and urged to inform future ophthalmologists about their surgery. Patients should be referred to a glaucoma specialist when indicated.

Other methods of measuring IOP appear to be more accurate than GAT after LASIK. Compared with GAT, the pneumotonometer has a smaller area of applanation, so it is less affected by the properties of the cornea and, thus, is less affected by LASIK. The Tono-Pen (Reichert Ophthalmic Instruments, Depew, NY), which uses the Mackay-Marg principle, also has a smaller area of applanation and is less affected by changes in ocular rigidity or corneal flattening than GAT after LASIK. Some studies have further found that Tono-Pen IOP measurements taken on the temporal, nonablated side of the cornea change the least after LASIK, compared with those of other devices used centrally or temporally.

In a small number of patients who have had LASIK, fluid accumulates in the flap interface due to elevated IOP, resulting in a condition that resembles diffuse lamellar keratitis (DLK) but has a later onset and is unresponsive to steroids. Fluid under the flap makes the GAT IOP measurement significantly lower than it actually is, thus masking an IOP elevation that can cause significant glaucomatous damage if not identified.

Retinal nerve fiber layer (RNFL) analysis and optic nerve head (ONH) analysis have developed into useful tools to diagnose glaucoma and monitor for glaucomatous progression. Although there are case reports of glaucomatous damage or progression following refractive surgery, several well-designed studies have been published that demonstrate no significant change in the RNFL or ONH analyses after either LASIK or LASEK. Some studies suggest that scanning laser polarimetry is sensitive to the corneal optical properties and may show transient changes in the RNFL after LASIK that resolve with corneal healing over time.

Patients with ocular hypertension can often safely undergo refractive surgery. Such patients must be counseled preoperatively that the refractive surgery treats only the refractive error and not the natural history of the ocular hypertension, which can sometimes progress to glaucoma, with optic nerve cupping and visual field loss. Particular attention should be paid to the risk factors for progression to glaucoma, including age, corneal thickness, cup–disc ratio, and IOP. The patient needs to understand that after excimer laser ablation it is more difficult to accurately assess IOP.

The decision about whether to perform refractive surgery in a patient with glaucoma is controversial. There are no long-term studies on refractive surgery in this population. LASIK is contraindicated in any patient with marked optic nerve cupping, visual field loss, or visual acuity loss. The refractive surgeon may ask the patient to sign an ancillary consent form that documents the patient's understanding that POAG may result in progressive visual loss independent of any refractive surgery and that IOP elevation during a LASIK or an epi-LASIK procedure or following LASIK or surface ablation (often due to a corticosteroid response) can cause glaucoma progression.

The surgeon should be aware that placement of a suction ring may not be possible if there is a functioning filtering bleb. Typically, glaucoma should be well controlled before refractive surgery is even considered. In the rare case in which filtering surgery and

LASIK are both being planned, it is preferable to perform LASIK before the filter is placed. Suction time should be minimized to decrease the chance of optic nerve damage from the transient increase in IOP. Alternatively, PRK or LASEK may be preferable because each avoids the IOP rise associated with LASIK flap creation. The surgeon must be cautious in using postoperative corticosteroids because of their potential for elevating IOP. The patient should be informed as to when he or she can resume postoperative topical medications for glaucoma.

To avoid trauma to the flap, IOP should generally not be checked for at least 72 hours. The patient should be told to inform any subsequent ophthalmologists of the prior LASIK, as well as the preoperative refractive error, so that post-LASIK IOP can be assessed more accurately.

Bashford KP, Shafranov G, Tauber S, Shields MB. Considerations of glaucoma in patients undergoing corneal refractive surgery. *Surv Ophthalmol.* 2005;50(3):245–251.

Bushley DM, Parmley VC, Paglen P. Visual field defect associated with laser in situ keratomileusis. *Am J Ophthalmol.* 2000;129(5):668–671.

Choplin NT, Schallhorn SC, Sinai M, Tanzer D, Tidwell JL, Zhou Q. Retinal nerve fiber layer measurements do not change after LASIK for high myopia as measured by scanning laser polarimetry with custom compensation. *Ophthalmology.* 2005;112(1):92–97.

Hamilton DR, Manche EE, Rich LF, Maloney RK. Steroid-induced glaucoma after laser in situ keratomileusis associated with interface fluid. *Ophthalmology.* 2002;109(4):659–665.

Lewis RA. Refractive surgery and the glaucoma patient: customized corneas under pressure. *Ophthalmology.* 2000;107(9):1621–1622.

Morales J, Good D. Permanent glaucomatous visual loss after photorefractive keratectomy. *J Cataract Refract Surg.* 1998;24(5):715–718.

Shaikh NM, Shaikh S, Singh K, Manche E. Progression to end-stage glaucoma after laser in situ keratomileusis. *J Cataract Refract Surg.* 2002;28(2):356–359.

Sharma N, Sony P, Gupta A, Vajpayee RB. Effect of laser in situ keratomileusis and laser-assisted subepithelial keratectomy on retinal nerve fiber layer thickness. *J Cataract Refract Surg.* 2006;32(3):446–450.

Whitson JT, McCulley JP, Cavanagh HD, Song J, Bowman RW, Hertzog L. Effect of laser in situ keratomileusis on optic nerve head topography and retinal nerve fiber layer thickness. *J Cataract Refract Surg.* 2003;29(12):2302–2305.

Wong TY, Klein BE, Klein R, Knudtson M, Lee KE. Refractive errors, intraocular pressure, and glaucoma in a white population. *Ophthalmology.* 2003;110(1):211–217.

Retinal Disease

All patients undergoing refractive surgery should have a preoperative dilated retinal examination. The patient should be informed of the significance, treatment, and prognosis of any vitreoretinal pathology.

High myopia

Highly myopic patients are at increased risk for retinal tears and detachment. The yearly incidence of retinal detachments has been estimated at 0.015% in patients with <4.75 D of myopia, increasing to 0.07% in patients with ≥5.00 D of myopia. A study of 1000 patients with myopia >6.00 D revealed a 3.2% incidence of retinal detachment. A thorough dilated retinal examination (including scleral depression, if indicated) should be performed on all patients with high myopia. Referral to a retina specialist should be considered in those with predisposing retinal pathology. One study of 4800 consecutive patients in a private refractive surgery practice found that 52 (1.1%) had posterior segment pathology that required intervention. Symptomatic retinal tears or subclinical retinal detachments should be treated. In the absence of other risk factors, asymptomatic lattice degeneration with or without atrophic holes generally does not require prophylactic treatment. Asymptomatic retinal flap tears or holes usually do not require treatment (see BCSC Section 12, *Retina and Vitreous*); however, tears or holes associated with high myopia and other risk factors should be considered for treatment. In a study of 29,916 myopic and hyperopic eyes undergoing LASIK, 1.5% required preoperative treatment of retinal pathology.

Brady J, O'Keefe M, Kilmartin D. Importance of fundoscopy in refractive surgery. *J Cataract Refract Surg.* 2007;33(9):1602–1607.

Retinal detachment

Patients with high myopia should be counseled that refractive surgery corrects only the refractive aspect of the myopia and not the natural history of the highly myopic eye with its known complications. Highly myopic patients remain at risk for retinal tears and detachment throughout their lives, despite refractive surgery.

Although no causal link has been established between retinal detachment and excimer laser refractive surgery, the potential adverse effects should be considered. The rapid increase and then decrease in IOP could theoretically stretch the vitreous base, and the acoustic shock waves from the laser could play a role in the development of a posterior vitreous detachment. Although the actual risk to eyes with high myopia or preexisting retinal pathology has not been determined through well-controlled, long-term studies, current data suggest that radial keratotomy, surface ablation, and LASIK do not appear to increase the incidence of retinal detachment. The occurrence of retinal detachment after LASIK has been reported to range from 0.034% to 0.250%. In a series of 1554 eyes that underwent LASIK for myopia with a mean refractive error of –13.52 ± 3.38 D, 4 eyes (0.25%) developed retinal detachments at 11.25 ± 8.53 months after the procedure. Three of the eyes had retinal flap tears and 1 eye had an atrophic hole. There was no statistically significant difference in BCVA before and after conventional retinal reattachment surgery. A myopic shift did result from the scleral buckle, however.

In a study of 38,823 eyes with a mean myopia of –6.00 D, the frequency of rhegmatogenous retinal detachments at a mean of 16.3 months after LASIK was 0.8%. The eyes that developed retinal detachments had a mean preoperative myopia of –8.75 D. Final BCVA after conventional scleral buckling procedures in such patients is usually good.

Using retrospective review, Blumenkranz reported that the frequency of retinal detachment after excimer laser was similar to the frequency in the general population, averaging 0.034% over 2 years. The operating retinal surgeon must be informed that LASIK has previously been performed because of the potential for flap dehiscence during retinal detachment surgery, especially during corneal epithelial scraping.

The risk of retinal detachment after cataract surgery is well described (see BCSC Section 11, *Lens and Cataract*). Cataract surgery is the intraocular surgical procedure most commonly complicated subsequently by retinal detachment. Highly myopic eyes undergoing phakic IOL procedures are at risk for retinal detachment from the underlying high myopia as well as from the intraocular surgery. A retinal detachment rate of 4.8% was reported in a study of phakic IOLs to correct high myopia.

Clear lens extraction has also been associated with retinal detachment. Colin reported an incidence of postoperative retinal detachment following clear lens extraction of 2.0% after 4 years and 8.1% at 7 years despite prophylactic laser photocoagulation of lattice degeneration, retinal tears, and holes. This study emphasized the need for prolonged surveillance: at 4 years, the rate of retinal detachment was similar to the rate seen in patients with myopia of greater than −10.00 D who did not undergo surgery; but at 7 years, the actual rate was double the predicted rate. In other studies, serious vitreoretinal complications also occurred despite preoperative prophylactic treatment of retinal lesions. In some cases, the postoperative retinal tears occurred at the edge of the treated zones. Longer-term follow-up is needed to determine whether these surgeries increase morbidity in the highly myopic eye.

Arevalo JF. Posterior segment complications after laser-assisted in situ keratomileusis. *Curr Opin Ophthalmol.* 2008;19(3):177–184.

Arevalo JF, Ramirez E, Suarez E, Cortez R, Ramirez G, Yepez JB. Retinal detachment in myopic eyes after laser in situ keratomileusis. *J Refract Surg.* 2002;18(6):708–714.

Blumenkranz MS. LASIK and retinal detachment: should we be concerned? [editorial]. *Retina.* 2000;5:578–581.

Colin J, Robinet A, Cochener B. Retinal detachment after clear lens extraction for high myopia: seven-year follow-up. *Ophthalmology.* 1999;106(12):2281–2284.

Loewenstein A, Goldstein M, Lazar M. Retinal pathology occurring after excimer laser surgery or phakic intraocular lens implantation: evaluation of possible relationship. *Surv Ophthalmol.* 2002;47(2):125–135.

Qin B, Huang L, Zeng J, Hu J. Retinal detachment after laser in situ keratomileusis in myopic eyes. *Am J Ophthalmol.* 2007;144(6):921–923.

Ruiz-Moreno JM, Alió JL, Pérez-Santonja JJ, de la Hoz F. Retinal detachment in phakic eyes with anterior chamber intraocular lenses to correct severe myopia. *Am J Ophthalmol.* 1999;127(3):270–275.

Sakurai E, Okuda M, Nozaki M, Ogura Y. Late-onset laser in situ keratomileusis (LASIK) flap dehiscence during retinal detachment surgery. *Am J Ophthalmol.* 2002;134(2):265–266.

Previous retinal detachment surgery

Patients who have had prior scleral buckle surgery or vitrectomy may want refractive surgery because of resultant myopia. Prior retinal detachment surgery can result in a myopic shift because of axial elongation of the eye from indentation of the scleral buckle. Refractive surgery can be considered in selected cases that have symptomatic anisometropia with good BCVA.

The retina should be extensively evaluated preoperatively. Referral to a retina specialist should be made when indicated. The surgeon should determine whether the scleral buckle or conjunctival scarring will interfere with placement of the suction ring in preparation for creation of the LASIK flap. If so, PRK or LASEK may be considered instead of LASIK.

The patient must be informed that the role of the surgery is solely to treat the refractive error to correct anisometropia or to reduce dependence on corrective eyewear. Preoperative pathology, including preexisting macular pathology, will continue to limit UCVA and BCVA after refractive surgery. There are no published long-term series of the results of excimer laser vision correction in patients who have had prior retinal detachment surgery. Both the patient and the doctor should realize that the final visual results may not be as predictable as after other refractive surgeries. Patients should also be aware that if the scleral buckle needs to be removed, the refractive error could change dramatically. Unexpected corneal steepening has been reported in patients undergoing LASIK with previously placed scleral buckles.

Barequet IS, Levy J, Klemperer I, et al. Laser in situ keratomileusis for correction of myopia in eyes after retinal detachment surgery. *J Refract Surg.* 2005;21(2):191–193.

Panozzo G, Parolini B. Relationships between vitreoretinal and refractive surgery. *Ophthalmology.* 2001;108(9):1663–1668.

Amblyopia and Strabismus in the Adult and Child

Amblyopia and anisometropic amblyopia

Amblyopia is defined as a decrease in visual acuity without evidence of organic eye disease, typically resulting from unequal visual stimulation during the period of visual development. The prevalence of amblyopia is 2%–4% of the US population, with up to half of these cases representing anisometropic amblyopia. In addition, a percentage of patients also have both anisometropia and strabismus. Anisometropia of >3.00 D between the 2 eyes is likely to induce amblyopia. Anisometropic amblyopia may be more resistant to traditional amblyopia therapy, such as glasses, contact lenses, patching, or atropine penalization therapy, partly because of the large aniseikonia induced.

Assessment of the amblyopic patient should include a thorough medical history to identify any known cause of amblyopia, a history of ocular disease or surgery, assessment of ocular alignment and motility, and a comprehensive anterior segment and retinal examination. Referral to a strabismus specialist should be made when indicated. Preoperative counseling of an amblyopic patient must emphasize that, even after refractive surgery, the vision in the amblyopic eye will not be as good as vision in the nonamblyopic eye. The patient should also understand that BCVA will be the same, or nearly so, with or without refractive surgery.

Typically, refractive surgery is performed in this group of patients to treat high anisometropia or astigmatism in 1 eye or high refractive error in both eyes. Laser vision correction and phakic IOL implantation have been successfully performed in the more myopic amblyopic eye in adult patients with anisometropic amblyopia. Some studies suggest that postoperative best spectacle-corrected visual acuities may even improve modestly compared with preoperative levels in a subset of adults who undergo refractive surgery. For example, 1 study examined phakic IOL implantation in 59 eyes of 48 patients with ≥3.00 D of anisometropia. An average of 3 lines of vision was gained, with 91% of eyes gaining ≥1 line and no eyes losing best-corrected vision. This increase in vision was attributed to an increase in magnification and a decrease in optical aberrations, rather than an actual improvement in the amblyopia.

Performing refractive surgery in the normal eye of the adult amblyopic patient, however, is controversial. The decision to do so depends on many factors, including the level of BCVA in the amblyopic eye and the normal eye and the ocular alignment. To increase safety, unilateral surgery in the amblyopic eye followed by surgery in the nonamblyopic eye can be considered. However, ocular deviation has been reported after unilateral LASIK for high myopia because of focus disparity resulting in esodeviation and impairment of fusion. A preoperative contact lens trial may be helpful in some cases to assess this potential risk.

A patient with anisometropic amblyopia, for example, who is corrected to 20/40 with –7.00 D in the right eye and to 20/20 with –1.00 D in the left eye may be an excellent candidate for refractive surgery in the amblyopic right eye. This patient likely cannot tolerate glasses to correct the anisometropic amblyopia and may not want or tolerate contact lenses. Even if the post-LASIK UCVA were less than 20/40 in the amblyopic eye, it would be better than the pre-LASIK UCVA of counting fingers.

If the postoperative UCVA in the amblyopic right eye improved to 20/40, the patient could consider laser vision correction in the left eye for –1.00 D. However, if the patient were presbyopic, some surgeons would discourage further intervention and discuss potential advantages of the low myopia. In a younger patient with accommodation, some surgeons would inform the patient of the potential risks associated with treating the better eye but would perform the excimer laser vision correction.

If BCVA in the amblyopic eye were 20/200 or worse, however, the patient would be considered legally blind if he were to lose significant vision in the normal fellow eye. In such cases, refractive surgery in the amblyopic eye may or may not offer much benefit, and refractive surgery in the nonamblyopic eye should be regarded as contraindicated in most cases. In the extenuating circumstances where such surgery might be considered, the physician and patient should have an extensive discussion of the potential risks. As a general rule of thumb, if the patient would not be happy with the vision in the amblyopic eye alone if something adverse happened to the better eye, then refractive surgery should not be performed on the better eye.

Persistent diplopia has been reported after bilateral LASIK in a patient with anisometropic amblyopia and a history of intermittent diplopia in childhood. Preoperatively, this type of patient can adjust to the disparity of the retinal image sizes with spectacle correction. Refractive surgery, however, can result in a dissimilar retinal image size that the patient cannot fuse, resulting in diplopia. This type of diplopia cannot be treated by prisms or muscle surgery.

Alió JL, Ortiz D, Abdelrahman A, de Luca A. Optical analysis of visual improvement after correction of anisometropic amblyopia with a phakic intraocular lens in adult patients. *Ophthalmology.* 2007;114(4):643–647.

Kim SK, Lee JB, Han SH, Kim EK. Ocular deviation after unilateral laser in situ keratomileusis. *Yonsei Med J.* 2000;41(3):404–406.

Sakatani K, Jabbur NS, O'Brien TP. Improvement in best corrected visual acuity in amblyopic adult eyes after laser in situ keratomileusis. *J Cataract Refract Surg.* 2004;30(12):2517–2521.

Refractive surgery in children

In children, refractive surgery is controversial because their eyes and refractive state continue to change. More studies on the growing eye and the effect of excimer laser and phakic IOLs on the pediatric corneal endothelium and lens are needed before the effect of refractive surgery in the pediatric age group can be fully understood. Consequently, these procedures are typically regarded as investigational.

In the literature, however, there are multiple reports of the successful performance of PRK, LASEK, LASIK, and phakic IOL implantation in children, mostly age 8 years and older, when conventional therapies have failed. Most of these children underwent treatment for anisometropic amblyopia in the more myopic eye. In these studies, refractive error was decreased and visual acuity was maintained or improved in moderately amblyopic eyes. Refractive surgery did not improve BCVA in older children with densely amblyopic eyes, and stereopsis did not improve in this group. The limited effect on visual acuity was generally attributed to the fact that the children were beyond amblyogenic age. Many authors have also reported a myopic shift and haze after PRK and LASIK, possibly related to the more vigorous wound-healing response that occurs in children. Thus, although these studies demonstrate the feasibility of performing keratorefractive surgery in this age group, its effectiveness in treating amblyopia cannot be adequately assessed, as amblyopia must typically be treated by the age of 8 years.

In one study involving a younger population, general anesthesia was used to perform PRK in 40 children, ages 1–6 years, who were unable to wear glasses or contact lenses for high myopia or anisometropic amblyopia from myopia. Patients were treated for existing amblyopia, and mean BCVA improved from 20/70 to 20/40. The study found that 60% of eyes developed posttreatment corneal haze, with most patients demonstrating "increasing corneal clarity" within 1 year, although 2 of 27 patients required PTK for the corneal haze. Regression of effect was attributed to a vigorous healing response and the axial myopic shift associated with growth.

There are also several reports of successful implantation of phakic IOLs in children with high anisometropia and amblyopia. This technique eliminates the previously mentioned corneal wound-healing problems associated with keratorefractive procedures and may be considered when the refractive error is high and other traditional methods of amblyopia therapy have failed. Depending on the type of phakic IOL, however, other potentially serious complications may ensue, including progressive corneal endothelial cell loss, cataract formation, and persistent inflammation, as well as the usual risks associated with intraocular surgery. Thus, phakic IOLs should also be approached as investigational in children, and larger clinical trials are necessary to adequately evaluate the safety and efficacy of this technique in this age group.

Agarwal A, Agarwal A, Agarwal T, Siraj AA, Narang P, Narang S. Results of pediatric laser in situ keratomileusis. *J Cataract Refract Surg.* 2000;26(5):684–689.

Astle WF, Huang PT, Ells AL, Cox RG, Deschenes MC, Vibert HM. Photorefractive keratectomy in children. *J Cataract Refract Surg.* 2002;28(6):932–941.

Astle WF, Huang PT, Ereifej I, Paszuk A. Laser-assisted subepithelial keratectomy for bilateral hyperopia and hyperopic anisometropic amblyopia in children: one-year outcomes. *J Cataract Refract Surg.* 2010;36(2):260–267.

Daoud YJ, Hutchinson A, Wallace DK, Song J, Kim T. Refractive surgery in children: treatment options, outcomes, and controversies. *Am J Ophthalmol.* 2009;147(4):573–582.e1.

Holland D, Amm M, de Decker W. Persisting diplopia after bilateral laser in situ keratomileusis. *J Cataract Refract Surg.* 2000;26(10):1555–1557.

Lesueur LC, Arne JL. Phakic intraocular lens to correct high myopic amblyopia in children. *J Refract Surg.* 2002;18(5):519–523.

Nemet P, Levenger S, Nemet A. Refractive surgery for refractive errors which cause strabismus: a report of 8 cases. *Binocul Vis Strabismus Q.* 2002;17(3):187–190.

Nucci P, Drack AV. Refractive surgery for unilateral high myopia in children. *J AAPOS.* 2001; 5(6):348–351.

Paysse EA, Coats DK, Hussein MA, Hamill MB, Koch DD. Long-term outcomes of photorefractive keratectomy for anisometropic amblyopia in children. *Ophthalmology.* 2006;113(2): 169–176.

Paysse EA, Hussein M, Koch DD, et al. Successful implementation of a protocol for photorefractive keratectomy in children requiring anesthesia. *J Cataract Refract Surg.* 2003;29(9): 1744–1747.

Phillips CB, Prager TC, McClellan G, Mintz-Hittner HA. Laser in situ keratomileusis for treated anisometropic amblyopia in awake, autofixating pediatric and adolescent patients. *J Cataract Refract Surg.* 2004;30(12):2522–2528.

Accommodative esotropia

Uncorrected hyperopia causes an increase in accommodation leading to accommodative convergence. Esotropia results because of insufficient fusional divergence. Traditional treatment includes correction of hyperopia with glasses or contact lenses and muscle surgery for any residual esotropia (see BCSC Section 6, *Pediatric Ophthalmology and Strabismus*). While glasses or contact lenses are being worn, the esotropia is usually kept in check. Hyperopia typically decreases in adolescence, so emmetropia and resolution of the accommodative esotropia may occur with age. If significant hyperopia persists, however, glasses or contact lenses continue to be needed to control the esotropia.

Before refractive surgery, it is important to perform an adequate cycloplegic refraction on patients younger than 35 years of age who have intermittent strabismus or phoria. Accurate refraction is necessary to avoid inducing postoperative hyperopia. Otherwise, the postoperative hyperopia may result in a new onset of esotropia with an accommodative element.

There have been reports outside the United States of PRK and LASIK for adults with accommodative esotropia. In 1 study, orthophoria or microesotropia was achieved after LASIK for hyperopia in accommodative esotropia in a series of 9 patients over 18 years of age. However, another study of LASIK in accommodative esotropia in patients 10–52 years of age found that 42% of patients had no reduction in their esotropia and that these patients could not have been predicted on the basis of preoperative sensorimotor testing.

Hoyos JE, Cigales M, Hoyos-Chacón J, Ferrer J, Maldonado-Bas A. Hyperopic laser in situ keratomileusis for refractive accommodative esotropia. *J Cataract Refract Surg.* 2002;28(9): 1522–1529.

Stidham DB, Borissova O, Borissov V, Prager TC. Effect of hyperopic laser in situ keratomileusis on ocular alignment and stereopsis in patients with accommodative esotropia. *Ophthalmology.* 2002;109(6):1148–1153.

Systemic Conditions

Human Immunodeficiency Virus

Little has been written on refractive surgery in patients with known human immuno-deficiency virus (HIV) infection, and individual opinions vary. It should be noted that the FDA recommends that patients with an immunodeficiency disease not have LASIK, regardless of the excimer platform, as the risk outweighs the benefit.

In a recent survey on the subject sent to members of the International Society of Re-fractive Surgery, 51% of respondents considered HIV-positive patients who did not have definite AIDS to be acceptable refractive surgery candidates. Only 13% felt that patients with definite AIDS were candidates for refractive surgery, while 44% felt the presence of AIDS was an absolute contraindication to refractive surgery. Some surgeons counsel these patients against refractive surgery because of concerns about postoperative complications, including the increased risk of infection associated with their immunosuppression, al-though, to date, only 1 case of keratitis (a bilateral infection with *Staphylococcus aureus*) following LASIK in an HIV-positive patient has been reported.

An additional concern is the potential for aerosolizing live virus during laser abla-tion, which could pose a risk to laser suite personnel. Because the refractive surgeon may operate on patients who do not know they have been infected with viruses such as HIV or hepatitis, universal precautions must be followed with all patients.

In 1 study, excimer laser ablation of pseudorabies virus, a porcine-enveloped herpes-virus similar to HIV and HSV, did not appear capable of causing infection by transmission through the air. The authors concluded that excimer laser ablation of the cornea in a pa-tient infected with HIV is unlikely to pose a health hazard to the surgeon or the assistants. In another study, after excimer laser ablation of infected corneal stroma, polymerase chain reaction did not detect viable varicella virus (200 nm) but did detect viable polio particles (70 nm).

Inhaled particles ≥5 µm are deposited in the bronchial, tracheal, nasopharyngeal, and nasal walls; and particles <2 µm are deposited in the bronchioles and alveoli. Even if viral particles are not viable, the excimer laser plume produces particles with a mean diameter of 0.22 µm that can be inhaled. Although the health effects of inhaled particles from the plume have not yet been determined, there have been anecdotal reports of respiratory ailments such as chronic bronchitis in busy excimer laser refractive surgeons. Canister filter masks can exclude particles down to 0.1 µm and may be more protective than con-ventional surgical masks. In addition, evacuation of the laser plume may potentially de-crease the amount of breathable debris. If a surgeon is considering performing excimer laser ablation in an HIV-infected patient who is not immunosuppressed and has a normal eye examination, extra precautions should be exercised. The surgeon should counsel the patient extensively about the visual risks of HIV and the lack of long-term follow-up on refractive surgery in this population. The surgeon may also consider consulting with the physicians, including infectious disease specialists, who are responsible for managing the patient's underlying disease. The surgeon may choose to treat 1 eye at a time on separate days and schedule the patient as the last patient of the day. In addition, the surgeon may consider implementing additional precautions for the operating room staff, such as wearing filter masks during the procedure and evacuating the laser plume.

Aref AA, Scott IU, Zerfoss EL, Kunselman AR. Refractive surgical practices in persons with human immunodeficiency virus positivity or acquired immune deficiency syndrome. *J Cataract Refract Surg.* 2010;36(1):153–160.

Hagen KB, Kettering JD, Aprecio RM, Beltran F, Maloney RK. Lack of virus transmission by the excimer laser plume. *Am J Ophthalmol.* 1997;124(2):206–211.

Hovanesian JA, Faktorovich EG, Hoffbauer JD, Shah SS, Maloney RK. Bilateral bacterial keratitis after laser in situ keratomileusis in a patient with human immunodeficiency virus infection. *Arch Ophthalmol.* 1999;117(7):968–970.

Taravella MJ, Viega J, Luiszer F, et al. Respirable particles in the excimer laser plume. *J Cataract Refract Surg.* 2001;27(4):604–607.

Diabetes Mellitus

In the newsletter of January 26, 2009, the National Institutes of Health reported a prevalence of nearly 13% for diabetes mellitus in adults aged 20 and older in the United States. With the increasing incidence of this condition, more and more patients with diabetes will be requesting refractive surgery. Diabetic patients present special problems, and those who are considering refractive surgery should have a thorough preoperative history and examination with special attention to the presence of active diabetic ocular disease. The blood sugar of diabetic patients must be well controlled at the time of examination to ensure an accurate refraction. A history of laser treatment for proliferative diabetic retinopathy or cystoid macular edema indicates visually significant diabetic complications that typically contraindicate refractive surgery. Any patient who has preexisting, visually significant diabetic ocular complications is not a good candidate for refractive surgery. Ocular examination should include inspection of the corneal epithelium to check the health of the ocular surface, identification of cataract if present, and detailed retinal examination. Preoperative corneal sensation should be assessed because corneal anesthesia can impede epithelial healing.

The most common problems associated with LASIK in the diabetic patient appear to be related to the corneal epithelium, but the magnitude of the relative risk is not clear. One retrospective review of 30 eyes of diabetic patients 6 months after LASIK revealed a complication rate of 47%, compared with a complication rate of 6.9% in the control group. The most common problems in this study were related to epithelial healing and included epithelial loosening and defects. A loss of ≥2 lines of BCVA was reported in <1% of both the diabetic group and the control group. However, 6 of the 30 eyes in the diabetic group required a mean of 4.3 months to heal because of persistent epithelial defects. These authors concluded that the high complication rate in diabetic patients was explained by unmasking subclinical diabetic keratopathy. Another retrospective review of 24 diabetic patients who underwent LASIK demonstrated that 63% achieved UCVA of 20/25 or better. Three of the 24 eyes had an epithelial defect after surgery, with epithelial ingrowth developing in 2 of these eyes. No eye lost BCVA. A review of 22 patients who developed epithelial ingrowth after LASIK suggested that type 1 diabetes might increase the risk of this condition. In contrast, Cobo-Soriano and colleagues evaluated 44 patients with diabetes (a mixture of insulin-dependent and non–insulin-dependent patients) in a retrospective, observational, case-controlled study and reported no significant difference in perioperative and postoperative complications, including epithelial defects, epithelial ingrowth, and flap complications between diabetic and control patients.

In light of these contradictory reports, refractive surgeons should exercise caution in the selection of diabetic patients for refractive surgery. Intraoperative technique should be adjusted to ensure maximal epithelial health. To reduce corneal toxicity, the surgeon should use the minimal amount of topical anesthetic immediately before performing the procedure. Diabetic patients should be counseled preoperatively about the increased risk of postoperative complications and the possibility of a prolonged healing time after LASIK. In addition, they should be informed that the procedure treats only the refractive error and not the natural history of the diabetes, which can lead to future diabetic ocular complications and associated visual loss.

Cobo-Soriano R, Beltran J, Baviera J. LASIK outcomes in patients with underlying systemic contraindications: a preliminary study. *Ophthalmology*. 2006;113(7):113.e1–e8.

Fraunfelder FW, Rich LF. Laser-assisted in situ keratomileusis complications in diabetes mellitus. *Cornea*. 2002;21(3):246–248.

Halkiadakis I, Belfair N, Gimbel HV. Laser in situ keratomileusis in patients with diabetes. *J Cataract Refract Surg*. 2005;31(10):1895–1898.

Jabbur NS, Chicani CF, Kuo IC, O'Brien TP. Risk factors in interface epithelialization after laser in situ keratomileusis. *J Refract Surg*. 2004;20(4):343–348.

National Institutes of Health. National Institute of Diabetes and Digestive and Kidney Diseases. New survey results show huge burden of diabetes. *NIH News*. January 26, 2009. Available at: http://www.nih.gov/news/health/jan2009/niddk-26.htm. Accessed July 27, 2010.

Connective Tissue and Autoimmune Diseases

Most surgeons consider active, uncontrolled connective tissue diseases such as rheumatoid arthritis, systemic lupus erythematosus, and polyarteritis nodosa to be contraindications to refractive surgery because of reports of corneal melting and perforation following cataract extraction in patients with these conditions. Late corneal scarring has been reported after PRK in a patient with systemic lupus erythematosus.

However, 2 retrospective series suggest that refractive surgery may be considered in patients with well-controlled connective tissue or autoimmune disease. One retrospective study of 49 eyes of 26 patients with inactive or stable autoimmune disease that underwent LASIK revealed no postoperative corneal melting or persistent epithelial defects after LASIK. Another retrospective study of 62 eyes of patients with autoimmune connective tissue disorders that had undergone LASIK revealed that these eyes had a somewhat worse refractive outcome compared with the controls, but otherwise no severe complications such as corneal melting or laceration or interface alterations were reported.

Because the risk from an underlying disease cannot be quantified, increased caution should be exercised if refractive surgery is considered in patients with well-controlled connective tissue disease or autoimmune diseases. Consultation with the treating physician, unilateral surgery, and ancillary informed consent should be considered.

Alió JL, Artola A, Belda JI, et al. LASIK in patients with rheumatic diseases: a pilot study. *Ophthalmology.* 2005;112(11):1948–1954.

Cobo-Soriano R, Beltran J, Baviera J. LASIK outcomes in patients with underlying systemic contraindications: a preliminary study. *Ophthalmology.* 2006;113(7):113.e1–e8.

Cua IY, Pepose JS. Late corneal scarring after photorefractive keratectomy concurrent with development of systemic lupus erythematosus. *J Refract Surg.* 2002;18(6):750–752.

Smith RJ, Maloney RK. Laser in situ keratomileusis in patients with autoimmune diseases. *J Cataract Refract Surg.* 2006;32(8):1292–1295.

CHAPTER 11

Considerations After Refractive Surgery

The number of patients who have had refractive surgery continues to grow, and ophthalmologists are increasingly confronted with the management of post–refractive surgery patients with other conditions, such as cataract, glaucoma, retinal detachment, corneal opacities, and irregular astigmatism. Calculation of the intraocular lens (IOL) power presents a particular challenge in this population.

IOL Calculations After Refractive Surgery

Although numerous formulas have been developed to calculate IOL power prior to cataract surgery in eyes that have undergone refractive surgery, these cases are still prone to refractive surprises. Currently, there is no infallible way to calculate IOL power in a patient who has undergone refractive surgery. Even though the measurement of axial length should remain accurate after refractive surgery, determining the keratometric power of the post–refractive surgery cornea is problematic. The difficulty arises from several factors. Small, effective central optical zones after refractive surgery (especially after radial keratotomy [RK]) can lead to inaccurate measurements because keratometers and Placido disk–based corneal topography units measure the corneal curvature several millimeters away from the center of the cornea. In addition, the relationship between the anterior and posterior corneal curvatures may be considerably altered after refractive surgery (especially after laser ablative procedures), leading to inaccurate results. Generally, if standard keratometry readings are used to calculate IOL power in a previously myopic patient, the postoperative refraction will be hyperopic because the keratometry readings are higher than the true corneal power.

A variety of methods have been developed to better estimate the central corneal power after refractive surgery. None of these methods is perfectly accurate, and different methods can lead to disparate values. As many methods as possible should be used to calculate corneal power, and these estimates should be compared with each other, with standard keratometric readings, and with corneal topographic central power and simulated K readings.

Newer corneal topography and tomography systems not based on the Placido disk claim to directly measure the central corneal curvature, and such technology may make direct calculation of IOL power after refractive surgery more accurate.

Eyes With Known Pre– and Post–Refractive Surgery Data

Theoretically, the most accurate way to calculate IOL power should be the *clinical history method,* in which pre–refractive surgery refraction and keratometry values are available along with the current refraction. However, the trend is moving away from this historical method as the gold standard because, in reality, the results are less than perfect. Nevertheless, pre–refractive surgery information should be kept by both the patient and the surgeon. To assist in retaining these data, the American Academy of Ophthalmology (AAO) has developed the K Card, which is accessible under the heading of Academy Resources at the following URL: http://one.aao.org/CE/GlobalONE/Default.aspx.

To use the historical method, the ophthalmologist should have the preoperative refraction and keratometry readings, and the change in spherical equivalent can be calculated at the spectacle plane or, better yet, at the corneal plane. The postoperative refraction used must be a stable refraction obtained several months after the refractive surgery but before any potential onset of induced myopia from a nuclear sclerotic cataract. For example:

> Preoperative average keratometry: 44.00 D
> Preoperative spherical equivalent refraction (vertex distance 12 mm): –8.00 D
> Preoperative refraction at the corneal plane: $-8.00 \, D/(1 - [0.012 \times -8.00 \, D]) = -7.30 \, D$
> Postoperative spherical equivalent refraction (vertex distance 12 mm): –1.00 D
> Postoperative refraction at the corneal plane: $-1.00 \, D/(1 - [0.012 \times -1.00 \, D]) = -0.98 \, D$
> Change in manifest refraction at the corneal plane: $-7.30 \, D - (-0.98 \, D) = -6.32 \, D$
> Postoperative estimated keratometry: $44.00 - 6.32 \, D = 37.68 \, D$

Eyes With No Preoperative Information

When no preoperative information is available, the *hard contact lens method* can be used to calculate corneal power. This method is quite accurate in theory but, unfortunately, not very useful in clinical practice. The BCVA needs to be at least 20/80 for this approach to work. First, a manifest refraction is performed. Then a plano hard contact lens of known base curve (power) is placed on the eye, and another manifest refraction is performed. If the manifest refraction does not change, then the cornea has the same power as the contact lens. If the refraction is more myopic, the contact lens is steeper (more powerful) than the cornea by the amount of change in the refraction; the reverse holds true if the refraction is more hyperopic. For example:

> Current spherical equivalent manifest refraction: –1.00 D
> A hard contact lens of known base curve (8.7 mm) and power (37.00 D) is placed
> Overrefraction: +2.00 D
> Change in refraction: $+2.00 \, D - (-1.00 \, D) = +3.00 \, D$
> Calculation of corneal power: $37.00 \, D + 3.00 \, D = 40.00 \, D$

The ASCRS Online Post-Refractive IOL Power Calculator

A particularly useful resource for calculating IOL power in a post–refractive surgery patient has been developed by Warren Hill, MD; Li Wang, MD, PhD; and Doug Koch, MD. It is available on the website of the American Society of Cataract and Refractive Surgery (ASCRS) (http://iol.ascrs.org/).

To use this IOL calculator, the surgeon selects the appropriate prior refractive surgical procedure and enters the patient data, if known (Fig 11-1). The IOL powers, calculated by a variety of formulas, are displayed at the bottom of the form, and the surgeon can compare the results to select the best IOL power for the individual situation. This spreadsheet is updated with new formulas and information as they become available and at this time probably represents the best option for calculation of IOL powers in post–refractive surgery patients.

Patients need to be informed prior to cataract surgery, however, that IOL power calculations are not as accurate when performed after refractive surgery and that additional surgery, such as surface ablation, LASIK, IOL exchange, or a piggyback IOL, may be required to attain a better refractive result despite maximum effort by the surgeon preoperatively to prevent such an outcome. It should be remembered that cataract surgery done after RK often induces short-term corneal swelling with flattening and hyperopic shift. For this reason, in the event of a refractive "surprise," an IOL exchange should not be performed in these patients until the cornea and refraction stabilize, which may take several weeks to months. As corneal curvature does not tend to change as much when cataract surgery is done after PRK or LASIK, it may be possible to perform an IOL exchange earlier in these patients.

Awwad ST, Manasseh C, Bowman RW, et al. Intraocular lens power calculation after myopic laser in situ keratomileusis: estimating the corneal refractive power. *J Cataract Refract Surg.* 2008;34(7):1070–1076.

Chokshi AR, Latkany RA, Speaker MG, Yu G. Intraocular lens calculations after hyperopic refractive surgery. *Ophthalmology.* 2007;114(11):2044–2049.

Feiz V, Mannis MJ. Intraocular lens power calculation after corneal refractive surgery. *Curr Opin Ophthalmol.* 2004;15(4):342–349.

Hill WE, Byrne SF. Complex axial length measurements and unusual IOL power calculations. *Focal Points: Clinical Modules for Ophthalmologists.* San Francisco: American Academy of Ophthalmology; 2004, module 9.

Latkany RA, Chokshi AR, Speaker MG, Abramson J, Soloway BD, Yu G. Intraocular lens calculations after refractive surgery. *J Cataract Refract Surg.* 2005;31(3):562–570.

Masket S, Masket SE. Simple regression formula for intraocular lens power adjustment in eyes requiring cataract surgery after excimer laser photoablation. *J Cataract Refract Surg.* 2006;32(3):430–434.

Retinal Detachment Repair After LASIK

Even if patients with highly myopic eyes become emmetropic as a result of refractive surgery, they need to be informed that their eyes remain at increased risk of retinal detachment. For this reason, the vitreoretinal surgeon should ask about prior refractive surgery. Eyes undergoing retinal detachment repair after LASIK are prone to flap problems, including flap dehiscence, microstriae, and macrostriae. The surgeon may find it helpful to mark the edge of the flap prior to surgery to aid in flap replacement in case it is dislodged. The risk of flap problems increases dramatically if the epithelium is debrided during the retinal detachment repair. If flap dehiscence occurs, the flap should be carefully repositioned and the interface irrigated. A bandage soft contact lens may be placed at the end of

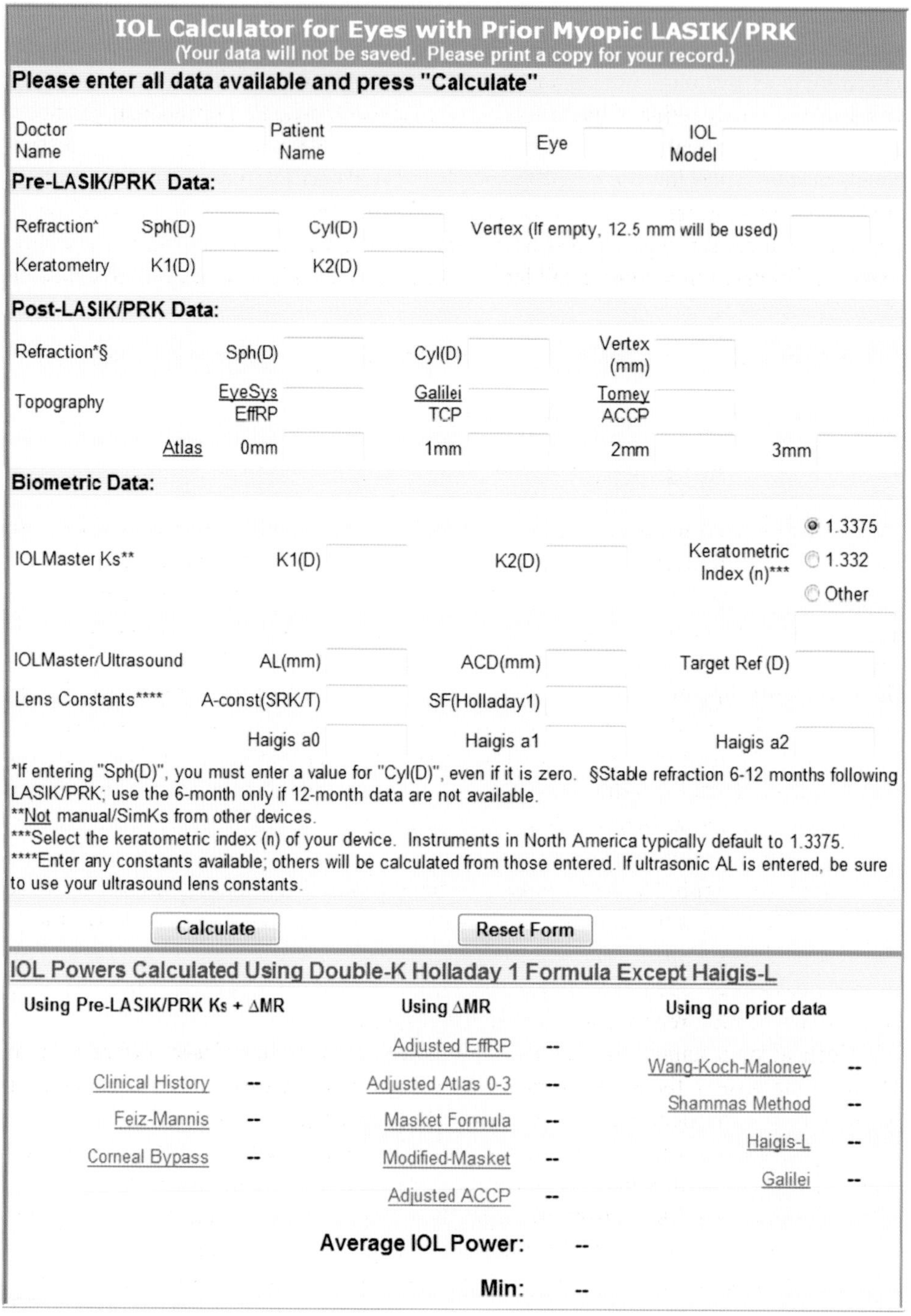

IOL Calculator for Eyes with Prior Myopic LASIK/PRK
(Your data will not be saved. Please print a copy for your record.)

Please enter all data available and press "Calculate"

Doctor Name   Patient Name   Eye   IOL Model

Pre-LASIK/PRK Data:

Refraction*   Sph(D)   Cyl(D)   Vertex (If empty, 12.5 mm will be used)

Keratometry   K1(D)   K2(D)

Post-LASIK/PRK Data:

Refraction*§   Sph(D)   Cyl(D)   Vertex (mm)

Topography   EyeSys EffRP   Galilei TCP   Tomey ACCP

   Atlas   0mm   1mm   2mm   3mm

Biometric Data:

IOLMaster Ks**   K1(D)   K2(D)   Keratometric Index (n)***   ⦿ 1.3375   ◉ 1.332   ○ Other

IOLMaster/Ultrasound   AL(mm)   ACD(mm)   Target Ref (D)

Lens Constants****   A-const(SRK/T)   SF(Holladay1)

   Haigis a0   Haigis a1   Haigis a2

*If entering "Sph(D)", you must enter a value for "Cyl(D)", even if it is zero. §Stable refraction 6-12 months following LASIK/PRK; use the 6-month only if 12-month data are not available.
**Not manual/SimKs from other devices.
***Select the keratometric index (n) of your device. Instruments in North America typically default to 1.3375.
****Enter any constants available; others will be calculated from those entered. If ultrasonic AL is entered, be sure to use your ultrasound lens constants.

Calculate		Reset Form

IOL Powers Calculated Using Double-K Holladay 1 Formula Except Haigis-L

Using Pre-LASIK/PRK Ks + ΔMR		Using ΔMR		Using no prior data	
		Adjusted EffRP	--	Wang-Koch-Maloney	--
Clinical History	--	Adjusted Atlas 0-3	--	Shammas Method	--
Feiz-Mannis	--	Masket Formula	--	Haigis-L	--
Corneal Bypass	--	Modified-Masket	--	Galilei	--
		Adjusted ACCP	--		

Average IOL Power: --

Min: --

Figure 11-1 The data screen of the IOL calculator. The surgeon enters the patient's pre–refractive surgery data (if known) and current data into the data form. After the "calculate" button at the bottom of the form is clicked, the IOL power calculated by a variety of formulas is displayed. (Note: In this illustration the "calculate" button was activated with no patient data entered so as to show the final appearance of the screen.) *(Used with permission from the American Society of Cataract and Refractive Surgery.)*

surgery. Postoperatively, the patient should be observed closely for flap problems such as epithelial ingrowth and diffuse lamellar keratitis, especially if an epithelial defect was present in the flap. Although the intraocular pressure (IOP) needs to be monitored carefully in all patients after retinal detachment repair, especially when an intraocular gas bubble is used, some potential problems are specific to post-LASIK patients. First, IOP measurements may be falsely low due to the surgically induced corneal thinning. Second, elevated IOP can cause a diffuse lamellar keratitis–like picture or even a fluid cleft between the flap and the stroma, resulting in a misleading, extremely low IOP measurement. These problems are discussed in greater detail later in this chapter under the heading of Glaucoma After Refractive Surgery.

> Wirbelauer C, Pham DT. Imaging interface fluid after laser in situ keratomileusis with corneal optical coherence tomography. *J Cataract Refract Surg.* 2005;31(4):853–856.

Corneal Transplantation After Refractive Surgery

Corneal transplantation is occasionally required after refractive surgery. Reasons for needing a corneal graft after refractive surgery include significant corneal scarring, irregular astigmatism, corneal ectasia, and corneal edema. Issues unrelated to refractive surgery, such as trauma or corneal edema after cataract surgery, can also necessitate corneal transplant surgery. The reasons why a graft may be required and ways to avoid problems with the corneal transplant are unique to each refractive surgical procedure. Corneal transplantation is discussed in greater detail in BCSC Section 8, *External Disease and Cornea.*

After RK, a graft may be required because of trauma resulting in incisional rupture or because of central scarring not responsive to phototherapeutic keratectomy; irregular astigmatism; contact lens intolerance; or progressive hyperopia. The RK incisions can gape or dehisce during penetrating keratoplasty trephination, preventing an even, uniform, and deep trephination. One method for avoiding RK wound gape or dehiscence during keratoplasty is to mark the cornea with the trephine and then to reinforce the RK incisions with interrupted sutures outside the trephine mark prior to trephination. If the old RK incisions do open during the corneal transplant surgery, then X, mattress, or lasso sutures may be required to close these stellate wounds.

Corneal transplantation may also be required after excimer laser surface ablation. However, because of the 6- to 8-mm ablation zones typically used, the corneal periphery is generally not thinned, and transplantation in this setting is usually routine.

After LASIK, corneal transplantation may be required due to central scarring (eg, after infection or with a buttonhole) or corneal ectasia. A significant challenge in this scenario is that most LASIK flaps are larger than a typical trephine size (8 mm). Trephination through the flap increases the risk that the flap peripheral to the corneal transplant wound may separate. This complication may be avoidable by careful trephination and a gentle suture technique that incorporates the LASIK flap under the corneal transplant suture. Femtosecond laser trephination may theoretically decrease the risk of flap separation during trephination.

A few cases of inadvertent use of donor tissue that had undergone prior LASIK have been reported. The risk of this untoward event will increase as the donor pool includes more individuals who have undergone LASIK. Eye banks need to develop better techniques to screen out such donor corneas. If a post-LASIK eye is inadvertently used for corneal transplantation, the patient should be informed. A regraft may be required to address significant anisometropia.

Corneal transplantation is occasionally required in a patient with intrastromal corneal ring segments. The polymethylmethacrylate ring segments are typically placed near the edge of a standard corneal transplant, so the ring segments should be removed prior to grafting, ideally well before the corneal transplant, to allow the cornea to heal.

Corneal transplantation is also rarely required after laser thermokeratoplasty or conductive keratoplasty. Trephination should be routine in such cases, and the thermal scars should generally be incorporated in the corneal button. Even if they are not, they should not significantly affect wound architecture, graft healing, or corneal curvature.

Contact Lens Use After Refractive Surgery

Indications

Contact lenses can be used before and after refractive surgery. For example, temporary soft contact lenses can allow a presbyopic patient to experience monovision before the procedure, thus reducing the risk of postoperative dissatisfaction. Contact lenses can also be used preoperatively in a patient with a motility abnormality to simulate what vision might be like after refractive surgery and to ensure that diplopia does not develop.

In the perioperative period, hydrophilic soft contact lenses help promote epithelialization, provide patient comfort, and perhaps reduce the risk of epithelial ingrowth and flap dehiscence in the case of a free cap. A soft contact lens can be used following a flap refloat. Rigid gas-permeable (RGP) contact lenses are the gold standard for the correction of reduced vision due to irregular astigmatism. In this case, RGP lenses are more effective than soft lenses. Night-vision problems caused by uncorrected refractive error or irregular astigmatism may also be reduced by using contact lenses. However, if the symptoms are associated with a scotopic pupil diameter that is larger than the treatment zone or related to higher-order aberrations, the symptoms may persist despite contact lens use.

General Principles

Contact lenses for refractive purposes should not be fitted until surgical wounds and serial refractions are stable. The most practical approach to fitting an RGP lens after refractive surgery is to do a trial fitting with overrefraction.

The clinician needs to discuss with the patient in lay terms the challenges of contact lens fitting after refractive surgery and align the patient's expectations with reality. A patient who successfully wore contact lenses before refractive surgery is more likely to be a successful contact lens wearer postoperatively than a patient who never wore contact lenses.

Contact Lenses After Radial Keratotomy

Centration is a challenge in fitting contact lenses after RK because the corneal apex is displaced to the midperiphery (Fig 11-2). Popular fitting techniques involve referring to the preoperative keratometry readings and basing the initial lens trial on the flatter curvature. Contact lens stability is achieved by adjusting the lens diameter. In general, larger-diameter lenses take advantage of the eyelid to achieve stability. However, they also increase the effective steepness of the lens due to increased sagittal depth. If preoperative keratometry is not available, the ophthalmologist can use a paracentral or midperipheral curve, as measured with postoperative corneal topography, as a starting point.

When a successful fit cannot be obtained with a standard RGP lens, a reverse-geometry lens can be used. The secondary curves can be designed as steep as necessary to achieve a stable fit. The larger the optical zone, the flatter the fit.

Hydrophilic soft lenses can also be used after RK. Toric soft lenses can be helpful when regular astigmatism is present. Soft lenses are less helpful in cases of irregular astigmatism because they are less able to mask an irregular surface. Newer lens designs, such as hybrid contacts, which consist of an RGP center surrounded by a soft contact lens skirt (eg, SynergEyes, Carlsbad, CA), and the Boston Scleral Lens (Boston Foundation for Sight, Needham, MA) may be helpful for patients with significant irregular astigmatism who are intolerant of conventional RGP lenses. The SynergEyes lens has a greater power range and a higher degree of oxygen permeability than earlier types of hybrid lenses.

Contact Lenses After Surface Ablation

Immediately after surface ablation, a soft contact lens is placed on the cornea as a bandage to help promote epithelialization and reduce discomfort. The lens is worn until the corneal epithelium has healed. Healing time depends on the size of the epithelial defect but is generally 4–7 days. A tight-fitting lens should be removed if there is evidence of corneal hypoxia (such as edema, folds in the Descemet membrane, or iritis).

Contact Lenses After LASIK

The indications for contact lens fitting after LASIK are similar to those following other types of refractive surgery. The corneal contour is usually stable by 3 months after LASIK

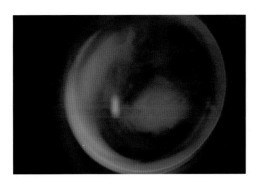

Figure 11-2 Fluorescein staining pattern in a contact lens patient following both RK and LASIK shows pooling centrally and touch in the midperiphery. This pattern is due to central corneal flattening and steepening in the midperiphery. *(Courtesy of Robert S. Feder, MD.)*

for myopia; however, it may take up to 6 months for the cornea to stabilize after LASIK for hyperopia.

A soft contact lens may be used immediately after LASIK surgery to promote epithelialization and to prevent epithelial ingrowth. It is generally used for several days on an extended-wear basis and then removed by the surgeon. Daily-wear contact lenses for refractive purposes should not be considered until the surgeon feels the risk of flap displacement is low. Hybrid contact lenses (such as the SynergEyes lens discussed earlier) are helpful in certain patients after keratorefractive surgery.

Glaucoma After Refractive Surgery

The force required for applanation of a Goldmann tonometer is proportional to the central corneal thickness. As a result, an eye that has a thin central cornea may have an artifactually low IOP as measured by Goldmann applanation tonometry. Patients with normal-tension glaucoma have significantly thinner corneas than patients with primary open-angle glaucoma. When a correction factor based on corneal thickness is applied, over 30% of these patients demonstrate abnormally high IOP. The correction factor may be less with both the Tono-Pen (Reichert Ophthalmic Instruments, Depew, NY) and the pneumotonometer.

An artifactual IOP reduction occurs following surface ablation and LASIK for myopia, both of which reduce central corneal thickness. Similar inaccuracies of IOP measurement can occur with surface ablation and LASIK for hyperopia. The mean reduction in IOP measurement following excimer laser refractive surgery is 0.63 mm Hg per diopter of correction, with fairly wide variation. Postoperatively, some patients may experience no change in IOP measurement, whereas others may have an increase. In general, the reduction of measured IOP is greater for LASIK than for surface ablation. Surface ablation patients with a preoperative refractive error ≤5.00 D may have a negligible decrease in IOP measurements.

Measuring IOP from the nasal side following LASIK surgery has been shown to lessen the artifactual IOP reduction by half (3.9 to 2.0 mm Hg). These data support the use of the Tono-Pen or pneumotonometer from the side (ie, over the untreated cornea) to minimize artifactual IOP reduction after excimer laser refractive surgery. The PASCAL Dynamic Contour Tonometer (Ziemer, Port, Switzerland) is capable of accurately measuring IOP independent of corneal thickness. Although some refractive surgeons cautiously measure IOP as soon as a few days after LASIK, others wait weeks or a month because of concerns about disrupting the flap.

Topical corticosteroids that are used after refractive surgery pose a serious risk of corticosteroid-induced IOP elevation, particularly because accurate IOP measurement is difficult to obtain. By 3 months postoperatively, up to 15% of surface ablation patients may develop IOP above 22 mm Hg. Men appear to be more vulnerable than women to the corticosteroid effect. If the actual elevation of IOP is not detected, optic nerve damage and visual field loss can occur.

In patients with diffuse lamellar keratitis following LASIK, aqueous fluid may accumulate in the flap interface and falsely lower IOP measurement. Glaucomatous optic nerve damage and visual field loss have been reported in this setting. A syndrome of a diffuse lamellar keratitis pattern (with onset after the first postoperative week) associated with elevated IOP has been described. The syndrome does not respond to increased corticosteroids but rather resolves when the IOP is lowered.

If topical corticosteroids are used postoperatively over a long time, periodic, careful disc evaluation is essential. Optic nerve and nerve fiber layer imaging may facilitate the evaluation. Periodic visual field assessment may be more effective than IOP measurement for identifying at-risk patients before severe visual field loss occurs (see Chapter 10, Fig 10-4).

Refractive surgery patients who develop glaucoma are initially treated with IOP-lowering medications, and their IOP is carefully measured. If medication or laser treatment does not adequately reduce the IOP, glaucoma surgery may be recommended. Patients who have had refractive surgery should be warned prior to glaucoma surgery of the potential for transient vision loss from inflammation, hypotony, or change in refractive error. The glaucoma surgeon should be made aware of the patient's previous LASIK in order to avoid trauma to the corneal flap.

Belin MW, Hannush SB, Yau CW, Schultze RL. Elevated intraocular pressure–induced interlamellar stromal keratitis. *Ophthalmology.* 2002;109(10):1929–1933.

Brandt JD, Beiser JA, Kass MA, Gordon MO. Central corneal thickness in the Ocular Hypertension Treatment Study (OHTS). *Ophthalmology.* 2001;108(10):1779–1788.

Dohadwala AA, Munger R, Damji KF. Positive correlation between Tono-Pen intraocular pressure and central corneal thickness. *Ophthalmology.* 1998;105(10):1849–1854.

Hamilton DR, Manche EE, Rich LF, Maloney RK. Steroid-induced glaucoma after laser in situ keratomileusis associated with interface fluid. *Ophthalmology.* 2002;109(4):659–665.

Kaufmann C, Bachmann LM, Thiel MA. Comparison of dynamic contour tonometry with Goldman applanation tonometry. *Invest Ophthalmol Vis Sci.* 2004;45(9):3118–3121.

CHAPTER 12

International Perspectives in Refractive Surgery

Introduction

For many years, refractive surgery was the fastest-growing ophthalmic subspecialty, with strong growth rates both in the United States and the rest of the world. That pattern changed in the past few years as a result of the global economic downturn. The decline averaged 20%–30% in most parts of the world, although it was mitigated by increasing demand in emerging markets in Asia. Global practice trends differ significantly according to ethnic variance in the prevalence of refractive errors, socioeconomic factors, and regulatory differences. This chapter presents information on international trends and perspectives in refractive surgery and summarizes medical device regulation in refractive surgery in different countries. In addition, this chapter reviews new clinical studies and refractive surgery therapies currently performed outside the United States.

Global Estimates of Refractive Surgery

It is estimated that 3.4 million refractive surgery procedures were performed worldwide in 2009. Of these, 785,000 (23%) were performed in the United States. This represents a 5.4% drop compared to 2008 (Fig 12-1). Volumes have been on the decline because of the global economic downturn, although Market Scope predicts that volumes will improve in 2010, with a return to previous levels and growth rates. A report by Alió and Pettersen predicted a 10% annual growth rate in 2010 based on economic recovery and weak 2009 comparisons. Outside the United States, the picture is mixed, with volumes in parts of western Europe (eg, United Kingdom and Scandinavia) continuing to grow or remain stable. Western Europe's share of global procedures expanded to 19.9%, growing by just under 2% compared to 2008. The report by Ewbank on trends in refractive surgery in the United Kingdom reported that growth had slowed in 2008–2009, with 10 new clinics opening during the survey period. This represents an 8% growth rate, compared with a 22% increase in 2007. Meanwhile, in Asia, demand continued to grow for refractive surgery in China and Japan.

Overall, global demand for laser refractive surgery is expected to grow at a compounded annual rate of 7.7% from 2009 to 2014, with the number of procedures increasing

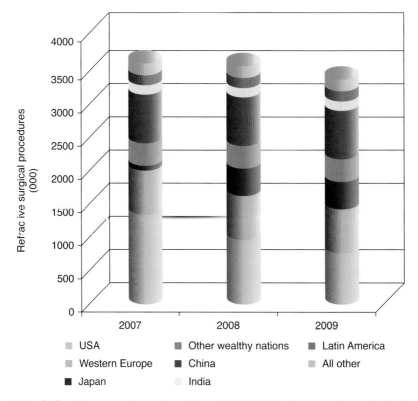

Figure 12-1 Refractive procedures by region, 2007–2009. *(Redrawn with permission from* Market Scope. *2009 Comprehensive report on the global refractive surgery market. Available at: http://dev.market-scope.com/ market_reports/2010/9/2010-comprehensive-report-on-t-7.html.)*

from 3.4 million to 4.9 million, with the majority of growth occurring in emerging Asian economies of China, Japan, and India. China remains one of the fastest-growing laser refractive markets, with an estimated 951 laser centers, accounting for 22% globally, fueled by a growing middle class and a highly myopic population. Refractive surgery in India is also rapidly growing, with approximately 128,000 procedures per year.

Alió JL, Pettersen P. LASIK volume and the future of refractive surgery. *Cataract and Refractive Surgery Today Europe.* Available at: http://www.crstodayeurope.com/Issues/0309/0309_04 .php. Accessed August 4, 2010.

Ewbank A. Trends in refractive surgery in the UK 2009. Available at: http://www.bsrs.co.uk/ Laser%20Survey%202009.pdf. Accessed August 4, 2010.

Harmon D. Global recession shadows 2009 refractive market. Market Scope January 2010. Available at: http://www.market-scope.com/market_scope/.

Market Scope. 2009 Comprehensive report on the global refractive surgery market. Available at: http://dev.market-scope.com/market_reports/2010/9/2010-comprehensive-report-on-t-7 .html.

International Trends in Refractive Surgery

Although international trends in refractive surgery are influenced by those in the US and in the developed nations in Europe and Asia, there are some distinct differences. For example, overall refractive surgery market statistics suggest that outside of the US, emerging lens-based refractive technologies are expected to make up approximately 10% of refractive procedures, while in the US, the percentages remain in the single digits.

Preferences for different types of excimer lasers for LASIK vary internationally. In the US, with a total of 1388 excimer lasers in use in 2009, the 3 major laser systems consisted of AMO/VISX lasers (65%), Alcon WaveLight and some remaining LADARVision lasers (25%), and Bausch & Lomb (B&L) Technolas lasers (8%). In contrast, outside the US, Alcon WaveLight lasers hold the largest market share (21%), followed by AMO/VISX and B&L (both 16%), and Schwind (15%). Unlike in the US, where wavefront-guided customized ablation continues to prevail, customized ablations are less popular internationally. Interestingly, in 2009, more than 4 times as many lasers were sold internationally (375 units) as in the US (82). In the US, adoption of wavefront-guided treatment in 2009 is estimated to be 50%–54%, while it is closer to 25%–30% outside the US, possibly because of the higher cost for this mode of treatment.

The choice of LASIK microkeratomes is changing because of the availability of femtosecond lasers, especially in the US, where they are currently used in approximately 63% of all LASIK procedures. Although their market share is much lower outside the US (32%), the use of femtosecond lasers is expected to grow internationally because of the perceived clinical advantages, the potential for increased surgeon revenue, and patient perceptions of a bladeless, "no-touch" procedure.

Among surface ablation procedures, photorefractive keratectomy (PRK) remains popular for the treatment of low myopia. There is an increasing use of mitomycin C for higher degrees of correction in Asia, which may also explain the resurgence in the interest in PRK globally. In Asian countries and other countries with relatively high rates of high myopia, PRK was extensively used in the mid- to late 1990s until the significant risk of corneal haze with greater amounts of ablation was recognized, and LASIK largely replaced PRK for treatment of high myopia. LASEK and epi-LASIK procedures are becoming increasingly popular in some European countries, such as Italy, and in the Middle East, which has a high prevalence of keratoconus.

The other major trend in the refractive market is expected to be the further development of lasers to treat presbyopia. The global presbyopic patient population is estimated to be 1.5 billion, and these patients represent an underserved market. Research is continuing in the use of excimer lasers for multifocal LASIK, or presbyLASIK. AMO, Schwind eyetech-solutions GmBH (PresbyMAX), Technolas Perfect Vision (PresbyONE), Carl Zeiss Meditec, Nidek, and WaveLight all have procedures in development, with clinical trials currently ongoing outside the US.

Femtosecond lasers now also offer possible presbyopia treatments. Though not yet approved for use outside the US, the LensAR FS laser (LensAR, Winter Park, FL) is claimed to restore compliance and elasticity to the crystalline lens by cutting tissue planes within the lens. A similar approach is being pursued by Laser Zentrum Hannover eV, based in

Germany. Data are still emerging on this technique. Technolas Perfect Vision received European approval in 2009 for its femtosecond laser–based presbyopic treatment, IntraCor. With this technique, the femtosecond laser is used to create concentric ring-shaped cuts within the cornea. The theory is that these cuts change the corneal curvature in a way that leads to improvement in near vision, without a trade-off in distance vision. The 18-month results, presented at the 2009 annual meeting of the European Society of Cataract and Refractive Surgeons (ESCRS), showed that visual outcomes were stable. The company is now working on expanding the range of treatments with the IntraCor procedure to include myopia, hyperopia, and astigmatism.

A third treatment area for presbyopia remains on the horizon: corneal inlays. Three companies are currently beginning to commercialize products: AcuFocus (Irvine, CA), ReVision Optics (Lake Forest, CA), and Presbia, Inc (Amsterdam, the Netherlands; and Los Angeles, CA).

The Kamra Inlay (formerly known as the AcuFocus Corneal Inlay) uses the small-aperture, or pinhole, effect to enhance depth of focus for the correction of emmetropic presbyopia; it can also be combined with bilateral LASIK and simultaneous implantation in ametropic presbyopia. Implanted only in the nondominant eye, with either a femtosecond LASIK–type flap or a femtosecond laser–generated pocket incision, the inlay is 3.8 mm in diameter, with a 1.6-mm opening, and is 5 μm thick. Data presented at the 2009 ESCRS meeting showed an average improvement in near vision of 4 lines and a mean near acuity of J1. The inlay is currently available in Singapore, Japan, and Europe; clinical studies are ongoing at 17 clinical sites in the US in an FDA study and at 9 international sites (Europe and Asia-Pacific). Further international trials are under way to perform Kamra implantation in post-LASIK and pseudophakic patients. It is anticipated that Kamra will be widely available outside the US by the end of 2010.

The PresbyLens from ReVision Optics is a 2-mm hydrogel inlay which is centered on the cornea under a flap or through a pocket incision. In clinical studies, PresbyLens showed an average improvement of 4 lines in uncorrected near vision. The company recently received clearance to market this device in Europe and is expected to begin a phase 3 clinical study in the US in 2010.

The third inlay under development is the Flexivue from Presbia, Inc. The inlay is 3 mm in diameter. Results presented at the 2009 ESCRS meeting showed that patients achieved less of an improvement in near vision compared with that gained with other inlays, while experiencing a trade-off in distance vision.

Minimal clinical data have been published to date on these 3 inlays, with only a sole study on the AcuFocus (now Kamra Inlay). In this study of 39 patients, mean uncorrected near visual acuity improved from J6 preoperatively to J1+ postoperatively and remained stable for up to 4 years. All eyes improved to J3 or better, while 85% improved to J1 or better. Mean uncorrected distance visual acuity did not change and remained at 20/20 throughout the follow-up. More than 1000 patients have now been implanted with Kamra in a total of 7 clinical studies.

Phakic intraocular lenses (PIOLs) are widely used in Europe and Asia, mainly for the treatment of high or extreme myopia, but their usage is lower in the US, partly due to regulatory issues. Intrastromal corneal ring segment (ICRS) surgery remains limited to treating keratoconus and post–refractive surgery keratectasia. As in the US, Intacs rings are the most commonly used ICRS in Europe and Asia, while the use of Ferrara rings is limited to South America.

In Europe, as in the US, there is strong interest in the convergence of refractive and cataract surgery, with PIOLs and presbyopia-correcting IOLs bridging the gap between cataract and refractive technologies. Over the past several years, there has been a growing interest in lens-related refractive surgery as an alternative to the established forms of keratorefractive laser surgery. In the US, the Verisyse and the Visian ICL are the only FDA-approved PIOLs (discussed in Chapter 8). In Scandinavia (Norway, Sweden) and Spain, posterior chamber IOLs (ICL and Toric ICL) are the most commonly used PIOLs. In contrast, anterior chamber phakic IOLs are mostly used in Germany and France, while approximately equal usage of anterior chamber and posterior chamber PIOLs is seen in Italy.

In Asia, LASIK continues to be the most common refractive procedure. In South Korea, arguably a major developed Asian country with the highest penetration of refractive surgery, a 2004 survey (unpublished data, Kyung Hwan Shin) conducted by the Korean Society of Cataract and Refractive Surgery revealed that for myopia <12 diopters, LASIK surgery accounted for 82% of all forms of refractive surgery, followed by LASEK (11%) and PRK (7%). For myopia >12 diopters, phakic IOLs were the preferred surgical option. In China, reports suggest that more LASIK is performed annually than cataract surgery, which is thought to be related to higher incomes in its major cities. In Japan, the prevalence of refractive surgery is lower because of the relatively conservative attitudes of ophthalmic surgeons and the public toward refractive surgery and also because of the stringent regulations governing medical devices and medical advertising. Alcon, B&L, and WaveLight have yet to attain regulatory approvals in Japan. Nidek lasers are naturally predominant, as Nidek is based in Japan. It is estimated that only 450 of the 11,200 Japanese ophthalmologists currently perform refractive surgery in Japan, although that country has the world's tenth-largest population, of almost 128 million. Nevertheless, refractive surgery growth continues in Japan; in 2009, an estimated 785,900 laser refractive procedures were performed, compared with 48,000 in 2003. Ironically, the world's largest chain of refractive clinics is in Japan. In 2007, 115,431 refractive procedures were performed in 2 Shinagawa LASIK clinics in Tokyo and Osaka; and in 2009, this figure rose to 241,781 procedures in 4 Shinagawa LASIK clinics. LASIK procedures accounted for 98% of procedures, using the IntraLase and WaveLight platforms.

Seyeddain O, Riha W, Hohensinn M, Nix G, Dexl AK, Grabner G. Refractive surgical correction of presbyopia with the AcuFocus small aperture corneal inlay: two-year follow-up. *J Refract Surg.* 2010;26(10):707–715.

International Regulation of Refractive Surgery Practices and Devices

Standards and levels of regulation differ among various countries, but many developing nations accept or conform to regulatory standards from established administrations such as the US FDA and the regulatory framework of the European Union (EU).

The concept of globalization has been adopted by medical device regulation at an international level, with the development of the International Harmonized System for medical devices control, established by the Global Harmonization Task Force (GHTF) in 1992. The 5 founding members are the European Union, the United States, Canada, Australia, and Japan.

The EU began medical regulation in 1990 and has adopted a risk-based classification comparable to that of the US FDA, consisting of 4 classes (I, II, III, and IV). Regulatory controls focus primarily on safety, with less emphasis on efficacy than for the FDA.

In Asia, regulatory controls vary considerably. Some countries use existing drug and food control legislation to regulate a limited range of medical devices. However, many countries (including China and South Korea) recognize or have adopted regulatory standards set by the EU or US FDA within their respective internal regulatory frameworks. In India, medical device regulation is still undergoing regulatory reorganization, while in Japan, strict internal regulatory controls have limited the importation of refractive surgical devices and procedures. Some Asian countries have adopted, or are in the process of adopting, a harmonized approach to device regulation through the Asian Harmonization Working Party (AHWP) a nongovernmental agency formed in 1996 with direct links to the GHTF.

Lachman M. ESCRS 2009: The next wave in cataract and presbyopia devices. Available at: http://www.medicaldevicestoday.com/2009/11/escrs-2009-the-next-wave-in-cataract-and -presbyopia-devices.html.

Market Scope. 2009 Comprehensive report on the global refractive surgery market. Available at: http://dev.market-scope.com/market_reports/2010/9/2010-comprehensive-report-on-t-7 .html.

The Role of the FDA
in Refractive Surgery

The field of refractive surgery is uniquely dependent on rapidly changing technology that dictates surgical technique. Some of the investigational devices discussed in the preceding chapters will receive Food and Drug Administration (FDA) approval by the time this book is published. Other "promising" devices or techniques may have already fallen out of favor.

Because of the continual introduction of new devices to the US market, the FDA approval process has particular influence in refractive surgery. Therefore, we have included this brief appendix to review the FDA approval process. A list of FDA-approved lasers for refractive surgery can be found on the FDA website (http://www.fda.gov/MedicalDevices/ProductsandMedicalProcedures/SurgeryandLifeSupport/LASIK/ucm168641.htm).

The FDA

The scope of the FDA's work is established by legislation. The Food, Drug, and Cosmetic Act, passed by Congress in 1938, required for the first time that companies prove the safety of new drugs before placing them on the market and required regulation of cosmetics and therapeutic devices. The Medical Device Amendments of 1976 authorized the FDA to ensure that medical devices are safe and effective before they come to market in the United States. This amendment also provided for classification of medical devices into 3 categories, depending on potential risk of the device; established 3 pathways to market; and established advisory panels to assist the FDA in the review of devices. The Ophthalmic Devices Panel, for example, evaluates and advises on marketing and device applications for ophthalmic devices (see discussion later in this appendix).

Device Classification

All manufacturers of medical devices distributed in the United States must comply with basic regulations, or general controls. These include

- establishment (company) registration
- medical device listing
- quality systems regulation

- labeling requirements
- medical device reporting (of problems)

In addition, devices are classified into 1 of 3 regulatory control groups (I, II, III). This classification of medical devices identifies any regulatory control specific to the class that is necessary to ensure the safety and effectiveness of a device.

Class I devices (eg, refractometers, perimeters, sunglasses, visual acuity charts) are usually considered minimal-risk devices. Although these devices are subject to general controls, most of them are exempt from premarket review by the FDA. With few exceptions, manufacturers can go directly to market with a class I device.

Class II devices (eg, phacoemulsification units, tonometers, vitrectomy machines, daily-wear contact lenses) are usually considered moderate-risk devices. Class II devices are those for which general controls alone are insufficient to ensure safety and effectiveness and for which methods exist to provide such assurances. These devices, in addition to general controls, are subject to special controls, which may include special labeling requirements, mandatory performance standards, and postmarket surveillance. With few exceptions, class II devices require premarket review by the FDA.

Class III devices (eg, excimer lasers, intraocular lenses, extended-wear contact lenses, intraocular fluids) are considered significant-risk devices that present a potential unreasonable risk of illness or injury. Class III devices are those for which insufficient information exists to ensure safety and effectiveness solely through general or special controls. Class III devices cannot be marketed in the United States until the FDA determines that there is a reasonable assurance of safety and effectiveness when used according to the approved indications for use. Most class III devices come to market through the *premarket approval (PMA)* process and require an extensive review by the FDA before approval is granted for marketing.

Collection of Clinical Data for an Unapproved Device

For all class III devices and many class II devices, clinical performance data are required to be included in the regulatory marketing submissions. An *investigational device exemption (IDE)* allows the investigational device to be shipped and used in a clinical trial to collect the safety and effectiveness data required to support an application to the FDA requesting clearance to market. The FDA has 30 days to review and grant approval of an IDE application. Applications containing deficiencies in such areas as bench testing, study design, or informed consent documents are denied or conditionally approved. The sponsor may begin enrollment and treatment of subjects for IDE applications that are conditionally approved, but the sponsor must respond to the deficiencies within 45 days of the date of the conditional approval letter. During the IDE process, the sponsor often meets with the FDA to discuss the details of the clinical trial in order to facilitate effective data collection for eventual review.

Pathways to Market

Premarket Notification 510(k)

Manufacturers of class I and class II devices that are not otherwise exempt from premarket review must submit a *premarket notification,* commonly referred to as a *510(k) application,* to the FDA before going to market. In the 510(k) application, a manufacturer must demonstrate that its device is substantially equivalent to a legally marketed device (commonly referred to as the "predicate device") of the same type and for the same intended use. The FDA must make its determination of substantial equivalence within 90 days. If a device is not found to be substantially equivalent, it is placed into class III, or alternatively, if the device is not of high risk, the sponsor may submit a de novo request stating that the device defines a new 510(k) device regulatory classification.

Humanitarian Device Exemption

Devices marketed under a *humanitarian device exemption (HDE)* are intended to treat or diagnose diseases or conditions that affect or are manifested in fewer than 4000 individuals per year in the United States. The sponsor is required to provide an HDE application to the FDA containing a reasonable assurance of safety. Efficacy information is limited to a demonstration of "probable benefits to health" rather than the higher standard of "reasonable assurance of effectiveness," as would be required for a PMA. These devices must be used in a facility with an institutional review board (IRB). The FDA has 75 days to review and make a decision on an HDE application.

Premarket Approval

The PMA process is the primary pathway to market for class III devices. Clinical data from the IDE study, along with manufacturing information, preclinical bench testing, animal data (if needed), and labeling, are submitted to the FDA as a PMA application. The FDA must decide within 180 days whether the information submitted in the application demonstrates the safety and effectiveness of the device in question. The time for making the decision is extended when the application lacks the required information or contains information that is incomplete or insufficient.

Ophthalmic Devices Panel

The Ophthalmic Devices Panel consists of 6 voting members, the chair (who votes in case of a tie), 1 nonvoting consumer representative, and 1 nonvoting industry representative. The panel includes ophthalmologists as well as other experts, such as vision scientists, biostatisticians, and optometrists. Consultants are included on the panel as the need for their expertise dictates. All panel members are considered "special government employees" and are subject to the conflict-of-interest rules and ethics requirements for government employees.

The Ophthalmic Devices Panel meets in open public session to evaluate and advise on marketing applications for first-of-a-kind devices and for previously approved devices for which a firm is seeking a new indication for use, as well as on device applications that raise significant issues of safety and effectiveness. The panel also provides clinical input in the development of FDA and industry guidelines for the study of new devices.

During a panel meeting scheduled to review a specific device, panel deliberations focus on the clinical study data and the proposed physician and patient labeling (if applicable). After deliberation, the panel members must determine their recommendation regarding whether the information in the PMA application demonstrates a reasonable assurance of safety and effectiveness. At the conclusion of the meeting, the panel votes on its recommendation. However, because the committee is advisory in nature, the FDA is not bound to follow its recommendation.

Labeling

The sponsor defines the inclusion and exclusion criteria for the clinical trial. Prior to approval, the FDA reviews and makes recommendations for changes in the device labeling using the data from the population studied. For example, if dry eyes are an exclusion criteria for the PMA study, there will be no data on subjects with dry eyes. Consequently, the device is not approved in this subset of patients, and the labeling will indicate that dry eyes are an exclusion criterion. This does not mean that the device is contraindicated in dry-eye patients but that the safety and effectiveness of the device cannot be evaluated in this population because there are no data. Some exclusion criteria may be contraindications to treatment. For example, keratoconus could be an exclusion criterion as well as a contraindication to laser in situ keratomileusis (LASIK).

The clinical trial is performed for a limited range of refractive errors. Safety and effectiveness data guide the range of refractive error that is approved for use in the PMA labeling.

If a treating clinician does not follow the labeling recommendations for the device, he or she is using the device "off-label." Some off-label uses reflect the PMA's lack of data on safety and effectiveness—for example, use of the device in a patient listed within the exclusion criterion; other off-label uses reflect decreased or unknown safety or effectiveness—for example, use of the device beyond the refractive range of the labeling. Any modifications to the device to enable an off-label use, such as the addition of unapproved software, adulterate the device and cause it to be unapproved.

In the United States, ophthalmologists very commonly use devices off-label because the FDA does not control the practice of medicine. In some cases, off-label use has actually become the standard of care. For example, topical fluoroquinolones are FDA approved to treat bacterial conjunctivitis; however, these medications are commonly used to treat corneal ulcers as well, even though they are not FDA approved for this indication. Consequently, although use of fluoroquinolones for corneal ulcer treatment may be off-label, in some situations it may also be the community standard of care.

Conversely, use of an FDA-approved device in an off-label fashion that deviates from the community standard of care may place an ophthalmologist at increased risk of legal scrutiny, particularly if there is a poor result. In such a situation, the physician should seriously consider both informing the patient and having the patient sign an ancillary consent form.

Delays in FDA Approval

At times, deficiencies in the clinical trials of a PMA application may delay its presentation to the Ophthalmic Devices Panel. Sometimes a PMA application may be recommended for approval by the panel, but the manufacturer must wait for final FDA approval before marketing. Usually, a panel recommendation for approval is granted with conditions that must be met before final FDA approval is granted. For example, the panel may request that data obtained on study subjects with certain ophthalmic characteristics be submitted to the FDA to determine whether visual results in this subset of patients demonstrate efficacy.

When delays occur, the public naturally wants to know why. The FDA and the Ophthalmic Devices Panel are legally bound to keep the result of the PMA application process confidential and are prohibited by law from revealing any information about the PMA, favorable or unfavorable. However, the company is not bound by these same rules and is not restricted in what it chooses to tell the public. The company's dissemination of information about the PMA often has financial motivation because such information may affect the company's stock price and the public's perception of the product. The FDA does not comment on statements made by the company; however, this does not indicate an FDA endorsement of any statement by the company. Even if a company releases incorrect or misleading information about the reasons for delay in FDA approval, the FDA is still prohibited from discussing details of the PMA application, which could include evidence contrary to statements made by the company. Only in the public sessions of the Ophthalmic Devices Panel is information about the PMA process legally allowed to be released to the public before a final decision on the application is made by the FDA. All other deliberations regarding the application, before and after the panel meeting, remain subject to FDA confidentiality rules. Consequently, before the FDA reaches its decision, the panel meeting is the best forum for the public to actually observe the true data from the PMA clinical trial. The executive summary minutes and a complete transcript of the panel meetings are placed on the FDA public website once the chair approves the minutes.

Reporting of Medical Device–Related Adverse Events

The FDA's involvement in medical devices is not limited to the premarket process. The FDA monitors postmarket reports of device-related adverse events (AEs), or product problems, through both voluntary and mandatory reporting. This monitoring is done to detect "signals" of potential public health safety issues.

Since 1984, device manufacturers and importers have been required to report device-related deaths, serious injuries, and malfunctions to the FDA. User facilities (hospitals, nursing homes, ambulatory surgical facilities, outpatient diagnostic and treatment facilities, ambulance services, and health care entities) are required to report deaths to the FDA and deaths and serious injuries to the manufacturer.

Voluntary reporting to the FDA of device-related problems is a critical professional and public health responsibility. Currently, voluntary reporting takes place under Med-Watch, an FDA product-reporting program. MedWatch allows health care professionals and consumers to report serious problems that they suspect are associated with the medical devices they prescribe, dispense, or use. Reporting can be done online at www.fda.gov/medwatch/getforms.htm, by phone (1-800-FDA-1088), or by submitting the MedWatch 3500 form by mail or fax. Voluntary reporting to the FDA is an easy, minimally time-consuming task that has an enormous impact on public health.

The FDA relies on AE reports to maintain a safety surveillance of all FDA-regulated devices. Physician reports may be the critical action that prompts a modification in the use or design of a product, improves the safety profile of a device, and leads to increased patient safety.

APPENDIX 2

Sample Informed Consent Forms

Example Informed Consent Form for PRK
(Courtesy of Ophthalmic Mutual Insurance Company, www.OMIC.com)

NOTE: THIS FORM IS INTENDED AS A SAMPLE FORM. IT CONTAINS THE INFORMATION OMIC RECOMMENDS YOU AS THE SURGEON PERSONALLY DISCUSS WITH THE PATIENT. IT DOES NOT CONTAIN INFORMATION ABOUT LIMBAL RELAXING INCISION (LRI). PLEASE REVIEW IT AND MODIFY TO FIT YOUR ACTUAL PRACTICE. GIVE THE PATIENT A COPY AND SEND THIS FORM TO THE HOSPITAL OR SURGERY CENTER AS VERIFICATION THAT YOU HAVE OBTAINED INFORMED CONSENT. (Version 04/09/07)

INFORMED CONSENT FOR PHOTOREFRACTIVE KERATECTOMY (PRK)

This information and the *Patient Information* booklet must be reviewed so you can make an informed decision regarding Photorefractive Keratectomy (PRK) surgery to reduce your nearsightedness, farsightedness, or astigmatism. Only you and your doctor can determine if you should have PRK surgery based upon your own visual needs and medical considerations. Any questions you have regarding PRK or other alternative therapies for your case should be directed to your doctor.

Alternatives to PRK Surgery

The alternatives to PRK include, among others, eyeglasses, contact lenses, and other refractive surgical procedures. Each of these alternatives to PRK has been explained to me.

Complications and Side Effects

I have been informed, and I understand, that certain complications and side effects have been reported in the post-treatment period by patients who have had PRK, including the following:

- **Possible short-term effects of PRK surgery:** The following have been reported in the short-term post-treatment period and are associated with the normal post-treatment healing process: *mild discomfort or pain (first 72 to 96 hours),* corneal swelling, double vision, feeling something is in the eye, ghost images, light sensitivity, and tearing.

- **Possible long-term complications of PRK surgery:**
  - *Haze:* Loss of perfect clarity of the cornea, usually not affecting vision, which usually resolves over time.
  - *Starbursting:* After refractive surgery, a certain number of patients experience glare, a "starbursting" or halo effect around lights, or other low-light vision problems that may interfere with the ability to drive at night or see well in dim light. Although there are several possible causes for these difficulties, the risk may be increased in patients with large pupils or high degrees of correction. For most patients, this is a temporary condition that diminishes with time or is correctable by wearing glasses at night or taking eye drops. For some patients, however, these visual problems are permanent. I understand that my vision may not seem as sharp at night as during the day and that I may need to wear glasses at night or take eye drops. I understand that it is not possible to predict whether I will experience these night vision or low-light problems, and that I may permanently lose the ability to drive at night or function in dim light because of them. I understand that I should not drive unless my vision is adequate. These risks in relation to my particular pupil size and amount of correction have been discussed with me.
  - *Loss of best vision:* A decrease in my best vision even with glasses or contacts.
  - *IOP elevation:* An increase in the inner eye pressure due to post-treatment medications, which is usually resolved by drug therapy or discontinuation of post-treatment medications.
  - *Mild or severe infection:* Mild infection can usually be treated with antibiotics and usually does not lead to permanent visual loss. Severe infection, even if successfully treated with antibiotics, could lead to permanent scarring and loss of vision that may require corrective laser surgery or, if very severe, corneal transplantation.
  - *Keratoconus:* Some patients develop keratoconus, a degenerative corneal disease affecting vision that occurs in approximately 1/2000 in the general population. While there are several tests that suggest which patients might be at risk, this condition can develop in patients who have normal preoperative topography (a map of the cornea obtained before surgery) and pachymetry (corneal thickness measurement). Since keratoconus may occur on its own, there is no absolute test that will ensure a patient will not develop keratoconus following laser vision correction. Severe keratoconus may need to be treated with a corneal transplant, while mild keratoconus can be corrected by glasses or contact lenses.
- **Infrequent complications.** The following complications have been reported infrequently by those who have had PRK surgery: itching, dryness of the eye, or foreign body feeling in the eye; double or ghost images; patient discomfort; inflammation of the cornea or iris; persistent corneal surface defect; persistent corneal scarring severe enough to affect vision; ulceration/infection; irregular astigmatism (warped corneal surface which causes distorted images); cataract; drooping of the eyelid; loss of bandage contact lens with increased pain (usually corrected by replacing with another contact lens); and a slight increase of possible infection due to use of a bandage contact lens in the immediate post-operative period.

In giving my permission for PRK surgery, I declare that I understand the following information:

The long-term risks and effects of PRK surgery are unknown. The goal of PRK with the excimer laser is to reduce dependence upon or need for contact lenses and/or eyeglasses; however, I understand that as with all forms of treatment, the results in my case cannot be guaranteed. For example:

1. I understand that an overcorrection or undercorrection could occur, causing me to become farsighted or nearsighted or increase my astigmatism and that this could be either permanent or treatable. I understand an overcorrection or undercorrection is more likely in people over the age of 40 years and may require the use of glasses for reading or for distance vision some or all of the time.
2. If I currently need reading glasses, I will likely still need *reading glasses* after this treatment. It is possible that dependence on reading glasses may increase or that reading glasses may be required at an earlier age if I have PRK surgery.
3. *Further treatment may be necessary,* including a variety of eye drops, the wearing of eyeglasses or contact lenses (hard or soft), or additional PRK or other refractive surgery.
4. My *best vision, even with glasses or contacts, may become worse.*
5. There may be a *difference in spectacle correction between eyes,* making the wearing of glasses difficult or impossible. Fitting and wearing *contact lenses* may be more difficult.

I understand there is a remote chance of partial or complete loss of vision in the eye that has had PRK surgery.

I understand that it is not possible to state every complication that may occur as a result of PRK surgery. I also understand that complications or a poor outcome may manifest weeks, months, or even years after PRK surgery.

I understand this is an elective procedure and that PRK surgery is not reversible.

FOR WOMEN ONLY: I am not pregnant or nursing. I understand that pregnancy could adversely affect my treatment result.

My personal reasons for choosing to have PRK surgery are as follows:

_____

_____

_____

_____

_____

I have spoken with my physician, who has explained PRK, its risks and alternatives, and answered my questions about PRK surgery. I therefore consent to having PRK surgery on:

_____ **Right eye**　　　　　_____ **Left eye**　　　　　_____ **Both eyes**

_____　　　　_____

Patient Signature　　　　　　　　　　　　　　　　　　　　　Date

I have been offered a copy of this consent form. _____

Example Informed Consent Form for LASIK
(Courtesy of Ophthalmic Mutual Insurance Company, www.OMIC.com)

> NOTE: THIS FORM IS INTENDED AS A SAMPLE FORM. IT CONTAINS THE INFORMATION OMIC RECOMMENDS YOU AS THE SURGEON PERSONALLY DISCUSS WITH THE PATIENT. IT DOES NOT CONTAIN INFORMATION ABOUT LIMBAL RELAXING INCISION (LRI). PLEASE REVIEW IT AND MODIFY TO FIT YOUR ACTUAL PRACTICE. GIVE THE PATIENT A COPY AND SEND THIS FORM TO THE HOSPITAL OR SURGERY CENTER AS VERIFICATION THAT YOU HAVE OBTAINED INFORMED CONSENT. (Version 07/19/06)

INFORMED CONSENT FOR LASER IN-SITU KERATOMILEUSIS (LASIK)

Introduction

This information is being provided to you so that you can make an informed decision about the use of a device known as a microkeratome, combined with the use of a device known as an excimer laser, to perform LASIK. LASIK is one of a number of alternatives for correcting nearsightedness, farsightedness, and astigmatism. In LASIK, the microkeratome is used to shave the cornea to create a flap. The flap then is opened like the page of a book to expose tissue just below the cornea's surface. Next, the excimer laser is used to remove ultra-thin layers from the cornea to reshape it to reduce nearsightedness. Finally, the flap is returned to its original position, without sutures.

LASIK is an elective procedure: There is no emergency condition or other reason that requires or demands that you have it performed. You could continue wearing contact lenses or glasses and have adequate visual acuity. This procedure, like all surgery, presents some risks, many of which are listed below. You should also understand that there may be other risks not known to your doctor, which may become known later. Despite the best of care, complications and side effects may occur; should this happen in your case, the result might be affected even to the extent of making your vision worse.

Alternatives to LASIK

If you decide not to have LASIK, there are other methods of correcting your nearsightedness, farsightedness, or astigmatism. These alternatives include, among others, eyeglasses, contact lenses, and other refractive surgical procedures.

Patient Consent

In giving my permission for LASIK, I understand the following: The long-term risks and effects of LASIK are unknown. I have received no guarantee as to the success of my particular case. I understand that the following risks are associated with the procedure:

Vision Threatening Complications

1. I understand that the microkeratome or the excimer laser could malfunction, requiring the procedure to be stopped before completion. Depending on the type of malfunction, this may or may not be accompanied by visual loss.

> Patient Initials: _____

2. I understand that, in using the microkeratome, instead of making a flap, an entire portion of the central cornea could be cut off, and very rarely could be lost. If preserved, I understand that my doctor would put this tissue back on the eye after the laser treatment, using sutures, according to the ALK procedure method. It is also possible that the flap incision could result in an incomplete flap, or a flap that is too thin. If this happens, it is likely that the laser part of the procedure will have to be postponed until the cornea has a chance to heal sufficiently to try to create the flap again.

3. I understand that irregular healing of the flap could result in a distorted cornea. This would mean that glasses or contact lenses may not correct my vision to the level possible before undergoing LASIK. If this distortion in vision is severe, a partial or complete corneal transplant might be necessary to repair the cornea.

4. I understand that it is possible a perforation of the cornea could occur, causing devastating complications, including loss of some or all of my vision. This could also be caused by an internal or external eye infection that could not be controlled with antibiotics or other means.

5. I understand that mild or severe infection is possible. Mild infection can usually be treated with antibiotics and usually does not lead to permanent visual loss. Severe infection, even if successfully treated with antibiotics, could lead to permanent scarring and loss of vision that may require corrective laser surgery or, if very severe, corneal transplantation or even loss of the eye.

6. I understand that I could develop keratoconus. Keratoconus is a degenerative corneal disease affecting vision that occurs in approximately 1/2000 in the general population. While there are several tests that suggest which patients might be at risk, this condition can develop in patients who have normal preoperative topography (a map of the cornea obtained before surgery) and pachymetry (corneal thickness measurement). Since keratoconus may occur on its own, there is no absolute test that will ensure a patient will not develop keratoconus following laser vision correction. Severe keratoconus may need to be treated with a corneal transplant, while mild keratoconus can be corrected by glasses or contact lenses.

7. I understand that other very rare complications threatening vision include, but are not limited to, corneal swelling, corneal thinning (ectasia), appearance of "floaters" and retinal detachment, hemorrhage, venous and arterial blockage, cataract formation, total blindness, and even loss of my eye.

Non–Vision Threatening Side Effects

1. I understand that there may be increased sensitivity to light, glare, and fluctuations in the sharpness of vision. I understand these conditions usually occur during the normal stabilization period of from one to three months, but they may also be permanent.

2. I understand that there is an increased risk of eye irritation related to drying of the corneal surface following the LASIK procedure. These symptoms may be tempo-

Patient Initials: _____

rary or, on rare occasions, permanent, and may require frequent application of artificial tears and/or closure of the tear duct openings in the eyelid.

3. I understand that an overcorrection or undercorrection could occur, causing me to become farsighted or nearsighted or increase my astigmatism and that this could be either permanent or treatable. I understand an overcorrection or under-correction is more likely in people over the age of 40 years and may require the use of glasses for reading or for distance vision some or all of the time.

4. After refractive surgery, a certain number of patients experience glare, a "star-bursting" or halo effect around lights, or other low-light vision problems that may interfere with the ability to drive at night or see well in dim light. The exact cause of these visual problems is not currently known; some ophthalmologists theorize that the risk may be increased in patients with large pupils or high de-grees of correction. For most patients, this is a temporary condition that dimin-ishes with time or is correctable by wearing glasses at night or taking eye drops. For some patients, however, these visual problems are permanent. I understand that my vision may not seem as sharp at night as during the day and that I may need to wear glasses at night or take eye drops. I understand that it is not possible to predict whether I will experience these night vision or low-light problems, and that I may permanently lose the ability to drive at night or function in dim light because of them. I understand that I should not drive unless my vision is adequate.

5. I understand that I may not get a full correction from my LASIK procedure and this may require future enhancement procedures, such as more laser treatment or the use of glasses or contact lenses.

6. I understand that there may be a "balance" problem between my two eyes after LASIK has been performed on one eye, but not the other. This phenomenon is called anisometropia. I understand this would cause eyestrain and make judg-ing distance or depth perception more difficult. I understand that my first eye may take longer to heal than is usual, prolonging the time I could experience anisometropia.

7. I understand that, after LASIK, the eye may be more fragile to trauma from im-pact. Evidence has shown that, as with any scar, the corneal incision will not be as strong as the cornea originally was at that site. I understand that the treated eye, therefore, is somewhat more vulnerable to all varieties of injuries, at least for the first year following LASIK. I understand it would be advisable for me to wear protective eyewear when engaging in sports or other activities in which the pos-sibility of a ball, projectile, elbow, fist, or other traumatizing object contacting the eye may be high.

8. I understand that there is a natural tendency of the eyelids to droop with age and that eye surgery may hasten this process.

9. I understand that there may be pain or a foreign body sensation, particularly dur-ing the first 48 hours after surgery.

Patient Initials: _____

10. I understand that temporary glasses either for distance or reading may be necessary while healing occurs and that more than one pair of glasses may be needed.
11. I understand that the long-term effects of LASIK are unknown and that unforeseen complications or side effects could possibly occur.
12. I understand that visual acuity I initially gain from LASIK could regress, and that my vision may go partially back to a level that may require glasses or contact lens use to see clearly.
13. I understand that the correction that I can expect to gain from LASIK may not be perfect. I understand that it is not realistic to expect that this procedure will result in perfect vision, at all times, under all circumstances, for the rest of my life. I understand I may need glasses to refine my vision for some purposes requiring fine detailed vision after some point in my life, and that this might occur soon after surgery or years later.
14. I understand that I may be given medication in conjunction with the procedure and that my eye may be patched afterward. I therefore understand that I must not drive the day of surgery and not until I am certain that my vision is adequate for driving.
15. I understand that if I currently need reading glasses, I will still likely need reading glasses after this treatment. It is possible that dependence on reading glasses may increase or that reading glasses may be required at an earlier age if I have this surgery.
16. Even 90% clarity of vision is still slightly blurry. Enhancement surgeries can be performed when vision is stable UNLESS it is unwise or unsafe. If the enhancement is performed within the first six months following surgery, there generally is no need to make another cut with the microkeratome. The original flap can usually be lifted with specialized techniques. After 6 months of healing, a new LASIK incision may be required, incurring greater risk. In order to perform an enhancement surgery, there must be adequate tissue remaining. If there is inadequate tissue, it may not be possible to perform an enhancement. An assessment and consultation will be held with the surgeon, at which time the benefits and risks of an enhancement surgery will be discussed.
17. I understand that, as with all types of surgery, there is a possibility of complications due to anesthesia, drug reactions, or other factors that may involve other parts of my body. I understand that, since it is impossible to state every complication that may occur as a result of any surgery, the list of complications in this form may not be complete.

For Presbyopic Patients (those requiring a separate prescription for reading)
The option of monovision has been discussed with my ophthalmologist.

Patient Initials: _____

Patient's Statement of Acceptance and Understanding

The details of the procedure known as LASIK have been presented to me in detail in this document and explained to me by my ophthalmologist. My ophthalmologist has answered all my questions to my satisfaction. I therefore consent to LASIK surgery on:

_____ **Right eye**   _____ **Left eye**   _____ **Both eyes**

I give permission for my ophthalmologist to record on video or photographic equipment my procedure, for purposes of education, research, or training of other health care professionals. I also give my permission for my ophthalmologist to use data about my procedure and subsequent treatment to further understand LASIK. I understand that my name will remain confidential, unless I give subsequent written permission for it to be disclosed outside my ophthalmologist's office or the center where my LASIK procedure will be performed.

_____   _____

Patient Name   Date

_____   _____

Witness Name   Date

I have been offered a copy of this consent form (please initial). _____

Basic Texts

Refractive Surgery

Azar DT, Gatinel D, Thanh Hoang-Xuan II, eds. *Refractive Surgery*. 2nd ed. Philadelphia: Elsevier Mosby; 2007.

Boyd BF, Agarwal S, Agarwal A, Agarwal A, eds. *LASIK and Beyond LASIK: Wavefront Analysis and Customized Ablations*. El Dorado, Panama: Highlights of Ophthalmology; 2001.

Feder R, Rapuano CJ. *The LASIK Handbook: A Case-Based Approach*. Philadelphia: Lippincott Williams & Wilkins; 2007.

Garg A. *Mastering the Techniques of Customized LASIK*. New Delhi: Jaypee Brothers; 2007.

Hardten DR, Lindstrom RL, Davis EA, eds. *Phakic Intraocular Lenses: Principles and Practice*. Thorofare, NJ: Slack; 2004.

Probst LE, ed. *LASIK: Advances, Controversies, and Custom*. Thorofare, NJ: Slack; 2003.

Troutman RC, Buzard KA. *Corneal Astigmatism: Etiology, Prevention, and Management*. St Louis: Mosby; 1992.

Related Academy Materials

Focal Points: Clinical Modules for Ophthalmologists

Klyce SD. Wavefront analysis (Module 10, 2005).
Koch DD. Cataract surgery following refractive surgery (Module 5, 2001).
Lawless MA. Surgical correction of hyperopia (Module 4, 2004).
Majmudar PA. LASIK complications (Module 13, 2004).
Packer M, Fine IH, Hoffman RS. Refractive lens exchange (Module 6, 2007).
Price FW Jr. LASIK (Module 3, 2000).
Schallhorn SC. Wavefront-guided LASIK (Module 1, 2008).
Wallace RB III. Multifocal and accommodating lens implementation (Module 11, 2004).

Print Publications

Arnold AC, ed. *Basic Principles of Ophthalmic Surgery* (2006).
Dunn JP, Langer PD, eds. *Basic Techniques of Ophthalmic Surgery* (2009).
Rockwood EJ, ed. *ProVision: Preferred Responses in Ophthalmology, Series 4*. Self-Assessment Program. 2-vol set (2007).
Wilson FM II, Blomquist PH, eds. *Practical Ophthalmology: A Manual for Beginning Residents*. 6th ed. (2009).

Academy Maintenance of Certification (MOC)

MOC Exam Review Course (2011).

Preferred Practice Patterns

Preferred Practice Patterns are available at http://one.aao.org/CE/PracticeGuidelines/PPP.aspx.

Preferred Practice Patterns Committee, Refractive Management/Intervention Panel. *Refractive Errors and Refractive Surgery* (2007).

Ophthalmic Technology Assessments

Ophthalmic Technology Assessments are available at http://one.aao.org/CE/Practice Guidelines/Ophthalmic.aspx and are published in the Academy's journal, *Ophthalmology*.

Ophthalmic Technology Assessment Committee. *Excimer Laser Photorefractive Keratectomy (PRK) for Myopia and Astigmatism* (1994).
Ophthalmic Technology Assessment Committee. *Intrastromal Corneal Ring Segments for Low Myopia* (2001; reviewed for currency 2009).

Ophthalmic Technology Assessment Committee. *LASIK for Hyperopia, Hyperopic Astigmatism, and Mixed Astigmatism* (2004; reviewed for currency 2009).

Ophthalmic Technology Assessment Committee. *LASIK for Myopia and Astigmatism: Safety and Efficacy* (2002; reviewed for currency 2009).

Ophthalmic Technology Assessment Committee. *Phakic Intraocular Lens Implantation for the Correction of Myopia* (2009).

Ophthalmic Technology Assessment Committee. *Safety of Overnight Orthokeratology for Myopia* (2008).

Ophthalmic Technology Assessment Committee. *Wavefront-Guided LASIK for the Correction of Primary Myopia and Astigmatism* (2008).

Complementary Therapy Assessments

Complementary Therapy Task Force. *Visual Training for Refractive Errors* (2004).

DVDs

Front Row View: Video Collections of Eye Surgery. Series 2 (DVD; 2007).
Front Row View: Video Collections of Eye Surgery. Series 3 (DVD; 2009).
Henderson BA, Afshari NA, eds. *Challenging Cases in Cataract Surgery* (DVD; 2009).

Online Materials

Complementary Therapy Assessments; http://one.aao.org/CE/PracticeGuidelines/Therapy.aspx

Focal Points modules; http://one.aao.org/CE/EducationalProducts/FocalPoints.aspx

ONE Network, Academy Grand Rounds, Refractive Management and Intervention; http://one.aao.org/CE/EducationalContent/Cases.aspx

ONE Network, Online Courses, Refractive Management and Intervention; http://one.aao.org/CE/EducationalContent/Courses.aspx

Ophthalmic Technology Assessments; http://one.aao.org/CE/PracticeGuidelines/Ophthalmic.aspx

Practicing Ophthalmologists Learning System (2011); http://one.aao.org/CE/POLS/Default.aspx

Preferred Practice Patterns; http://one.aao.org/CE/PracticeGuidelines/PPP.aspx

Rockwood EJ, ed. *ProVision: Preferred Responses in Ophthalmology, Series 4.* Self-Assessment Program. 2-vol set (2007); http://one.aao.org/CE/EducationalContent/Provision.aspx

---

To order any of these materials, please order online at www.aao.org/store or call the Academy's Customer Service toll-free number, 866-561-8558, in the U.S. If outside the U.S., call 415-561-8540 between 8:00 AM and 5:00 PM PST.

Requesting Continuing Medical Education Credit

The American Academy of Ophthalmology is accredited by the Accreditation Council for Continuing Medical Education to provide continuing medical education for physicians.

The American Academy of Ophthalmology designates this enduring material for a maximum of 10 *AMA PRA Category 1 Credits™*. Physicians should claim only credit commensurate with the extent of their participation in the activity.

The American Medical Association requires that all learners participating in activities involving enduring materials complete a formal assessment before claiming continuing medical education (CME) credit. To assess your achievement in this activity and ensure that a specified level of knowledge has been reached, a posttest for this Section of the Basic and Clinical Science Course is provided. A minimum score of 80% must be obtained to pass the test and claim CME credit.

To take the posttest and request CME credit online:

1. Go to www.aao.org/cme and log in.
2. Select the appropriate Academy activity. You will be directed to the posttest.
3. Once you have passed the test with a score of 80% or higher, you will be directed to your transcript. *If you are not an Academy member, you will be able to print out a certificate of participation once you have passed the test.*

To take the posttest and request CME credit using a paper form:

1. Complete the CME Credit Request Form on the following page and return it to the address provided. *Please note that there is a $20.00 processing fee for all paper requests.* The posttest will be mailed to you.
2. Return the completed test as directed. Once you have passed the test with a score of 80% or higher, your transcript will be updated automatically. To receive verification of your CME credits, be sure to check the appropriate box on the posttest.

   Please note that test results will not be provided. If you do not achieve a minimum score of 80%, another test will be sent to you automatically, at no charge. If you do not reach the specified level of knowledge (80%) on your second attempt, you will need to pay an additional processing fee to receive the third test.

Note: Submission of the CME Credit Request Form does not represent claiming CME credit.

• Credit must be claimed by June 30, 2014 •

For assistance, contact the Academy's Customer Service department at 866-561-8558 (US only) or 415-561-8540 between 8:00 AM and 5:00 PM (PST), Monday through Friday, or send an e-mail to customer_service@aao.org.

**AMERICAN ACADEMY
OF OPHTHALMOLOGY**
The Eye M.D. Association

CME Credit Request Form
Basic and Clinical Science Course, 2011–2012
Section 13

Please note that requesting CME credit with this form will incur a fee of $20.00. (Prepayment required.)

☐ Yes, please send me the posttest for BCSC Section 13. I choose not to report my CME credit online for free. I have enclosed a payment of **$20.00** for processing.

Academy Member ID Number (if known): _____

Name: _____
     First   Last

Address: _____

_____
     City   State/Province   ZIP/Postal Code   Country

Phone Number: _____   Fax Number: _____

E-mail Address: _____

Method of Payment: ☐ Check   ☐ Credit Card   Make checks payable to AAO.

Credit Card Type: ☐ Visa   ☐ MasterCard   ☐ American Express   ☐ Discover

Card Number: _____   Expiration Date: _____

Credit must be claimed by June 30, 2014. Please note that submission of this form does not represent claiming CME credits.

Test results will not be sent. If a participant does not achieve an 80% pass rate, one new posttest will be sent at no charge. Additional processing fees are incurred thereafter.

Please mail completed form to:
American Academy of Ophthalmology, CME Posttest
Dept. 34051
PO Box 39000
San Francisco, CA 94139

Please allow 3 weeks for delivery of the posttest.

Academy use only:

PN: _____   MC: _____

Study Questions

Please note that these questions are *not* part of your CME reporting process. They are provided here for self-assessment and identification of personal professional practice gaps. The required CME posttest is available online or by request (see "Requesting CME Credit").

Following the questions are a blank answer sheet and answers with discussions. Although a concerted effort has been made to avoid ambiguity and redundancy in these questions, the authors recognize that differences of opinion may occur regarding the "best" answer. The discussions are provided to demonstrate the rationale used to derive the answer. They may also be helpful in confirming that your approach to the problem was correct or, if necessary, in fixing the principle in your memory. The Section 13 faculty would like to thank the Self-Assessment Committee for working with them to provide these study questions and discussions.

1. The most common technique used clinically to measure wavefront aberrations employs the Hartmann-Shack wavefront sensor. Wavefront analysis is affected by which of the following ocular structures?
   a. cornea, anterior chamber, and lens
   b. cornea and anterior chamber
   c. cornea, anterior chamber, lens, and vitreous
   d. cornea

2. A limitation of the Munnerlyn formula that is used to calculate ablation depth in laser in situ keratomileusis (LASIK) or photorefractive keratectomy (PRK) is that
   a. it assumes a linear relationship between the optical zone and ablation depth
   b. it does not account for the amount of myopia
   c. it does not account for transition zones or wavefront-guided treatments
   d. it relies on optical zones which cannot be accurately measured

3. The primary disadvantage of increasing the optical zone in LASIK and PRK is that
   a. it increases night-vision complaints
   b. it increases the ablation depth
   c. it decreases predictability of the refractive outcome of the treatment
   d. it increases laser treatment time

4. A 45-year-old patient with myopia desires monovision correction with LASIK. The nondominant right eye is chosen for near vision and has a refraction of −5.00 sphere. Assuming no nomogram adjustment is required, what is the most appropriate laser treatment setting?
   a. +3.50 sphere
   b. −6.50 sphere
   c. −3.50 sphere
   d. +6.50 sphere

5. The residual thickness of the stromal bed following LASIK equals
    a. preoperative corneal thickness minus the amount of tissue ablated
    b. preoperative corneal thickness minus the flap thickness
    c. preoperative corneal thickness plus flap thickness minus the amount of tissue ablated
    d. preoperative corneal thickness minus the sum of the flap thickness and the amount of tissue ablated

6. Which of the following is an indication that adequate suction has been obtained with a microkeratome?
    a. pupil dilation
    b. changes in size and color of the patient's fixation target
    c. eye rotation within the keratome
    d. hand-held tonometer reading of 40 mm Hg

7. Epithelial basement membrane dystrophy (map-dot-fingerprint dystrophy) is best diagnosed by which one of the following?
    a. broad-beam tangential evaluation at the slit lamp
    b. Hruby lens evaluation at the slit lamp
    c. lissamine green staining
    d. rose bengal staining

8. When obtaining proper informed consent for LASIK, the discussion regarding the procedure should include which of the following explanations?
    a. explanation that the procedure will eliminate the need for reading glasses in patients younger than 40 years
    b. explanation of the medical alternatives to the procedure
    c. explanation that intraocular pressure (IOP) measurements will likely read artificially high after the procedure
    d. explanation that the procedure will eliminate the need for distance glasses

9. A 21-year-old patient presents for a LASIK evaluation. At his first visit, he is wearing 1-year-old glasses that measure −3.00 +1.00 × 25 OD and −3.25 +0.75 × 10 OS. The patient reads 20/25 OD and 20/30 OS. Manifest refraction results in 20/15 acuity in each eye with −3.75 +1.00 × 180 OD and −3.75 +1.00 × 170 OS. Cycloplegic refraction confirms the new manifest refraction. The most appropriate next step is
    a. schedule the patient for LASIK and treat an additional diopter more than the manifest to compensate for potential progression of myopia
    b. schedule the patient for a repeat examination in 1 month to ensure the stability and accuracy of the manifest refraction
    c. schedule the patient for LASIK and treat the new manifest refraction
    d. schedule the patient for a repeat evaluation in 6–12 months to ensure the stability of the manifest refraction

10. The most common complication of dry eye after LASIK is

    a. diffuse lamellar keratitis (DLK)

    b. epithelial basement membrane dystrophy

    c. dislocation of the flap

    d. decreased vision

11. A patient with a decentered ablation in 1 eye complains of poor vision and glare at night. Three months after surgery, the uncorrected vision in the affected eye is 20/40 and corrects to 20/30 with −0.50 +0.50 × 47. The affected eye reads 20/25 through a pinhole. An appropriate next step in the management of this patient is

    a. a contact lens trial

    b. reassuring the patient of a good surgical result

    c. enhancement

    d. amputation of the flap

12. In which of the following refractive procedures is corneal sensation best maintained?

    a. epikeratoplasty

    b. LASIK

    c. refractive lens exchange

    d. surface ablation

13. What are the advantages of phakic intraocular lens procedures compared to excimer laser–based surgeries?

    a. removability of the intraocular lens

    b. less risk of a serious infection

    c. can be performed in a surgery center

    d. less risk of endothelial cell loss

14. What do phakic intraocular lenses require?

    a. intraoperative dilation

    b. preoperative lens calculations

    c. preoperative Schirmer testing

    d. general anesthesia

15. Which of the following patients is a good candidate for LASIK?

    a. a 25-year-old pregnant woman

    b. a 25-year-old woman with amblyopia

    c. a 25-year-old woman with asthma

    d. a 25-year-old woman with pellucid marginal degeneration

16. Conductive keratoplasty is an FDA-approved procedure for which one of the following?

    a. the treatment of postkeratoplasty astigmatism

    b. the treatment of low amounts of hyperopia and/or presbyopia

    c. patients who have progressive hyperopia after radial keratotomy (RK)

    d. the early treatment of post-LASIK corneal ectasia

17. What can multifocal intraocular lenses (IOLs) be associated with?

    a. a higher than average rate of posterior capsule opacity than the rate with monofocal IOLs

    b. symptoms of poor contrast sensitivity

    c. less glare and fewer halos than with surface ablation or LASIK

    d. excellent uncorrected distance, intermediate, and near vision

18. What is the most common indication for the use of intrastromal corneal ring segments?

    a. hyperopia

    b. keratoconus

    c. Fuchs dystrophy

    d. astigmatism

19. Intrastromal corneal ring segments are made from which material?

    a. collamer

    b. silicone

    c. polymethylmethacrylate (PMMA)

    d. porcelain

20. What is a complication of intrastromal corneal ring segments?

    a. extrusion

    b. implosion

    c. contusion

    d. endophthalmitis

21. What is a common complication of RK?

    a. infection

    b. progressive hyperopia

    c. loss of best-corrected visual acuity (BCVA)

    d. globe perforation

22. Why is surface ablation such as PRK preferred over LASIK after RK?

    a. LASIK is a more difficult procedure to perform than PRK.

    b. PRK uses mitomycin C.

    c. LASIK is associated with an increased risk of epithelial ingrowth.

    d. PRK uses a bandage contact lens.

23. What is the correct definition of coupling?

    a. similar to snuggling

    b. a corneal change that occurs only with arcuate keratotomy (AK) incisions

    c. when 1 meridian is steepened by astigmatic incisional surgery, which induces flattening in the meridian 90° away from the axis of incision

    d. when 1 meridian is flattened by astigmatic incisional surgery, which induces steepening in the meridian 90° away from the axis of incision

24. A 45-year-old man develops grade 1 reticular haze 4 weeks after bilateral PRK. Which of the following therapies is the most appropriate initial management?

    a. repeat ablation with mitomycin C

    b. topical antibiotics

    c. observation alone

    d. topical mitomycin C therapy

25. One week following LASIK, a patient is asymptomatic but is found to have an area of epithelial ingrowth extending 1 mm into the flap interface. The most appropriate management for this complication is

    a. lifting of the flap and use of alcohol to facilitate removal of the epithelium

    b. lifting of the flap and treatment with mitomycin C to facilitate removal of the epithelium

    c. lifting of the flap and mechanical removal of the epithelium

    d. observation

26. The use of a bandage contact lens is most appropriate for which one of the following conditions?

    a. persistent epithelial defect

    b. severe dry eye

    c. acute microbial keratitis

    d. ocular rosacea

27. Which of the following is an absolute contraindication for performing LASIK?

    a. myopic patient with flat keratometry of 39 D

    b. connective tissue or autoimmune disease

    c. predicted residual corneal bed less than 250 μm

    d. myopic patient with steep keratometry of 48 D

28. After excimer laser refractive surgery, a patient develops herpes simplex virus (HSV) epithelial keratitis. Which of the following treatment regimens is *least* appropriate?

    a. oral acyclovir alone

    b. oral acyclovir with topical trifluridine or ganciclovir

    c. debridement alone

    d. topical trifluridine or ganciclovir alone

29. What has been noted when performing PRK in a patient with a history of strabismus?

    a. Hyperopic PRK to reduce accommodative convergence may improve esotropia.

    b. Patients rarely need prism postoperatively.

    c. Improved best-corrected vision is seen in older children with dense amblyopia.

    d. Diplopia can be treated with extraocular muscle surgery post-PRK.

30. A 42-year-old obese, adult-onset diabetic patient complains of blurred vision at distance. He inquires about LASIK surgery. He has not previously worn eyeglasses or contact lenses. He indicates that his glucose levels have ranged from about 270 to 350 mg/dL over the past few days. An HbA$_{1c}$ was 8.5 last week. He refracts to 20/15 in each eye (OD: −2.50 sphere; OS: −2.00 sphere). Ophthalmologic evaluation is otherwise normal. Which one of the following is the best option for this patient?

    a. LASIK

    b. contact lens wear

    c. distance eyeglass correction

    d. advising better glucose control and scheduling a repeat refraction

31. Corneal laser surface ablation may have specific advantages over LASIK in

    a. corneas with ultrasonic pachymetry readings greater than 580 μm

    b. patients with proptotic globes

    c. patients with small palpebral fissures

    d. patients with shallow orbits

32. Progression of refractive effect is seen after which one of the following?

    a. LASIK for myopia less than 3 D

    b. LASIK for hyperopia for more than 3 D

    c. radial keratotomy

    d. conductive keratoplasty

33. When LASIK is performed, slightly undercorrecting a myopic spectacle prescription may

    a. be better than monovision since the patient can still use both eyes together

    b. aggravate strain when the patient reads

    c. reduce stereopsis at near

    d. postpone presbyopic symptoms in the middle-aged patient

34. Which of the following statements about collagen crosslinking is true?

    a. Corneal crosslinking treatments have been shown to be safe and effective by the FDA.

    b. Corneal crosslinking compacts the stromal lamellae, changes the refractive index of the cornea, and results in increased corneal clarity.

    c. Corneal crosslinking is appropriate even for advanced keratoconus patients with thin corneas (<250 μm central pachymetry).

    d. Corneal crosslinking is often effective at stabilizing the corneal curvature and preventing further steepening and bulging of the corneal stroma in patients with keratoconus and ectasia following corneal refractive surgery.

35. A 48-year-old woman had uncomplicated bilateral LASIK. One month postoperatively, she notes blurred and fluctuating vision. Examination reveals diffuse corneal punctate epitheliopathy in the interpalpebral fissure. Which of the following is the best initial mode of therapy?

    a. frequent application of topical antibiotics

    b. frequent application of topical nonsteroidal anti-inflammatory agents

    c. frequent application of preservative-free artificial tears

    d. frequent application of topical corticosteroids

36. Findings that are suggestive of forme fruste keratoconus include all *except* which one of the following?

    a. best spectacle correction at 20/40

    b. average keratometry of 48 D

    c. 2 D of increased cylinder at 180°

    d. asymmetric bow-tie astigmatism

37. IOL selection in patients who develop cataract after LASIK is complicated because of which one of the following?

    a. Axial length measurements inaccurately reflect axial length.

    b. Keratometry measurements inaccurately reflect corneal refractive power.

    c. Anterior chamber depth measurements inaccurately reflect postoperative IOL position.

    d. Lens thickness measurements inaccurately reflect postoperative IOL position.

38. Five years ago, a patient underwent bilateral 16-incision RK with a 3-mm optical zone. This patient has now developed 4-mm posterior subcapsular cataracts in each eye. His vision is limited to 20/50 visual acuity OU due to the cataracts, and IOL implantation is planned. The least accurate method for determining the corneal K readings to be used for IOL calculation in this patient is

    a. calculation of K readings from preoperative radial keratometry K readings and the change in refraction

    b. calculation of change in refraction with and without a hard contact lens

    c. automated keratometry

    d. manual keratometry

39. An appropriate initial management option for myopic astigmatism induced by corneal ectasia after LASIK is

    a. wavefront-guided enhancement

    b. refractive lens exchange

    c. radial and astigmatic keratotomy

    d. rigid gas-permeable contact lens

40. A patient has irregular astigmatism following creation of a severely decentered LASIK flap. Which of the following treatment options is the safest initial option to correct the vision?

a. transepithelial phototherapeutic keratectomy

b. rigid gas-permeable contact lenses

c. lamellar keratoplasty

d. recutting of the flap followed by a custom LASIK procedure

Answer Sheet for Section 13
Study Questions

Question	Answer	Question	Answer
1	a b c d	21	a b c d
2	a b c d	22	a b c d
3	a b c d	23	a b c d
4	a b c d	24	a b c d
5	a b c d	25	a b c d
6	a b c d	26	a b c d
7	a b c d	27	a b c d
8	a b c d	28	a b c d
9	a b c d	29	a b c d
10	a b c d	30	a b c d
11	a b c d	31	a b c d
12	a b c d	32	a b c d
13	a b c d	33	a b c d
14	a b c d	34	a b c d
15	a b c d	35	a b c d
16	a b c d	36	a b c d
17	a b c d	37	a b c d
18	a b c d	38	a b c d
19	a b c d	39	a b c d
20	a b c d	40	a b c d

Answers

1. **c.** Wavefront analysis with a Hartmann-Shack aberrometer measures the wavefront error of the entire visual system, from the tear film to the retina. With this device, a low-power laser beam is focused on the retina, and the reflected light is then propagated back through the optical elements of the eye, at which point it is measured and analyzed.

2. **c.** The amount of tissue removed centrally for myopic treatments is estimated by the Munnerlyn formula:

   Ablation depth in micrometers (μm) ≈ diopters (D) of myopia
   multiplied by the square of the optical zone diameter (mm), divided by 3

   The formula is therefore a reliable approximation for tissue removal with conventional laser treatments. However, the formula does not account for variable transition zone ablation depths or ablation depths generated by wavefront-guided laser platforms, which tend to be greater than those generated by conventional laser treatments with equivalent manifest refractions.

3. **b.** The amount of ablation increases by the square of the optical zone, while glare, halos, and the potential for regression increase when the size of the optical zone decreases. The treatment time for larger optical zones is only slightly longer than the treatment time for smaller zones.

4. **c.** To create monovision in a myopic patient, it is necessary to undercorrect 1 eye (usually the nondominant eye). The amount of desired undercorrection is determined by a combination of the patient's requirements for near vision and the amount of anisometropia that is tolerable. In a 45-year-old patient, 1.5 D is generally the appropriate amount of undercorrection for providing functional near vision without generating significant problems with anisometropia, in the event that the nondominant eye requires correction with glasses for activities such as driving at night. This refraction allows good uncorrected distance vision in the dominant eye and good near vision in the nondominant eye. If a postoperative refraction of −1.5 D is desired in a patient who has a preoperative refraction of −5.0 D, then a correction of −3.50 D needs to be programmed into the laser.

5. **d.** Residual stromal bed thickness (RSBT) is relevant in LASIK because only the residual stromal bed provides biomechanical strength following LASIK. RSBT is determined by subtracting the flap thickness and laser ablation depth from the preoperative corneal thickness.

6. **a.** Suction obtained during flap creation with a mechanical microkeratome or a femtosecond laser causes a transient but significant rise in intraocular pressure (well over 80–100 mm Hg) with accompanying temporary vision loss and pupillary dilation. The suction causes the globe to be fixated during flap creation, thus preventing the formation of incomplete flaps. Before proceeding with flap creation, the surgeon must verify that suction is appropriate. This can be done by measuring the intraocular pressure (frequently done with a Barraquer tonometer to ensure that the pressure is much higher than 60 mm Hg), by observing pupillary dilation, and by confirming with the patient that his or her vision is blacked out.

7. **a.** Epithelial basement membrane dystrophy (EBMD; also called *anterior basement membrane dystrophy*) occurs when the epithelial layer of the cornea is not well attached to

the Bowman layer. Eyes with EBMD are predisposed to epithelial loosening or sloughing and even frank epithelial defects during the LASIK procedure. Epithelial problems after LASIK increase the risk of diffuse lamellar keratitis and epithelial ingrowth under the flap. The best method to detect EBMD is using a broad slit beam from the side to see the irregular epithelium. Other techniques include using retroillumination or fluorescein dye to identify subtle changes in the epithelium. Eyes with significant EBMD may do best with a surface ablation procedure rather than LASIK.

8. **b.** The informed consent discussion should include nonsurgical alternatives for correcting the patient's refractive error, including glasses and contact lenses. It should also include the variety of surgical options, including surface ablation, phakic intraocular lenses, and refractive lens exchange when appropriate. These procedures, their benefits, and their risks should be discussed. For prepresbyopic and presbyopic patients, the surgeon should make a special effort to explain that they will need to use reading glasses immediately after surgery or in the near future for all tasks performed up close, if they achieve good uncorrected distance vision in both eyes.

9. **d.** Although surface ablation and LASIK are FDA approved for patients 21 years and older, in many patients the refraction has not stabilized by this age. Refractive surgery is FDA approved for use in eyes with stable refractions, which generally means no more than a 0.5 D change in sphere or cylinder in at least the past year. Refractive stability can be checked by reviewing old medical records or measuring old glasses/contact lenses. When it is unclear whether the patient's refraction is stable, it is best to recheck the refraction in 6–12 months. Rechecking in 1 month is too short a time to ascertain refractive stability when the refraction has changed by this degree over the past year. This patient has experienced a 0.75 D increase in his myopia OD, and a 0.50 D increase in his myopia OS. If his myopia is continuing to progress, it is ill-advised to proceed with LASIK until his refraction stabilizes.

10. **d.** Dry eye is one of the most frequent transient adverse effects of LASIK, but occasionally it may persist for months or years; it has been reported in 60%–70% of all patients, to varying degrees. Corneal sensitivity decreases after LASIK because of the surgical amputation of nerves during flap formation and the destruction of superficial nerve fibers during the laser ablation. The cornea overlying the flap is significantly anesthetic for 3 to 6 months. As a result, most patients experience a decrease in tear production. Patients who had dry eyes before surgery or whose eyes were marginally compensated before surgery will have the most severe symptoms. In addition, most patients with dry eyes following LASIK or surface ablation will experience tear-film and ocular surface disruption and will often complain of fluctuating vision between blinks and at different times of the day.

11. **a.** In the scenario presented, the pinhole vision is better than the best spectacle-corrected vision in a patient with a known decentered ablation. It is reasonable, therefore, to consider irregular astigmatism as a cause of the patient's decreased spectacle-corrected vision. Rigid gas-permeable (RGP) contact lenses are the gold standard for the correction of reduced vision due to irregular astigmatism. Contact lenses for refractive purposes should not be fit until the cornea has healed and serial refractions are stable. The best approach to fitting an RGP lens after refractive surgery is to do a trial fitting with overrefraction. The physician needs to discuss with the patient in practical terms the challenges of contact lens fitting after refractive surgery and match the patient's expectations with reality. A patient who wore contact lenses successfully before refractive surgery is more likely to be a successful contact lens wearer postoperatively than a patient who never wore contact lenses.

12. **c.** Corneal sensation can be affected by any surgical procedure involving the cornea. Generally, the greater the disruption to the cornea, the greater the damage to the corneal nerves and the greater the reduction in corneal sensation. Epikeratoplasty (also called *epikeratophakia*) involved the creation of a 360° partial-thickness incision in which to place the lenticule that reshaped the cornea. LASIK involves a partial-thickness incision of approximately 300° to create the flap, and then a large-diameter central stromal ablation. Surface ablation involves epithelial removal, followed by a large-diameter central stromal ablation. Refractive lens exchange involves only a small peripheral full-thickness corneal incision, which results in a smaller area of neurotrophic cornea than the other procedures.

13. **a.** Phakic intraocular lenses (PIOLs) are removable. The term *reversible* is sometimes used in connection with PIOLs, but it is not ideal, as the process of placing and removing a PIOL can cause some permanent changes to the eye. Although the risk of endophthalmitis is low, it exists with a PIOL but not with excimer laser–based surgery. Excimer laser–based surgeries can be performed in an appropriate office-type setting, which is considered an advantage. There is more risk of endothelial cell loss with a PIOL than with excimer laser–based surgeries, not less.

14. **b.** Posterior chamber PIOLs require intraoperative pupillary dilation in order to be inserted behind the iris, whereas iris-fixated and anterior chamber PIOLs do not. As PIOLs are not associated with significant dry eye, a preoperative Schirmer test is not required in patients who are not suspected of having dry eye. PIOLs can be inserted under topical anesthesia, making general anesthesia unnecessary. All PIOLs currently require a peripheral iridotomy/iridectomy either preoperatively or intraoperatively to prevent pupillary block. All PIOLs require preoperative calculations to determine the correct lens power.

15. **c.** Pregnancy can cause a temporary change in the refraction, which makes refractive surgery potentially less accurate. It is generally recommended to wait approximately 3 months after delivery to obtain a stable preoperative refraction and perform refractive surgery. Since nursing may also affect the refraction, many surgeons also recommend waiting for several months after nursing has stopped before proceeding with refractive surgery. As LASIK has a small but definite risk of vision loss, it is not typically recommended for patients with good vision in only 1 eye. Consequently, LASIK is not typically recommended in the "good" eye when amblyopia is causing decreased visual acuity of worse than 20/40 in the "bad" eye. The visual results of LASIK in eyes with pellucid marginal degeneration are often quite poor. LASIK may also hasten the progression of ectasia. Controlled asthma is not a contraindication to LASIK.

16. **b.** Conductive keratoplasty (CK) uses radio waves to heat the midperipheral cornea to cause scarring, which secondarily steepens the central cornea. A steeper central cornea will correct low degrees of hyperopia or, in emmetropic individuals, induce myopia, which corrects presbyopia. While the technology of collagen shrinkage by heat would seem to be applicable to a variety of ocular conditions, CK was FDA approved in 2002 only for the temporary treatment of mild to moderate hyperopia (+0.75 to +3.25 D) with astigmatism of 0.75 D or less. In 2004, CK received FDA approval for the treatment of presbyopia in the nondominant eye of a presbyopic patient with an endpoint of –1.00 to –2.00 D. For both treatments, patients are typically 40 years of age or older and have had a stable refraction for at least 12 months. CK is not FDA approved to treat regular or irregular astigmatism. It is not advised in eyes after radial keratotomy (RK), as the procedure can cause the RK incisions to gape and cause significant irregular astigmatism and foreign-body sensation.

17. **b.** All multifocal IOLs are designed to provide very good uncorrected distance vision. Depending on the specific lens, they generally also provide good intermediate or near vision, but typically not both. While multifocal IOLs are not associated with higher than average rates of capsular opacity than are monofocal IOLs, a mild capsular opacity tends to affect the quality of vision more in an eye with a multifocal IOL than in one with a monofocal IOL. Because light entering an eye with a multifocal IOL is divided into more than 1 focal point, patients with a multifocal IOL tend to notice more glare and halos than do patients who had standard corneal refractive surgery, such as surface ablation or LASIK, and also may have symptoms of poor contrast sensitivity.

18. **b.** Initially, intrastromal corneal ring segments (ICRS) were FDA approved and used for the correction of myopia, but, because of reduced predictability, they have fallen out of favor for myopia. They are now used almost exclusively in patients with keratoconus.

19. **c.** Intrastromal corneal ring segments have always been made of polymethylmethacrylate (PMMA).

20. **a.** Segment placement that is too shallow can cause corneal stromal thinning and, ultimately, anterior extrusion of the segment, characterized by chronic foreign-body sensation, which requires segment explantation.

21. **b.** While infection, loss of BCVA, and globe perforation can occur in rare instances after RK, progressive hyperopia due to progressive corneal flattening is much more common. The Prospective Evaluation of Radial Keratotomy study found that, 10 years postoperatively, 23% of eyes were overcorrected by more than 1 D. Also, diurnal fluctuation of vision is a common side effect of RK.

22. **c.** LASIK after RK can cause micro or macro splaying open of the RK incisions, which provides a track for the epithelium to migrate down and into the interface. Epithelial removal in these cases can be very challenging.

23. **d.** When 1 meridian is flattened from an astigmatic incision, an amount of steepening occurs in the meridian 90° away; this is the concept of coupling.

24. **c.** Mild corneal haze after a surface ablation procedure is not uncommon and will usually resolve without treatment over time. If the haze were to persist, causing a reduction in vision or recurrent myopia, then treatment might be indicated and consist of either an increase in the topical steroid regimen or a corneal epithelial scraping with topical application of mitomycin C.

25. **d.** Epithelial ingrowth typically occurs in the first few weeks after LASIK. Surgical intervention is indicated only if the ingrowth is progressive and invading the central cornea, reducing the uncorrected vision, causing astigmatism, or triggering overlying flap melting. Usually, lifting the LASIK flap and scraping the epithelium from both the stromal bed and the underside of the flap are adequate as a first treatment, if indicated.

26. **a.** It is important to expedite the healing of the defect to reduce the risk of infectious keratitis, and a bandage contact lens is an excellent device. Acute microbial keratitis may be caused by contact lenses, and contact lenses may delay the healing and reduce the penetration of topical antibiotics. Bandage contact lenses may increase the risk of infectious keratitis in patients with severe dry eye.

27. **c.** Although the "safe" minimum residual corneal stromal bed thickness has not been definitively established, it should not be thinner than 250 μm, as this increases the risk of corneal ectasia, unstable corneal curvature, and poor visual results. Connective tissue and

autoimmune diseases are relative contraindications to refractive surgery, because these conditions can adversely affect healing. However, good results can be achieved in some patients with stable, inactive, well-controlled connective tissue and autoimmune diseases. Surgery in such patients may be considered "off-label." The potential increased risk and possible "off-label" status should be discussed with the patient and documented in the medical record. Keratometry readings lower than approximately 34 D and higher than approximately 50 D increase the risk of poor-quality vision after refractive surgery. A patient with low myopia who has a preoperative keratometry reading of 39 D would probably have a postoperative keratometry reading above 34 D. A myopic patient with a preoperative keratometry reading of 48 D would very likely have a postoperative keratometry reading above 34 D.

28. **c.** Herpes simplex virus (HSV) keratitis may develop following any refractive surgery, even in patients without any known history of HSV infections. Aggressive treatment is indicated, for many reasons, including the fact that many patients may be using topical steroid drops, and one wants to minimize the risk of corneal scarring, which may cause a permanent reduction in the uncorrected and even the best-corrected vision. Epithelial debridement alone is not sufficient to eradicate the HSV infection, although it may help reduce the viral load.

29. **a.** PRK is an effective means to treat hyperopia. In patients with a history of strabismus, especially esotropia, reducing or eliminating the hyperopia should reduce accommodative convergence and decrease the tendency for esotropia. Strabismus surgery may not always be indicated or possible after PRK surgery, despite the persistence or worsening of diplopia. Patients need to be warned about this possible postoperative complication. Prism correction may still be necessary following PRK in patients with strabismus. PRK will usually not significantly improve dense amblyopia.

30. **d.** Elective ocular surgery should not be performed in a diabetic patient with poor or erratic control. In a diabetic patient, the refraction may fluctuate until the patient's blood glucose levels have stabilized, thereby making any refractive surgery risky. For the same reason, it is risky to prescribe eyeglasses or contact lenses in a diabetic patient with labile control. The diabetes needs to be under control, and the refraction needs to be stable before refractive surgery can be performed or eyeglasses or contact lenses prescribed.

31. **c.** LASIK is not ideal in eyes with thin corneas, as it is more difficult to maintain an adequate residual stromal bed thickness (RSBT) with this procedure. Although the minimum acceptable RSBT has not been definitively established, the RSBT should be greater than 250 μm. LASIK is also not ideal in patients with deep-set eyes or small palpebral fissures, as it is more difficult to establish and maintain good suction. If good suction cannot be achieved, then a LASIK flap should not be attempted. If adequate suction is achieved, then flap creation can be initiated. However, if good suction cannot be maintained throughout the entire creation of the flap, a poor-quality flap can result. Issues with flap creation are avoided with a surface ablation procedure.

32. **c.** Like LASIK, conductive keratoplasty (CK) and laser thermokeratoplasty (LTK) treatments have a tendency for the regression of effect. Unlike LASIK, however, the regression seen with CK and LTK occurs quickly (within months to a year) and may result in an almost total loss of refractive effect. In some studies, there was an overall loss of 20% of effect after 2 years. Progression of effect was found in many eyes after radial keratotomy, between 1 and 10 years postoperatively.

33. **d.** The advantages of slight undercorrection are that it achieves good uncorrected distance vision while allowing good uncorrected near (reading) vision in middle-aged (early presbyopic) patients and it also maintains stereopsis. However, the uncorrected distance vision is not perfect. Monovision (ideally) achieves excellent uncorrected distance vision in one eye and good to excellent uncorrected near vision in the fellow eye, but there is often a loss of some stereopsis.

34. **d.** Corneal collagen crosslinking combines riboflavin (vitamin B_2), which is a naturally occurring photosensitizer found in all human cells, and ultraviolet A (UVA) light to strengthen the biomechanical properties of the cornea. Although there may also be a slight flattening of the cornea, the most important effect of the crosslinking is that it stabilizes the corneal curvature and prevents further steepening and bulging of the corneal stroma. There is no significant change in the refractive index or the clarity of the cornea. Clinically, collagen crosslinking can be used to prevent the progression of keratoconus and ectasia following corneal refractive surgery. In the presence of riboflavin, approximately 95% of the UVA light irradiance is absorbed anteriorly in the first 300 μm of the corneal stroma; therefore, to prevent endothelial damage, most studies require a minimum corneal thickness of 400 μm after epithelial removal. Thinner corneas may be thickened temporarily with application of a hypotonic riboflavin formulation prior to UVA treatment. Corneal collagen crosslinking is not currently FDA approved.

35. **c.** Dry-eye symptoms after LASIK are the most common adverse effects of refractive surgery. Corneal nerves are severed when the flap is made, and the cornea overlying the flap is significantly anesthetic for 3 to 6 months. As a result, most patients experience a decrease in tear production. Patients who had dry eyes before surgery or whose eyes were marginally compensated before surgery will have the most severe symptoms. In addition, most patients with dry eyes after LASIK or surface ablation will find the tear film and ocular surface disrupted and will often complain of fluctuating vision between blinks and at different times of the day. Frequent application of preservative-free artificial tears is often successful at improving patients' symptoms. Additional treatments include topical cyclosporine and punctal occlusion.

36. **c.** Keratoconus is generally considered a contraindication to LASIK and surface ablation. Weakening of the cornea as a result of the loss of structural integrity involved in creating the LASIK flap and removal of tissue significantly increase the risk of progressive ectasia, even if the keratoconus was stable prior to treatment. It is, therefore, very important to recognize early or forme fruste keratoconus during the screening examination for refractive surgery. Although different stages of keratoconus can be diagnosed by slit-lamp examination, more sensitive analyses using corneal topography and corneal pachymetry can reveal findings ranging from clearly normal to clearly pathologic. No specific agreed-upon test or measurement is diagnostic of a corneal ectatic disorder, but both of these diagnostic tests should be part of the evaluation because subtle corneal thinning or curvature changes can be overlooked on slit-lamp evaluation. Findings suggestive of forme fruste keratoconus include reduced best spectacle acuity, steep keratometry readings, and asymmetric astigmatism (usually steep vertically) on corneal mapping.

37. **b.** Even though the measurement of axial length should remain accurate after refractive surgery, determining the actual keratometric power of the post–refractive surgery cornea is problematic. The difficulty arises from several factors. Small, effective central optical zones after refractive surgery (especially after RK) can lead to inaccurate measurements,

because keratometers and Placido disk–based corneal topography units measure the corneal curvature several millimeters away from the center of the cornea. Also, the relationship between the anterior and posterior corneal curvatures may be altered after refractive surgery (especially after laser ablative procedures), leading to inaccurate results. Generally, if standard keratometry readings are used to calculate intraocular lens power in a previously myopic patient, the postoperative refraction will be hyperopic because the keratometry readings are higher than the true corneal power.

38. **d.** There are numerous ways to perform IOL calculations after refractive surgery. Unfortunately, none is perfect. Small, effective central optical zones after refractive surgery (especially after RK) can lead to inaccurate measurements, because keratometers and Placido disk–based corneal topography units measure the corneal curvature several millimeters away from the center of the cornea. Also, the relationship between the anterior and posterior corneal curvatures may be altered after refractive surgery (especially after laser ablative procedures), leading to inaccurate results. Historical methods and rigid contact lens overrefractions are often fairly accurate. Manual keratometry is often less accurate than automated keratometry. Technology that allows measurements from the central cornea (eg, Scheimpflug imaging) appears to provide more accurate results than does manual keratometry.

39. **d.** Rigid gas-permeable (RGP) contact lenses are the gold standard for the correction of reduced vision due to ectasia. Surgical procedures that either thin or destabilize the cornea (eg, LASIK, PRK, incisional procedures) are inappropriate. As ectasia may be a progressive condition, refractive lens exchange is also contraindicated. Because the contact lens fit and power can be modified as the ectasia progresses, RGP contact lenses are the most appropriate treatment. In the future, corneal crosslinking may become the treatment of choice, but it is not currently FDA approved.

40. **b.** Although severely decentered flaps and ablations are uncommon, they represent a significant management problem because of the irregular astigmatism that results. The goal of vision rehabilitation in these patients is to "regularize" the anterior refractive surface of the cornea. While in very mild cases custom LASIK procedures may offer some benefit, in significant irregular astigmatism further LASIK, even custom treatment, is generally not helpful in improving the patient's vision. Lamellar keratoplasty and recutting of the flap are also somewhat risky and may not improve the vision. Fitting an RGP contact lens, on the other hand, can provide the patient with significant visual improvement. It should be remembered that contact lenses for refractive purposes should not be fit until surgical wounds and serial refractions are stable. The most practical approach to fitting an RGP lens after refractive surgery is to do a trial fitting with overrefraction. The clinician needs to discuss with the patient in lay terms the challenges of contact lens fitting after refractive surgery and align the patient's expectations with reality. A patient who successfully wore contact lenses prior to refractive surgery is more likely to be a successful contact lens wearer postoperatively than a patient who never wore contact lenses.

Index

(*f* = figure; *t* = table)